Sacred Sexuality in Ancient Egypt

Hathor transmitting vital energy to the king by presenting him with the *menat,* symbol of the female element necessary to his rebirth. This is how she proves her love to the deceased king, who is mysteriously joined to the goddess by the touch of the *menat* and their interlaced hands (see fig. 4.14 for more on these gestures). (From a relief in the tomb of Seti I, Nineteenth Dynasty, Louvre Museum, Paris.)

Sacred Sexuality in Ancient Egypt

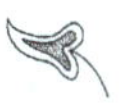

THE EROTIC SECRETS OF THE FORBIDDEN PAPYRUS

A look at the unique role of Hathor, the goddess of love

RUTH SCHUMANN ANTELME
AND STÉPHANE ROSSINI

Translated by Jon Graham

Inner Traditions
Rochester, Vermont

Inner Traditions International
One Park Street
Rochester, Vermont 05767
www.InnerTraditions.com

Originally published in French under the title *Les Secrets d'Hathor* by Éditions du Rocher

Library of Congress Cataloging-in-Publication Data

Schumann Antelme, Ruth.
[Secrets d'Hathor. English]
Sacred sexuality in ancient Egypt : the erotic secrets of the forbidden Papyrus / Ruth Schumann Antelme and Stéphane Rossini ; translated by Jon Graham.
p. cm.
"Originally published in French under the title Les Secrets d'Hathor."
Includes bibliographical references and index.
ISBN 978-0-89281-863-1 (pbk.)
1. Sex customs—Egypt—History. 2. Sex—Egypt—Philosophy. 3. Erotic art—Egypt. 4. Erotic drawing—Egypt. 5. Egypt—Social life and customs—To 332 B.C. 6. Civilization, Egyptian. I. Rossini, S. (Stéphane) II. Title.
HQ13 .S38 2001
306.7'0932—dc21
2001003252

Printed and bound in the United States

10 9 8 7 6 5 4 3 2

Text design and layout by Virginia L. Scott Bowman
This book was typeset in Garamond with Centaur as the display typeface

The images for the color plates in this book were provided courtesy of Art Resources (plates 12, 14, and 21), Réunion des musées nationaux (plate 1: ©RMN–Hervé Lewandowski and plate 4: ©RMN–Chuzeville), and M. François Gourdon (plates 2, 3, 5, 6, 7, 8, 9, 10, 11, 13, 15, 16, 17, 18, 19, 20, 22, 23).

Chorus mysticus:

Alles Vergängliche
Ist nur ein Gleichnis
Das Unzulängliche,
Hier wird's Ereignis;
Das Unbeschreibliche,
Hier ist's getan!
Das Ewig-Weibliche
Zieht uns hinan.

Mystical chorus:

All the ephemeral
Is naught but a symbol.
The insufficient,
Here becomes event;
The indescribable,
Here becomes fact!
The eternal feminine
Attracts us, exalts us.

—Johann W. von Goethe,
(*Faust* bk. 2, finale)

Contents

Acknowledgments **viii**

Introduction **1**

Chapter One: Sexuality, Engine of the Divine World **3**

The Heliopolitan and Hermopolitan Creation Myths 3

The Cosmic Children of the Demiurge 11

The Time Space Dimension: The Cursed Gods 13

The Osirian Cycle 15

The Memphis Triad 22

The Eye of Ra: The Myth of the Distant One 22

Amun the Theban 26

Hathor 27

Chapter Two: The Sexuality of the Human World **50**

The Socio-Legal Framework 50

Sexuality and Ritual Purity 63

The Earthly Harem of the Demiurge 65

Prostitution 66

Chapter Three: Love, Eroticism, and Sexuality in Literature **69**

Sarcasm, Insults, and Blasphemy 70

The Moral Literature 72

Love Poetry and Erotic Literature 75

Chapter Four: The Code of Love 94
The Code of Love in Figurative Art 94
Components of the Code of Love 102
Chapter Five: Medicine and Sexuality 132
The Primary Sources 132
Gynecology and Obstetrics 133
Venereal Diseases 137
Sexual Mutilations 137
Chapter Six: Uncommon Sexual Practices 139
Male and Female Homosexuality 139
Other Practices 148
Chapter Seven: The Erotic Papyrus of Turin 150
Conclusion 162

Appendix One: A Simplified Chronology 163
Appendix Two: Egyptian Deities 166
Appendix Three: Egyptian Place-Names 183
Appendix Four: Egyptian Hieroglyphics 187
Notes 203
Glossary 216
Bibliography 222
Index 225

Acknowledgments

The authors wish to express their thanks to the following persons:

Monsieur Jean-Paul Bertrand, president and general manager of the imprint that bears his name at Éditions du Rocher, for the confidence he has again shown to us by giving us the task of discussing for the public at large, on artistic and scientifically sound foundations, this delicate and poorly known subject, which is still often considered taboo.

Mademoiselle Catherine Bridonneau, archivist at the Department of Egyptian Antiquities at the Louvre Museum; Madame Christiane Hachet, editorial advisor; Madame Sylvie Lalague, M.D., and Madame Sibylle Lennoz, for their kind assistance with documents and archives.

To the secretarial staff and everyone else at Éditions Jean-Paul Bertrand for their constant monitoring of this work during its preparation, particularly to Madame Danielle Charpentier, Mademoiselle Charlotte Debiolles, and to Monsieur Frédéric Brument, who, by their patient and energetic professionalism, have contributed to the successful completion of this work.

Monsieur Wilfred Lauhon for his friendly assistance on the computer.

Madame Béatrice Antelme for graciously providing the archaeological drawings from the Papyrus of Turin.

Introduction

What's that? The ancient Egyptians had erotic obsessions? That people—whom Herodotus dubbed the most religious in the whole world—devoted themselves to the subtleties of love? But of course! The reader need not feel any alarm, for in this domain, as in all others, the Ancients followed divine example. It may be asked, however, to what extent the divine model is simply a projection of behavior that is all too human. Obviously this model is completely different from current Western concepts—to the degree that even Champollion was shocked by certain extremely explicit depictions. Yet, the decoder of the hieroglyphs had a profound grasp of the marvelous civilization that lived along the banks of the Nile. So we feel compelled to provide the reader with some introductory information to this book, which has been conceived as a film, or as a CD-ROM with different menus the reader can "unroll" skimming through the pages and then "zoom in on" for details. All illustrate an aspect of the civilization of the pharaohs that is practically unknown to the public at large, who, until the present, did not have a work dealing with the topic to which it could refer. It is obvious that the many facets of this theme can only be presented in a summary fashion within the confines of a single volume. In fact a general glimpse behind the shutter of the private life of the ancient dwellers along the Nile is the authors' only ambition for this book.

The primary sources of our general knowledge of ancient Egypt are principally derived from the religious sphere—setting aside certain objects from daily life that nonetheless also frequently reflect beliefs. Revelatory documents on the sexuality and eroticism of the ancient Egyptians are not lacking though, but one must know how to "read" them. The most important are the images and inscriptions found in the temples. They are currently displayed out in the open, but were inaccessible to the profane in the times of antiquity, as the common people were not permitted to go beyond the enclosing walls of the sanctuaries. On the other hand, the figurative sketches of the ancient draughtsmen on the ostraca that circulated freely at that time are today still struck by a taboo and carefully hidden from the sight of the public. The literary, medical, and judicial papyri constitute a valuable source of information, primarily reserved for specialists. Finally, the ancient Greek travelers[1] left us interesting narratives, although they are difficult to verify. Thus the first task is to turn toward that divine model concerning the creation of the universe, a grandiose work bringing forces into play that go well beyond the human. To formulate and illustrate in an understandable format the cosmogonic concepts, the priests appealed to the strongest impulse of all living creatures, the reproductive instinct. All human societies, from the most primitive to the most modern, have attempted to submit this instinct and its corollary to more or less strict regulations, which were generally dictated by religious ideas. Pharaonic society was no exception. Its sages were concerned with the question of the origin of the universe, and their consideration of the matter led them to define the Creation as a sexual act.

CHAPTER ONE

Sexuality, Engine of the Divine World

THE HELIOPOLITAN AND HERMOPOLITAN CREATION MYTHS

The divine sexuality of the origin rendered sacred the reproductive instinct, making sexuality the basis of the dogmatic principles that were formulated and conveyed in the creation myths whose broad outlines should be known if one wants to understand certain aspects of ancient Egyptian life. Several of the oldest texts, such as those of the Pyramids,[1] testify to rather uncouth manners and customs.

For the ancients, before all of Creation existed, there was chaos, what astrophysicists today call the "cosmic soup." This "Nun" (fig. 1.1) contained the ancestral gods (fig. 1.2), and according to the priests of Hermopolis, the four primordial couples, the Ogdoad (fig. 1.3), who crafted the initial egg. This egg emerged from the abyssos and opened at the call of the god Thoth (fig. 1.4), keeper of all science. This was the birth of the core energy of our local star system, in other words, the birth of the sun, the big bang of the first atomic blast.[2] At this point the baton was passed to the Heliopolitan myth. This initial sun then became a divine entity under the name of Atum (fig.1.5) and shone under the

Figure 1.1: Nun, divine image of the uncreated matrix-reservoir of the primordial waters. The hieroglyph of this god's name represents the sky surmounted by three vases.

Figure 1.2: The ancestral gods hail the cosmos in becoming, a prospect that awakens their generative forces. They must facilitate the entry of the king into life ceaselessly renewed, in this instance the king is Ramses IX (Twentieth Dynasty). They are depicted on the ceiling of his tomb in the Valley of the Kings.

Figure 1.3: The Ogdoad, the "Eight of Hermopolis," consist of four couples. The males are frogs, and the females, snakes. They are the only deities whose human feet are equipped with raised claws. Forces diffused within chaos, a veritable cosmic laboratory, these uncreated beings are nevertheless the conceivers and creators of the solar egg, whose hatching signals the birth of the universe. Their male and female names and attributions are:

- Nun and Nunet (or Naunet), the original chaotic waters;
- Hehu and Hehet, indeteminate space, infinity;
- Keku and Kekut, the darkness, the Tenebrae;
- Tenemu and Tenemut, movement, agitation, wandering with no goal or order. They were later replaced by the couple Niau and Niaut, lack, absences, the void. When the Theban god Amun rose to the rank of god of the empire, his priests replaced Niau and Niaut with the couple Amun and Amunet, that which is hidden.

Figure 1.4: Thoth, the Hermopolitan, is god of knowledge and all science, "the First of the Eight," the inventor of writing and the calendar. He is depicted here as an ibis-headed man holding his two attributes, the scribe's palette and the calamus, or reed pen. He can also assume the shape of a baboon.

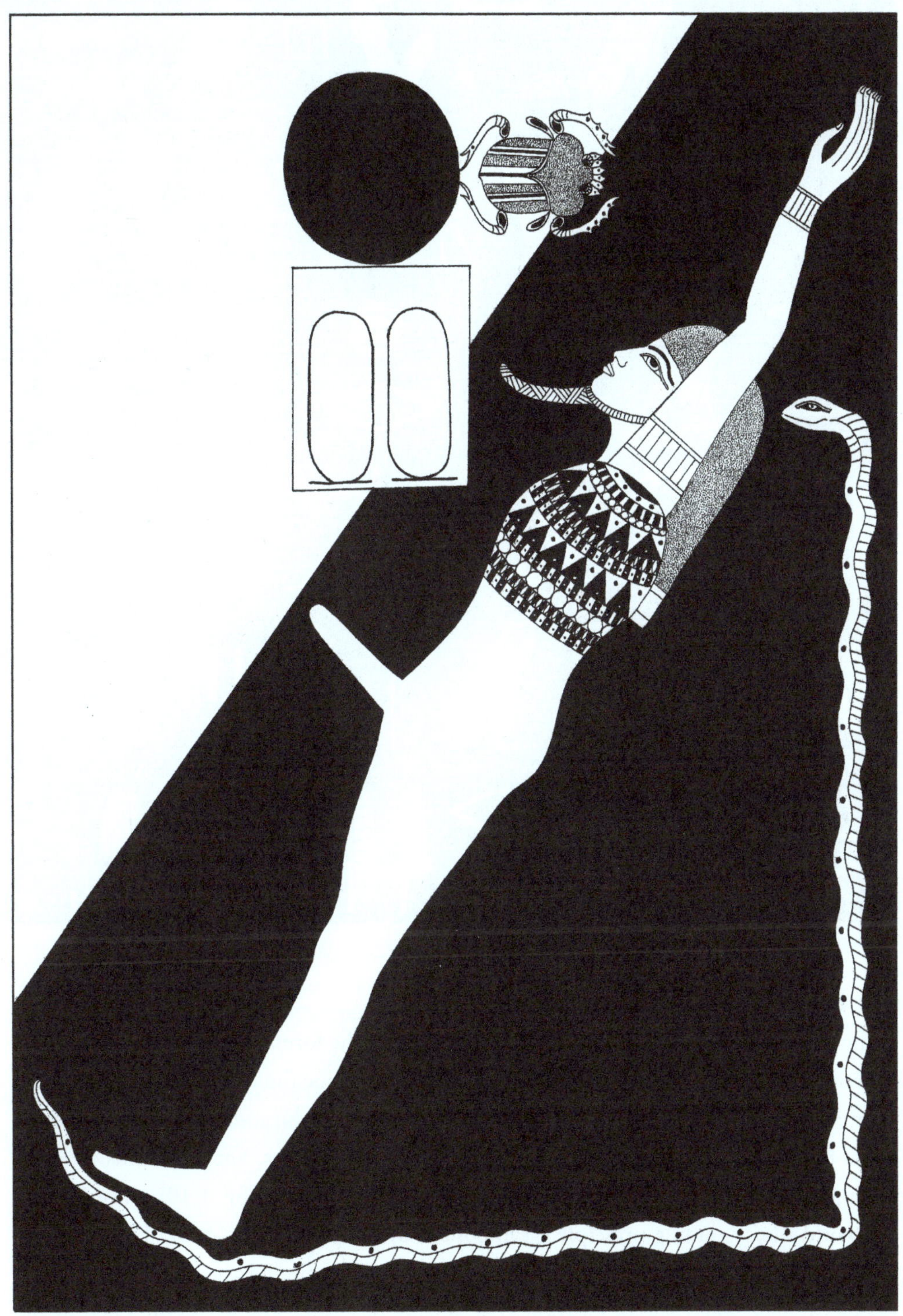

Figure 1.5: Atum, propped by the abyssal serpent who has taken the shape of a set square in order to support the god as he emerges from the darkness. The demiurge contains within his body the semen of all the future "Sons of the Sun" who are to rule over Egypt. The as of yet unrevealed sun is leaving the shadows; its passage into existence is indicated by the scarab, joining day to night, one of the images of the eternity into which Pharaoh would enter. (Tomb of Ramses IX, Twentieth Dynasty.)

Figure 1.6: The text of the Creation, reproducing the words of Atum: "I joined with my own hand, I [my phallus] stiffened in my fist [and] my heart came into my hand. My semen squirted into my mouth. I spit out Shu and expectorated Tefnut. I became these [three] gods, it was out of me that these two gods came into existence on this earth."

name of Ra at its zenith. Atum is a demiurge; he took the form of himself and created his descendents by masturbating (figs. 1.6 and 1.7). A feminine force that was as universal as his masculine strength inspired this act—Hathor (fig. 1.8), the goddess of love and joy in all its forms, but also the goddess of death and new becomings. She surrounds the Sun, Ra (fig. 1.9), like a halo and endeavors to stimulate his sexuality (fig. 1.10), the engine of the world whose guiding principle is symbolized by the goddess Maat (fig. 1.11).[3] Under various names and attributes these three divine entities maintain the equilibrium of the ceaselessly renewing cycle of creation. The reserve of cosmic energy is contained in the Nun, awaiting a future big bang, a new universe—for even the gods are subject to the cosmic cycle.

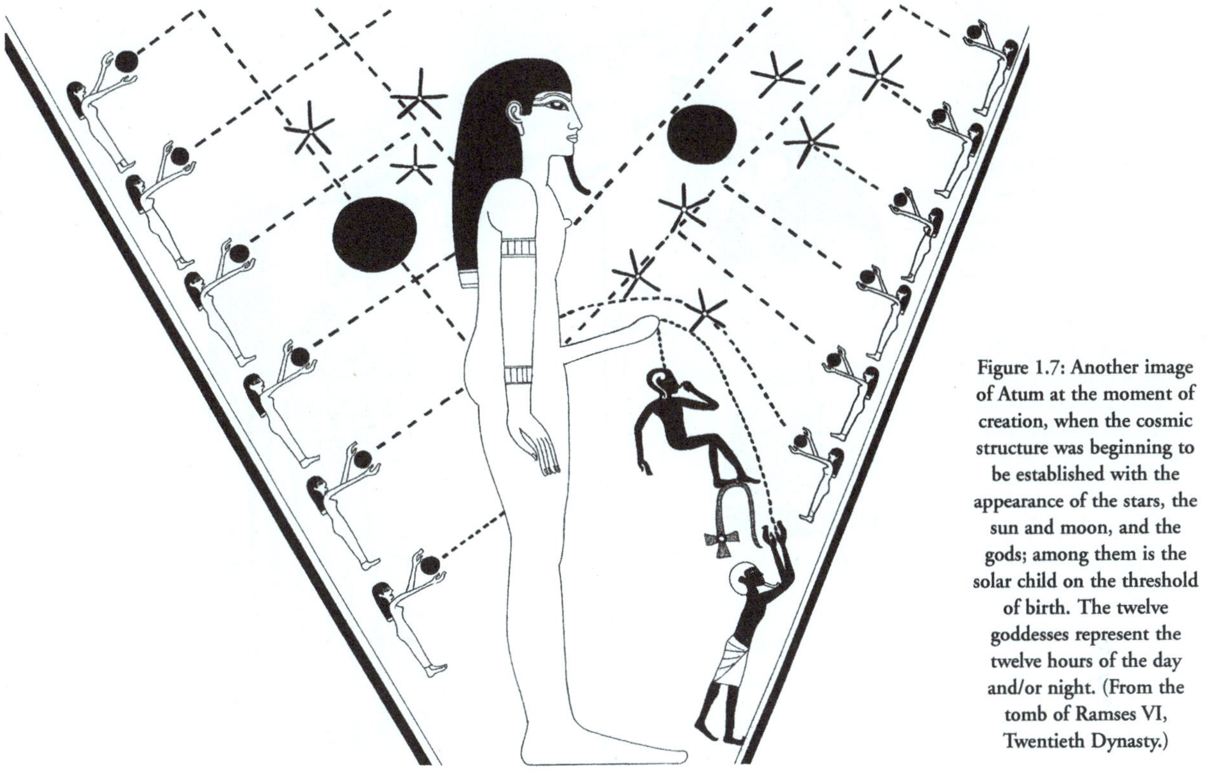

Figure 1.7: Another image of Atum at the moment of creation, when the cosmic structure was beginning to be established with the appearance of the stars, the sun and moon, and the gods; among them is the solar child on the threshold of birth. The twelve goddesses represent the twelve hours of the day and/or night. (From the tomb of Ramses VI, Twentieth Dynasty.)

Figure 1.8: The goddess Hathor in her guise as Nebet-Hetepet, with the attributes of her sexual prowess, necessary for the liberation of the creational forces of the demiurge. (From a relief in the temple of Hibis, the Kharga Oasis, Twenty-seventh Dynasty.)

Figure 1.9: Ra, the sun at its zenith, here sends his vivifying rays to a worshiper. These ray-flowers could be interpreted today as an image of photosynthesis. Ra is holding the insignia of both the divine and terrestrial throne, as well as the ankh, the sign of life. (Stele of the lady Taperet, Twenty-second Dynasty?, Louvre Museum, Paris.)

Figure 1.10: Mystical representation of the reinvigoration of the sun Atum by strange divine entities, one of which is an ithyphallic, starry-sky god in the customary place of the goddess Nut, who is depicted in the adjoining image, but without her stars, leaning over a snake-headed man who is in the posture of Geb, the Earth. Could this be an allusion to the god Sata, the "Son of the Earth," the serpent of the depths? As for the curious male figure performing fellatio upon himself, he could be either Geb or Osiris emerging or also Atum in the act of re-creating himself. The image of an Atum in his dotage is contained within the setting sun. (Papyrus no. 7312, British Museum, London.)

THE COSMIC CHILDREN OF THE DEMIURGE

Let's return to the myth. Following this first bout of sexual activity, Atum swallowed his semen and either spit or breathed out his children, the texts differ on this point. The version of the expectoration is based principally on a play on words, whereas the exhalation corresponds to the demiurge's nature. The creator's first respiration projected life breath into the universe. Born of the potent solar wind, his children, the god Shu and the goddess Tefnut, then got to work and shared the task of organizing space and filling it with air, light, and a soothing humidity. Shu and Tefnut are the Two Lions, the Ruty (fig. 1.12), who are the guardians of the solar horizon, among other things. These two inseparable deities are brother and sister as well as husband and wife. This first couple introduced normal sexual procreation into the universe at the same time as incest! Their children were the Sky, the goddess Nut, and the Earth, the god Geb; their male and female roles are reversed with regard to our perceptions of these cosmic elements. The two deities of the new generation were aligned according to parental example. But their union was more ardent and fecund than that of their elders. The nocturnal Sky met the

Figure 1.11: Maat, the goddess of balance and the right path for the achievement of the cosmic plan. In this capacity she also keeps watch over human behavior. She is wearing the hieroglyph of her name on her head; it is an ostrich feather that stirs at the slightest breath. She shares this attribute with Shu.

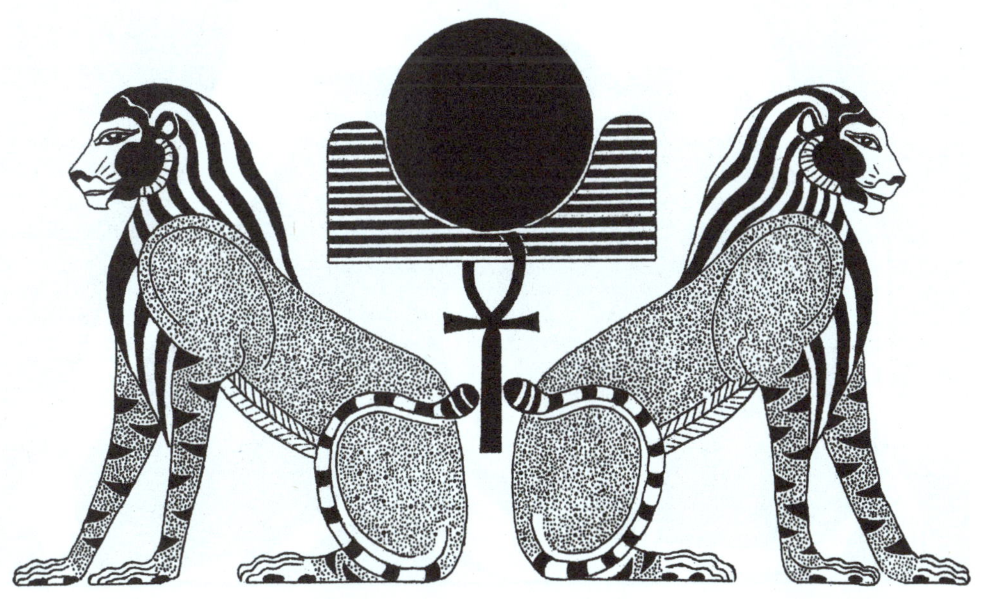

Figure 1.12: Shu and Tefnut, the Two Lions of the solar horizon, the Ruty. The children of Ra were worshiped under this aspect in Leontopolis. Both are of solar essence and connected to the Heliopolitan dogma.

Figure 1.13: The ardent embrace of Nut and Geb, image of the merging of Heaven and Earth, which bore such illicit and undesirable fruits. (Papyrus of the lady Tameniu, British Museum, London.)

Earth in an endless embrace (fig. 1.13), preventing Ra, the Sun, from circulating and shedding light and energizing the world that he was in the midst of creating, and thus provoking his anger. In response he commanded Shu to separate the two lovers, and Shu lifted up his own daughter to form the celestial vault. Geb twisted and turned in fury, spitting out fire and flames—but to no avail (fig. 1.14). These "upheavals of Geb" formed the moun-

Figure 1.14: Shu separating his overly amorous children. For this reason the sky will always be separated from the earth, but existing between them will be a space of life, breath, and light in which the two solar barques will navigate. (From the papyrus of Nespakashuty, Twenty-first Dynasty, Louvre Museum, Paris.)

tains and the volcanoes. To prevent similar annoyances from arising in the future, Ra cursed the children that Nut had conceived with Geb, wishing to prevent their birth during the course of the year—the solar year, of course. It will be noted that it was the feminine element of the couple that was considered dangerous and thus punished, whereas Geb does not seem to have been bothered. It would have been pointless to strike him anyway inasmuch as the four elements—air, water, fire, and earth—were in place and the universal program could continue to unfold.

THE TIME SPACE DIMENSION: THE CURSED GODS

Thoth the Hermopolitan, who possessed an ape-like cunning, insinuated himself into this fault in the cosmic edifice. No doubt he found Ra took up too much space, and it was necessary to create a counterweight to his power. He won five additional solar days (the epagomenal days) gaming with the Moon. This precarious delay allowed Nut to give birth to her quintuplets, who are Osiris, Isis, and Nephthys (fig. 1.15), Seth (fig. 1.16), and Horus, the elder (fig. 1.17). These children, born against the will of Ra, were cursed

Figure 1.15: Osiris, Isis, and Nephthys. The elder couple of the"epagomenal" children and Nephthys, a renegade; the wife of Seth, she forms an illicit couple with Osiris, the legitimate husband of Isis. Their legitimate son, Horus, will be born posthumously. The adulterine son, Anubis, will put the body of his father back together again.

Figure 1.16 (left): Seth, here depicted as a man with the head of an as of yet unidentified animal—one that will apparently remain unidentifiable. He represents the turbulent forces of nature. Inspite of his insatiable erotic appetite, he will have no children with his sister-wife Nephthys.

Figure 1.17 (right): Horus, the elder—but also, in the second generation, the son of Isis and Osiris. Along with Seth, he is one of the protectors of the throne. These two deities represent the double aspect of the pharaoh, something that explains the title conferred upon the queen: She who sees her Horus and her Seth.

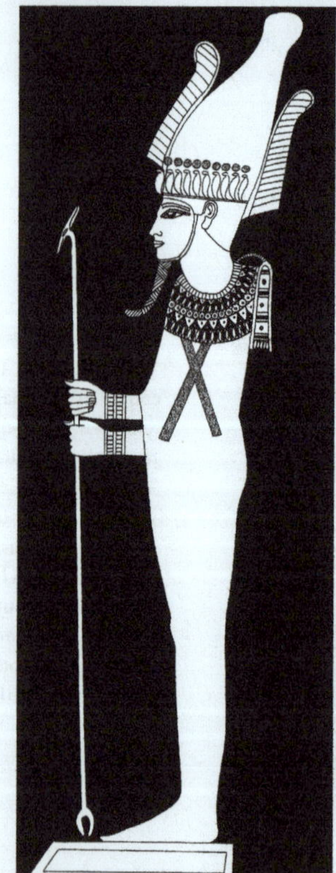

Figure 1.18: Osiris, king of the netherworld and master of transmutations. He is the "First of the Westerners," which is to say, the dead, who enter his kingdom in the west with the setting sun to wait in expectation of a new life.

in a certain way, as is told by the myth. Moreover, their existence had obliged the sun to lengthen and accelerate its course with respect to the moon, to which feminine sexuality would remain linked. Nevertheless, the children of Nut completed the divine group of the Heliopolitan cosmogony, which thus consists of nine members, the Ennead, all emanations of the demiurge Atum-Ra who rules them.

These dramatic events had one important consequence: the subtle maneuver by Thoth to introduce time into the divine sphere.[4] Henceforth the gods could no longer live outside space and time. They could no longer be immortal in a continuous manner, but were subject to cycles just like their creatures, as we have seen, even if the time and space of gods is of a totally different dimension than that of those who live in the terrestrial sphere. The checkered journey of the children of Nut (a house of Atreus, before the fact) reveals other implications. The first born, Osiris (fig. 1.18), and his twin, Isis, formed a couple and ruled peacefully over the earth, that is to say, over Egypt. Seth and Nephthys formed a sterile couple, although Seth embodied the turbulent and uncontrollable forces of nature and showed evidence of an overweening but utterly disorganized sexuality. Nephthys appeared to be more attracted to Isis as well as to Osiris; with him she conceived a child who is the fruit of a relationship that is both incestuous and adulterous. This child is the dark dog Anubis (figs. 1.19 and 1.20), the divine mummifier.

Figure 1.19: Anubis the mummifier leans over the reconstituted cadaver of the one who gave him life, in order to reanimate it by opening a passage to the organs of the senses with his magic adze.

THE OSIRIAN CYCLE

Seth, who was jealous of Osiris for more than one reason, decided to overthrow him and rule in his place. He used a ruse to draw him out and sealed him within a chest that he sunk into the flooded Nile. Isis and Nephthys, in distress, went off in search of the missing one, whom the waves have carried off to the banks of Byblos, where the chest had been caught in the roots of a tamarisk tree. They returned to Egypt with the chest, but Seth discovered it. He hurled himself upon his brother a second time and cut his body into sixteen pieces,[5] which he again threw into the Nile, convinced he had eliminated his rival once and for all. But Seth failed to take into account the determination of the faithful Isis, who was, moreover, a magician in her own right. She gathered together all the pieces of her husband, with the exception of the phallus swallowed by a fish, the oxyrhynchus (fig. 1.21). It is at this

Figure 1.20: Scene of the psychostasia at the tribunal of Osiris where the heart of the deceased and the feather of Maat balance on the scales. The entire lifetime of the deceased prepares for this balance, but it can only be obtained and observed after death. If such is the case, the deceased can hope to become one "righteous of voice" and to ascend into the kingdom of transformations. The inscription above the two divine witnesses of the weighing provides ample proof that Horus, the falcon, is the son of Isis, and Anubis, the black dog, is the son of Osiris. The text passes over the name of his mother in discreet silence—and for good reason!

point of the legend where the sources diverge—either Isis finally rediscovered Osiris's virile member, or she manufactured a substitute; in any event the divine body was reconstituted through her efforts with the help of Anubis (fig. 1.19). Isis then took the form of a bird and magically revived the generative ardor of Osiris, to whom the beating of her wings restored the vital breath (fig. 1.22).[6] Isis and Osiris finally obtained an heir, the god Horus, the young Sun. Meanwhile Osiris returned to the bowels of the earth in order to recharge his energies with an eye to a new cycle, symbolized by the image of a germinating Osiris (fig. 1.23).

Figure 1.21: The oxyrhynchus, with its long "phallic" nose, is the fish that allegedly swallowed Osiris's virile member. In the eighth nome of Upper Egypt, where the principal sanctuary of Osiris was located, it was forbidden under penalty of death to eat this fish, which was the mythical receptacle of the murdered god's procreative organ.

In this way Osiris, who shares the same energies as

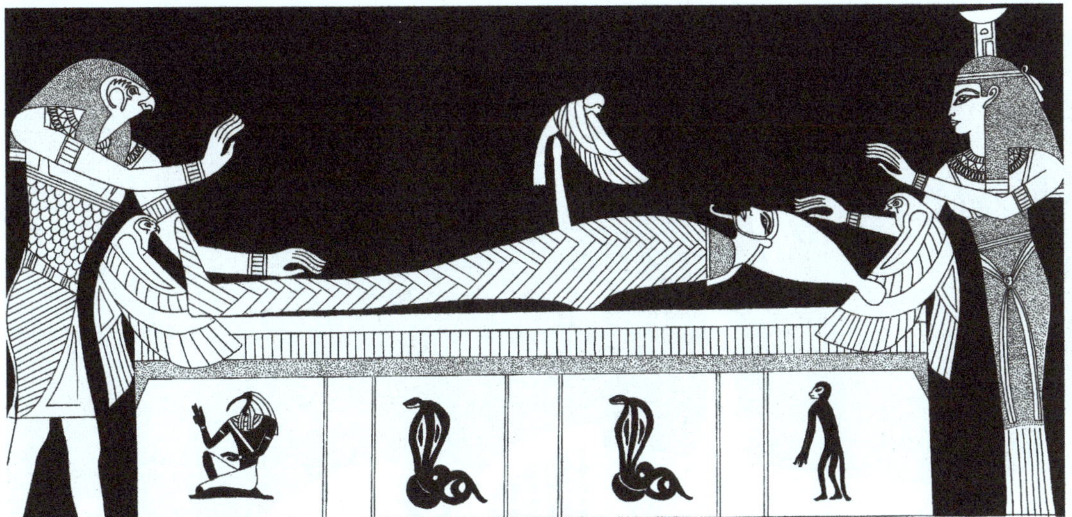

Figure 1.22: The "awakening of Osiris." The small bird Isis receives the sperm of Osiris, previously reanimated by Anubis (see fig. 1.19). The scene unfolds between Nephthys and Horus—no doubt this is the form he wore in space-time before conception. The receptacle of the sarcophagus is magically protected by two uraei, the two powers, and by the two forms of Thoth. The latter, in his ibis-headed form, is making the same sign with his hand as the god Khnum when he created all beings on his potter's wheel. The sign of the sky surmounts these four protective deities.

Ra, incarnates his terrestrial, latent potential in Anubis and reveals his dynamic, celestial face in Horus (fig. 1.24).

Isis raised her son alone and in hiding in the Chemmis Swamp (fig. 1.25) in order to evade the attacks of Seth. On reaching adulthood, Horus reclaimed his father's throne and immediately entered into conflict with his uncle Seth (fig. 1.26). The Pyramid Texts recount this ferocious combat engaged in by the two divine powers for domination of the cosmos.[7] The images used are partially of a sexual nature. Seth does not hesitate to tear

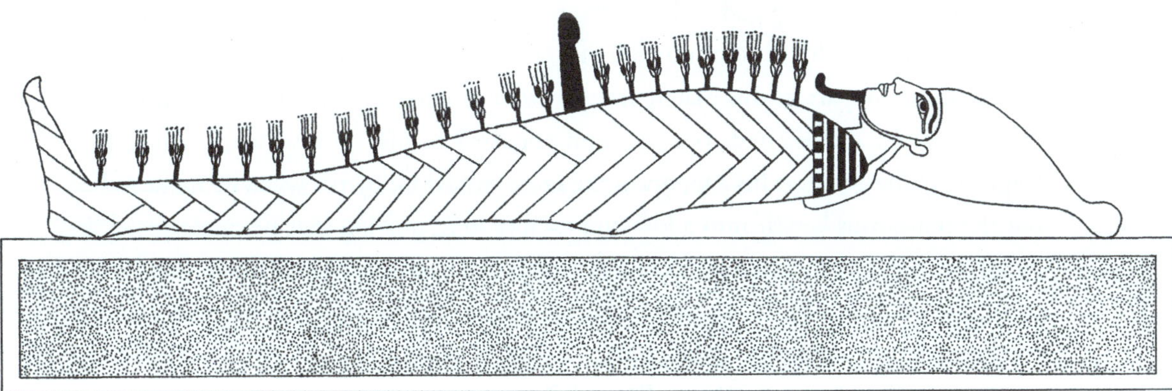

Figure 1.23: The image of Osiris "germinating" recalls his function as god of nature who prompts the growth of plants. Heads of wheat are emerging from his mummified body in alignment with his semen-charged phallus, the image of fertility. The god is not in a sarcophagus, rather his figure commingles with the earth, recalling the images of Osiris made from silt, seeded with grains of wheat, then watered and placed in the tombs.

Figure 1.24: This other phase of the "awakening of Osiris" places the sexual act within space-time and anticipates the coming into the world of Horus, whose image as a crowned king appears in transparency over the mummified body of his father. The god is resting on a bed-vehicle in the form of a lion.

out Horus's lunar eye, and Horus gets his revenge by tearing off Seth's testicles. Thoth heals the two contending gods. The mistreated divine eye will be completely restored and recover its good health as is indicated by its name *wedjat,* "healthy" (fig. 1.27).

Isis also took part in this match and, in order to make Seth admit the legitimacy of Horus's claims, she resorted to a ruse and appeared to him as a seductive young girl. Captivated, the god gave his support in the sense wished for by Isis when he spoke to her, but she transforms herself into a kite and escapes him, proving that he pronounced the judgment himself. It may be asked if Isis remained so aloof throughout their entire encounter because "Seth [. . .] saw her coming from afar. She uttered a magic spell and transformed into a beautiful young girl [. . .] and he loved her much. After which he rose [. . .] and ate bread with the Great Ennead."[8]

Seth was constantly in quest of new erotic adventures. To seduce his sister—and sister-in-law—Isis, he took the form of a bull and ran after the goddess who changed into a greyhound. "Seth could not catch her, so he ejaculated on the ground. She told him,

'You are disgusting, bull, to ejaculate that way!' But his sperm sprouted in the desertlike soil and became the *bedded-kaou* plant."[9] Seth was more successful when he surprised the goddess Anat bathing in the river. The subsequent scene was witnessed by Ra, who addressed some scornful reproaches to the divine warrior.[10]

None of this prevented Seth from giving free rein to his homosexual tendencies, with the intention of discrediting Horus who would thus be stripped of his birthright. "Seth said to Horus, 'Come, let us spend a delightful time together at my place!' Horus responded, 'With pleasure!' When evening fell, a bed was prepared for them and they slept together. During the night, Seth excited himself and inserted his stiffened member between Horus's thighs, [but] Horus put his hands between his thighs and caught Seth's semen." Horus returned to his mother's home to complain of this outrage and showed her his soiled hands. Horrified, Isis cut them off and threw them into the water—but replaced them with

Figure 1.25: Isis and her son Horus in the Chemmis Swamps. Swamps, as suggested by the plants, are the evocation of the amniotic fluid. The breast-feeding gesture is the symbol of the life protected in utero of the evolving being.

Figure 1.26: Image of the opposition of Horus and Seth. Both gods are wearing the royal garb of a warrior and are holding the *was* scepter of power, as well as the ankh, symbol of life. They can take on different forms during their confrontations.

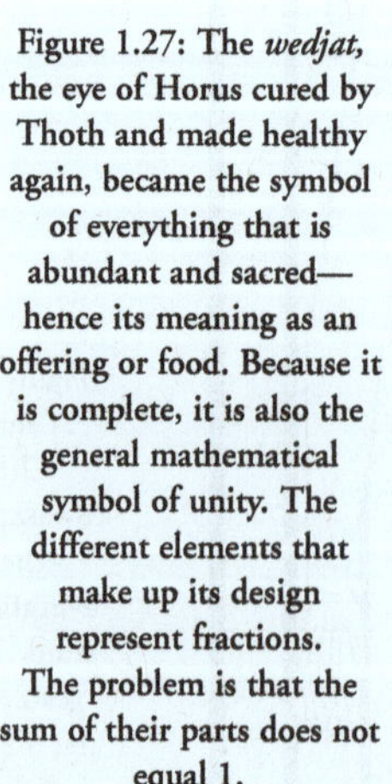

Figure 1.27: The *wedjat,* the eye of Horus cured by Thoth and made healthy again, became the symbol of everything that is abundant and sacred—hence its meaning as an offering or food. Because it is complete, it is also the general mathematical symbol of unity. The different elements that make up its design represent fractions. The problem is that the sum of their parts does not equal 1.

Figure 1.28: Horus and Seth face each other as battling hippopotami.

another set of hands!—and then prepared to take her revenge. "She took a small amount of a sweet balm and applied it to Horus's member. She placed it in a jar and gave him an erection, then made his sperm flow into the jar."[11] The following morning she made her way to Seth's gardens and spread Horus's sperm over the lettuces that Seth had the habit of eating. In this way the latter swallowed his nephew's sperm and became "pregnant"—without his knowledge, given the fact he had not noticed what Horus had done the previous night. Seth, believing his strategy had succeeded and proud of his feat, then hauled Horus before the tribunal of the Ennead. The gods noisily and quite vulgarly made known their disgust at the passive attitude of Horus, though not similarly reprimanding Seth. But Horus laughed at them, accused Seth of lying, and maintained that the opposite had occurred—for proof, it sufficed to summon each of their sperms and see from where they answered! Thoth undertook the test, and it was obviously Horus's sperm that emerged from Seth's forehead like a golden disk, which Thoth took for his own to wear on his head. The Ennead then declared Horus the legitimate successor to the throne of Osiris. Seth did not accept their verdict, however, and the two adversaries continued their necessary cosmic struggle; because that is what it truly is, in spite of the uncouth imagery and a political backdrop that speaks volumes about what has occurred on earth.

The problem of the litigious succession of Osiris was resolved by Ra, but only after long reflection, for it must be admitted that the young Horus often did thoughtless things—such as cutting off his mother's head, for example—and that he lacked the sangfroid necessary for a sovereign. In fact, following the countless quarrels between the Two Companions who were transformed into hippopotami (fig. 1.28), Isis, wishing to help her son, struck him by accident with a magic harpoon that she then pulled out immediately to throw at Seth. But, moved by the painful cries from her brother, she removed it. Horus, furious at his mother's compassion, decapitated her! Thoth, on the orders of Ra, grafted a cow's head upon her, which she evidently retransformed into a human head.[12] The incident facilitated her mythological assimilation, under the name of Hezat, into the goddess of love as Isis-Hathor.

Seizing his opportunity, Seth rushed at the perturbed Horus and gouged out his eyes, which he buried. Perhaps this is the image of a particularly distressing solar-lunar total eclipse—Horus did merit a severe punishment. As was customary, Thoth took care of matters. However, Ra had had more than enough of the follies committed by these two mad dogs and, after having Osiris consulted (by Thoth naturally), he decided that Horus would mount the throne of Osiris—who could finally rule in peace over the netherworld, the place of rest and of the recharging of solar energy, and the kingdom of transformations. As for Seth, he was enlisted into Ra's personal guard. Ra, in any event, preferred this warrior to his adversary and thus thought to benefit from the aggressive nature of the "red sun" for his defense. Finally, Horus had to reincarnate in each pharaoh as the Son of the Sun: a mystical adoption that was quite opportune for the royalty.

THE MEMPHIS TRIAD

In the former royal residence and holy city of Memphis, another demiurge came into existence: the god Ptah, master of the bowels of the earth and its treasures. He formed a family with his formidable wife, the lioness Sekhmet (fig. 1.29), and their son, Nefertum, a form of the solar infant emerging from the lotus and assimilated to Harpocratus (fig. 1.30).

THE EYE OF RA: THE MYTH OF THE DISTANT ONE

Sekhmet is also a daughter of the Sun—his eye, in fact—and an embodiment of both the destructive force of the day star and untamed feminine sexuality. Her name means "the powerful one." She is the heroine of two myths that later merged into one.[13] To begin with, Ra was faced by the rebellion of certain humans, although they are his creation. He sent his Hathoric eye to chase them out of Egypt. Mission accomplished, the goddess returns to Ra to give him a detailed account of how she defeated the insurgents who sought refuge in the desert. Satisfied, Ra decided henceforth to limit the numbers of men upon the earth. Putting this wise decision into practice required some strong methods; the play on words between the name of the goddess Sekhmet and the word for "power," *sekhem,* provides a forecast of what was to come. The destructive power of the solar eye struck humanity; the enraged lioness, Sekhmet, caused dreadful carnage not only in Egypt but even in the very heart of Africa. The results of his scheme caused Ra to undergo a change of heart, but the lioness Tefnut-Sekhmet was drunk on blood. The great god then gave the command for an enormous quantity of beer to be brewed, which he then

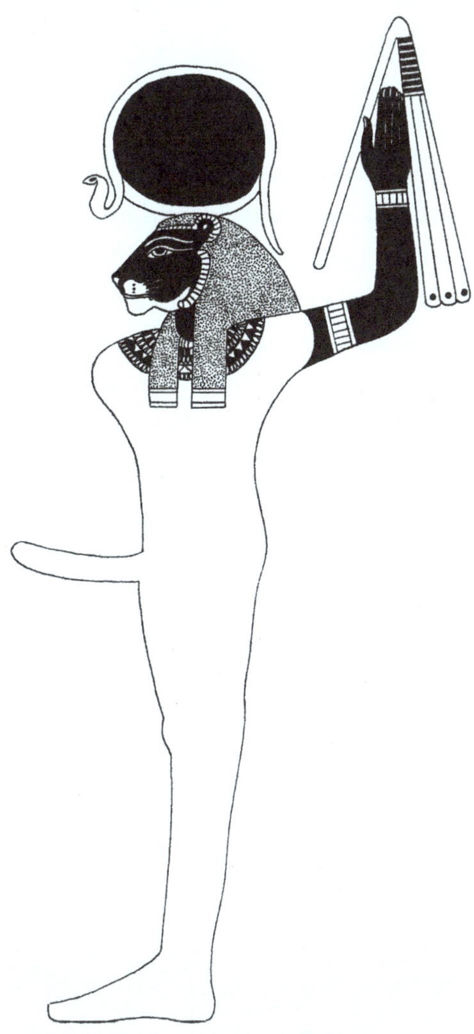

Figure 1.29: Here the goddess Sekhmet appears in the rare aspect of an ithyphallic deity, revealing both the masculine and feminine potential of this aggressive form of the demiurge's eye. Her mummylike garment, raised arm, and flail belong more to the god Min than to the wife of Ptah and mother of Nefertum. There would even be doubts as to her identity if the inscription on the wall of the temple of Karnak did not specify that this was indeed Sekhmet, who is customarily depicted as a lion-headed woman crowned by a solar globe.

Figure 1.30: Nefertum-Harpocratus, the just born solar child, is already the bearer of the divine and royal flail. Here he is not crowned by a lotus (which in reality is a water lily) but is emerging from one. This aquatic plant draws its strength out of the abyssal reservoir and transmits this energy to the regenerated sun.

had dyed red (with the extract of a red plant or clay, according to the various texts) and spread throughout the land while the goddess slept. On awakening she delightedly marched into this sea of what she thought was blood and drank copiously. Having been pacified this way she returned to Egypt—only to see that Ra had put another eye in her place! Again she grew wrathful and again she was pacified. Ra placed her over his forehead in the form of the uraeus (fig. 1.31), in this way she could discharge her aggression

Figure 1.31: The uraeus, one of the forms taken by the eye of Ra, representing the destructive, even fatal power of the sun. It is the guardian of the supreme power and will only let itself to be tamed by the deserving. Coiling on the forehead of her father, Ra, she also encircles the head of the divine son, Pharaoh, as protection.

on the enemies of the demiurge. But Ra, aging and weary, climbed upon the back of his daughter Hathor (fig. 1.32), the celestial cow, who carried him away to the depths of the universe, no doubt toward another galaxy, for another cycle.

Ra left the governing of the world to his son and successor Shu, who, a good and just ruler, had his power usurped by his son Geb. This latter coveted the ultimate weapon of royalty, the uraeus, which was locked within a chest. Geb tried every means to gain possession of the sacred serpent, who slipped away, no doubt judging the violator of his own mother, Tefnut, unworthy of royalty's supreme attribute.

Here is where this story joins with the myth of the Distant One. It again concerns the divine lioness, Tefnut-Sekhmet, an independent, untamed, and zealous deity, who left her father and Egypt to romp as she pleased in the remote lands of Africa, where she could satisfy her amorous desires, as is shown by the lion cubs who accompanied their bellicose but tender mother. Ra missed his daughter, Shu missed his sister, and all Egypt missed the goddess who brought joy and abundance into the

Figure 1.32: Hathor, as the celestial cow, in the solar barque. The goddess is sailing on the celestial ocean—or is it the Nile?—bringing either Ra or the dead toward a new destiny. She is shown with her essential attributes: lyre-shaped horns clutching the solar disk (globe); two curved ostrich feathers; and the *menat* necklace with its counterweight, which characterizes her as mother and divine wet nurse.

land but obstinately refused to return and threatened to kill any and all emissaries sent to her for this purpose. Shu, in his lion form, and Thoth in the shape of an ape (fig. 1.33), successfully managed to drag her away with them. When they arrived at the first cataract, they plunged the ferocious beauty into the sacred waters of the abaton, from which she emerged tamed and in the form of a ravishing young woman—or a charming and cuddly cat. She then took the name of Bastet (fig. 1.34). Her sexuality—still beyond control—and her fertility were now at the service of human couples and families. In the two legends the

Figure 1.33: Hathor-Tefnut and Thoth. The lioness is the aggressive form of the daughter of the Sun and represents the mortal glance of his eye, which is reinforced still further by the presence of the sacred cobra encircling the incandescent globe. Thoth, who has taken the form of a monkey, tries, with his gift of gab, to convince the Distant One to return to Egypt with him and Shu. The lioness hesitates; her teats engorged with milk indicate she will have to leave a whole litter of lion cubs behind. The vulture goddess protects the Distant One while indicating to her the direction she should take.

return from the beyond is celebrated with general merrymaking, including music, dance, and lots of alcoholic libations, in honor of the Lady of Drunkenness—on Ra's orders, naturally! Furthermore, everyone has free time for celebrating, because it is the season of the annual flooding and there is a respite from agricultural tasks. The entire country is covered by a sheet of red-colored water. This myth is also a cosmic parable: the unbridled eroticism of Hathor-Tefnut is the mirror image of the life-giving inundation, whose impetuous waters

Figure 1.34: Bastet, the cat. Following her somewhat forced bath in the waters of the abaton, the ferocious lioness was transformed into a cuddly cat. The savage has been civilized by contact with Egypt—but she still remains as untameable as ever and ready to brandish her dreadful claws.

come down from the heart of Africa and subside at the southern frontier of Egypt, and, becoming slack in her valley, deposit their fertile silt there.

AMUN THE THEBAN

Let's now complete this pantheon in which each entity has a role to play, sometimes against a background of political developments.

In Thebes, a local god, Amun, "the Hidden One," rose to the rank of creator during the time of the Middle Kingdom when Theban princes took power. He is cloaked with solar qualities and worshiped under the name of Amun-Ra as a universal god. The most important feast in his honor was the *opet* (or *ipet*). It celebrated the visit of the god to his "harem of the South," in the company of his consort, Mut (fig. 1.35), and the renewal of his generative powers. The Theban demiurge is thus represented as an ithyphallic masturbator (fig. 1.36) or as Min (fig. 1.37).

Figure 1.35: An aspect of the goddess Mut—normally depicted as a woman wearing the *pschent* but is here three-headed, winged, and ithyphallic—that is particularly appropriate for the subject of this book. The image shows that the goddess, the maternal element of the Theban triad, also carries within her the violence of Sekhmet and the primordial power of Nekhbet, who rules the South. Her wings bestow the vivifying wind; her phallus makes her a demiurge though a predominantly feminine one. Mut is flanked by two odd little spirits, both dwarfish and ithyphallic, who are standing in the traditional pose of the god Min.

HATHOR

And Hathor? We have seen that she was present at the moment of creation in the company of Atum. She is his preponderantly female alter ego, his emanation, his shining shield, his protection, and also his eye, his daughter—we could also even say she is, in a certain manner, his mother, since she surrounded him at the very first moment of existence. She aided him—and will always assist him—in the act of creation, which cannot be accomplished without her. For even though Atum is a demiurge and bears within himself the potential to be female as well as male (a trait shared by the majority of his creatures), this still does not make him a hermaphrodite, properly speaking, in contrast to Hapy, the deity of the flood (fig. 1.38) who "recalls all the fathers and mothers of Egypt." Atum has need of a revealing complement, who like him is made up of one part that is

Figure 1.36: The god Amun as a demiurge assimilated to the masturbating Atum. His human body has been replaced by a scarab, the hieroglyph for "becoming." He is standing in the traditional attitude of the god Min, which emphasizes his powers of fertility.

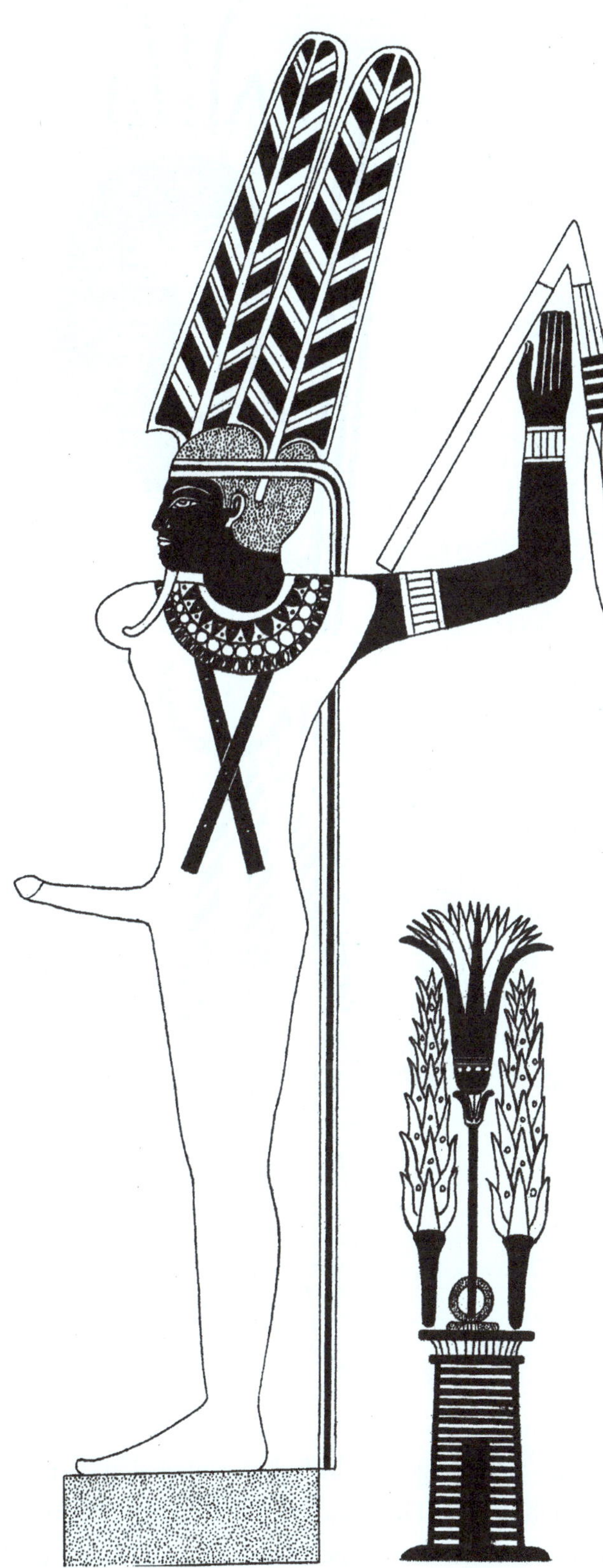

Figure 1.37: The classic image of Min, the agrarian god of fertility, suggested by his ritual "kitchen garden" always depicted behind him. The lower half of his body is constrained by a sheath, giving him a mummylike appearance, but, like Osiris upon his awakening, his virile member, the key of fertility, is prominent. His raised arm and flail betray the impetuous nature of his enthusiasms; his other arm is invisible but is supposed to be held tightly to his body with his hand clutching his phallus.

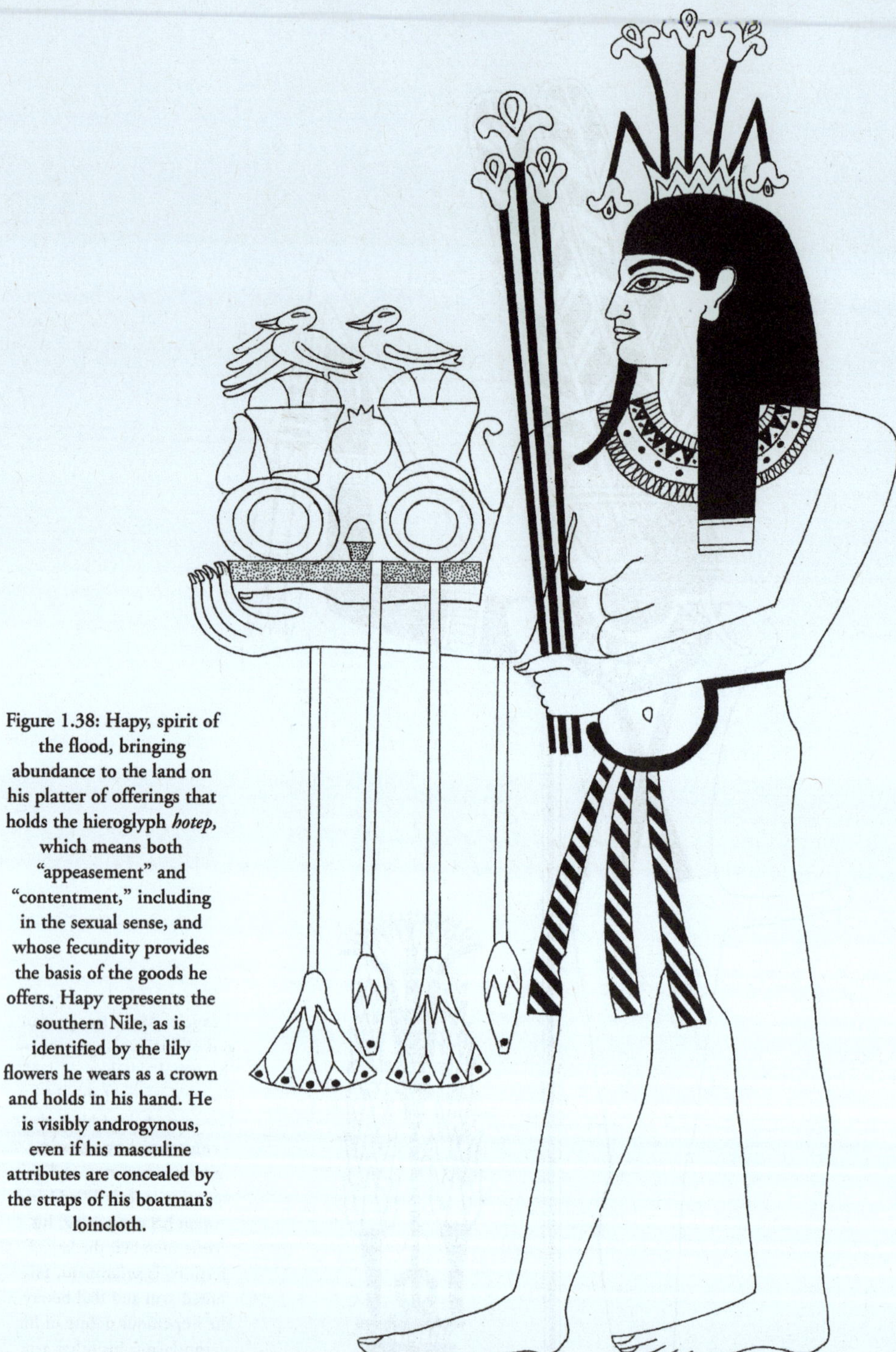

Figure 1.38: Hapy, spirit of the flood, bringing abundance to the land on his platter of offerings that holds the hieroglyph *hotep,* which means both "appeasement" and "contentment," including in the sexual sense, and whose fecundity provides the basis of the goods he offers. Hapy represents the southern Nile, as is identified by the lily flowers he wears as a crown and holds in his hand. He is visibly androgynous, even if his masculine attributes are concealed by the straps of his boatman's loincloth.

masculine and one part that is feminine. The Ancients have expressed this mysterious connection with the term "hand of god," which they conferred upon Hathor and consequently used in illustrations of her. This hand becomes a separate deity in its own right, sometimes under the name of Nebet-Hetepet (fig. 1.39), sometimes Iusaas (which is a

Figure 1.39: Nebet-Hetepet, literally, "mistress of appeasement" (or "contentment"), is the "hand of the creator," the feminine power, the emanation of Hathor who aided Atum in successfully realizing the first act of creation, thanks to her erotic vibrations, which surround the serpent, an ancient sexual symbol. The Hathor-headed sistrum (note the ears of the celestial cow) is flanked by two cats, the tame forms of Shu and Tefnut. (From a relief in the temple of Hibis, Kharga Oasis, Twenty-seventh Dynasty.)

fairly crude play on words) (fig. 1.40).[14] Later, the "divine worshipers," priestesses and mystic brides of the demiurge Amun, as well as certain queens who held this title, will give evidence of their high sarcedotal role.[15]

But generally Hathor is depicted as an attractive young woman (fig. 1.41) who causes the hearts of all the gods to rejoice, especially that of her father, Ra, who is quite susceptible to the sex appeal of this goddess, if we are to believe this passage from the Chester Beatty Papyrus: "The great god spent an entire day lying on his back beneath the arbor. His heart was very sad, because he was alone. After a long while came Hathor, lady of the sycamore of the South, and she stopped before her father, the master of the universe. Standing before

Figure 1.40: Iusaas, the other manifestation of the "hand of the creator" that triggers the act of creation. Her name is as significant as that of Nebet-Hetepet (see note 14). She is presented here in her more refined guise of a charming young woman, clad in an archaic sheath dress and adorned with a goodly number of jewels (*ousekh* neklace, wrist and ankle bracelets). Her divine wig is surmounted with the skin of the vulture of the mother goddesses crowned by *uraei* embodying the rays of the day star.

Figure 1.41: Here is an entirely gynomorphic (woman-shaped) Hathor in all her feminine beauty. Only her crown, with its lyriform horns holding the solar globe around which is coiled the uraeus, is reminiscent of her celestial cow form. The mystical mother of all humanity, she is sporting the skin of a vulture, a privilege she confers upon the queen mothers, with whom she likewise shares the floral scepter. The sign of life, the ankh, emphasizes her divine status.

Figure 1.42: Hathor, "the Curly-haired One," with her signature abundant hairstyle that is artfully braided and terminates in enticing curls. She looks out with a hypnotic gaze that dominates her face, stretched into a triangle by the bovine ears that recall her origin as the celestial cow. This is how she appears, in pairs, on the capitals of her temples of the Middle Kingdom.

him she uncovered her sex to his face and the great god smiled [. . .]." How could we then be surprised that Hathor was also called "Lady of the Vulva" who was invoked by lovers?[16]

Hathor could take on a variety of shapes and forms and make do with an impressive repertoire of titles. Foremost of these, she is the Daughter of Ra, the Golden One, or even simply the Gold, with all the sparkle of her solar essence. The epithet "Curly-haired One" (fig. 1.42) is an allusion to her elaborate hairstyle, with its very distinctive coiled braids, an element of erotic seduction. In the ritual domain, the Two Weepers, Isis and Neph-

Figure 1.43: Isis and Nephthys, activating the sign of magical protection in favor of Osiris. They are the Two Divine Weepers and, here, primarily the Two Women of the Braids. Their hair is gathered and held back at the neck with a ribbon, forming the *khaït* hairstyle. Evidence for the erotic connotation of this hairstyle can be found in writings as well as in figurative art. The goddesses are wearing the hieroglyphs of their respective names on their heads: Nephthys on the left, Isis on the right.

thys, who magically call Osiris back to life, are the Two Women of the Braids (fig. 1.43), and their words leave no doubt about their role:

> *Great God, take back your appearance!*
> *Do not withdraw from your place, Osiris!*
> *Come in peace, would you, toward your place, master of terror,*
> *pleasing in his form, the great bull, master of pleasure!*
> *Lie down with your sister Isis,*
> *And chase the sorrows from her body,*
> *So that she may embrace you, and you can not withdraw from her (. . .)*
> *Great God who provokes an abundance of love (. . .)*
> *Powerful male, the chief of perfection.*[17]

Figure 1.44: The genie Bes striking a dance rhythm on his tambour. Half man and half monkey, his capers accompany the divine mistress of the dance and contribute to enlivening life in the gynaeceum.

Other titles refer to the goddess's activities: Lady of Joy, Lady of Music, and Lady of Dance. When bearing these titles she is escorted by Bes, the deity of musicians (fig. 1.44), and also by young women playing lyres, flutes, harps, and drums (fig. 1.45), who perform surrounded by female dancers. A similar scene takes place during the funeral banquet. The divine Lady of Drunkenness presides over the ceremony, in which nothing is ever eaten, but the guests drink copious amounts in her honor and that of the *ka* of the

Figure 1.45: There should be no lack of female musicians in the joyous parade that accompanies the return of the Distant One. A lutist and tambourine player are here seen in ritual nudity, accented by the jewels that also adorn their abundant tresses. The mandrake bush, fruit of love, completes the erotic atmosphere.

deceased, in order to stimulate their generative powers. Hathor thereby forms a mystic couple with the departed, and the guests at the banquet are their ardent "supporters."

In Ancient Egypt, music always accompanied worship of the gods but seems to have had particular importance in the worship of Hathor. A particularly heartfelt example of this was provided by Intef II, no doubt a music lover, who felt the need to institute a musical celebration for "all days," a veritable sonorous offering in Hathor's honor. Addressing the Great Ones of the West who delighted in Hathor's beauty, he swore the oath that follows.

I wish to make known her nature,
I wish to speak by her side
That I am overjoyed by the sight of her,

Figure 1.46: Hathor, the divine cow, emerging from the western Theban mountain where the tombs (one of which is depicted here) of the great necropoli have been dug. This image is charged with symbolism: Hathor is grasping the solar disk with her horns, which is surmounted by two ostrich feathers, evocation of the vital breath. The papyrus thicket, concealing the mountainous desert, evokes prenatal existence, comparable to the swamps of legend. Finally, the *wedjat* eye is an allusion to the cure of the "sick one," the deceased, and the reconstitution of his body with a view to his rebirth, of which the goddess assures him by the intermediary of the *menat,* gestation in the universal matrix.

My two hands say to her: "Come to me, come to me!"
While my body says,
And my lips repeat:
"A pure music for Hathor,
Music a hundred million times!"
Because you love music
A million times music for your Ka wherever you dwell.
For it is I who will look after the adoration and the music of
Hathor each day,
At every hour she loves (. . .)
You may count upon me for that, each day.[18]

This is how Pharaoh prepared for himself a "Happy West" in the company of the Lady of Life, another title for Hathor who not only ruled love, but also death and renewal, or rebirth, for she is the cosmic mother of humanity. All the deceased are her future children, who Hathor in her guise of the divine cow (fig. 1.46) has introduced into the universal fold, the earth, where transformations take place under the aegis of Osiris (fig. 1.47). This aspect of her activity makes Hathor comparable to the maternal Isis under the name of Isis-Hathor.

The mystical son of Hathor is the young Ihy, assimilated to Osiris in transformation. Ihy is nude and his skin is black (fig. 1.48), because the son of the god Tatenen stands on the threshold between darkness and light, between death-nothingness-gestation and solar birth, which he summons with all his strength by brandishing the sparkling naos sistrum, evocation of the birth canal, decorated with the image of his mother. But as Isis-Hathor she is also the sister and lover of Ihy-Osiris, as is indicated by the text of an Osirian ceremony in which Isis and Nephthys call Ihy-Osiris so that he may join physically with them.

O perfect Ihy, come toward your domain!
So that the Two Sisters may join with your body, even when there
is no longer any activity within you (. . .)
The child, the premature young man,
May you travel the heavens and earth in your earlier appearance,
As you are the bull of the Two Sisters.
Come, if you would, child who peacefully grows younger,
Our master, so that we may gaze upon you
And that you may join with us as a male.[19] *(See fig. 1.49)*

Figure 1.47: Queen Nefertari, the favorite "Great Royal Wife" of Ramses II, and her *ba* in adoration (b), after having been welcomed to the world of the gods by Hathor (a). Following death, the *ba* reveals itself by virtue of the funeral rituals, and this "soul" accompanies the deceased into the beyond, where it will face various tests and encounter deities. (Tomb of Nefertari, Valley of the Queens.)

Plate 1: Painted limestone bas-relief from a pillar of the tomb of Seti I showing the goddess Hathor bestowing the renewal of life upon Seti I with her *menat*. Their affectionately entwined hands and the pearl necklace, which the king touches delicately, are gestures of the code of love. The *menat* is a refined and symbolic edition of the prehistoric crude wooden female idols, deprived of legs and having only short stumps instead of the arms, but always showing very large hips and voluminous breasts. These idols became the counterpoise of the *menat*. The lush head of hair of the idols was suggested by many strings of pearls, which developed into the so-called necklace. The whole idols themselves became the graceful "concubines of the dead." We might therefore consider that Hathor presenting her *menat* to the king, plays the role, on a sublimated level, of the "concubine of the dead," so that he can recreate himself for a new life. New Kingdom, 19th Dynasty. Louvre Museum, Paris. (see fig. 1.54, p. 46)

Plate 2. This scene is from a funerary papyrus that belonged to the lady Her-uben as part of her "passport" to the beyond. It shows the great god Osiris awakening by his own creative power on his mound in the netherworld. The Osirian mound is firmly anchored by the abyssal serpent. While such a suggestive male image may appear surprising in this instance (as the deceased is a woman) after funerary rites every deceased individual became an Osiris with the same possibilities for rebirth in the afterlife. New Kingdom. Egyptian Museum, Cairo.

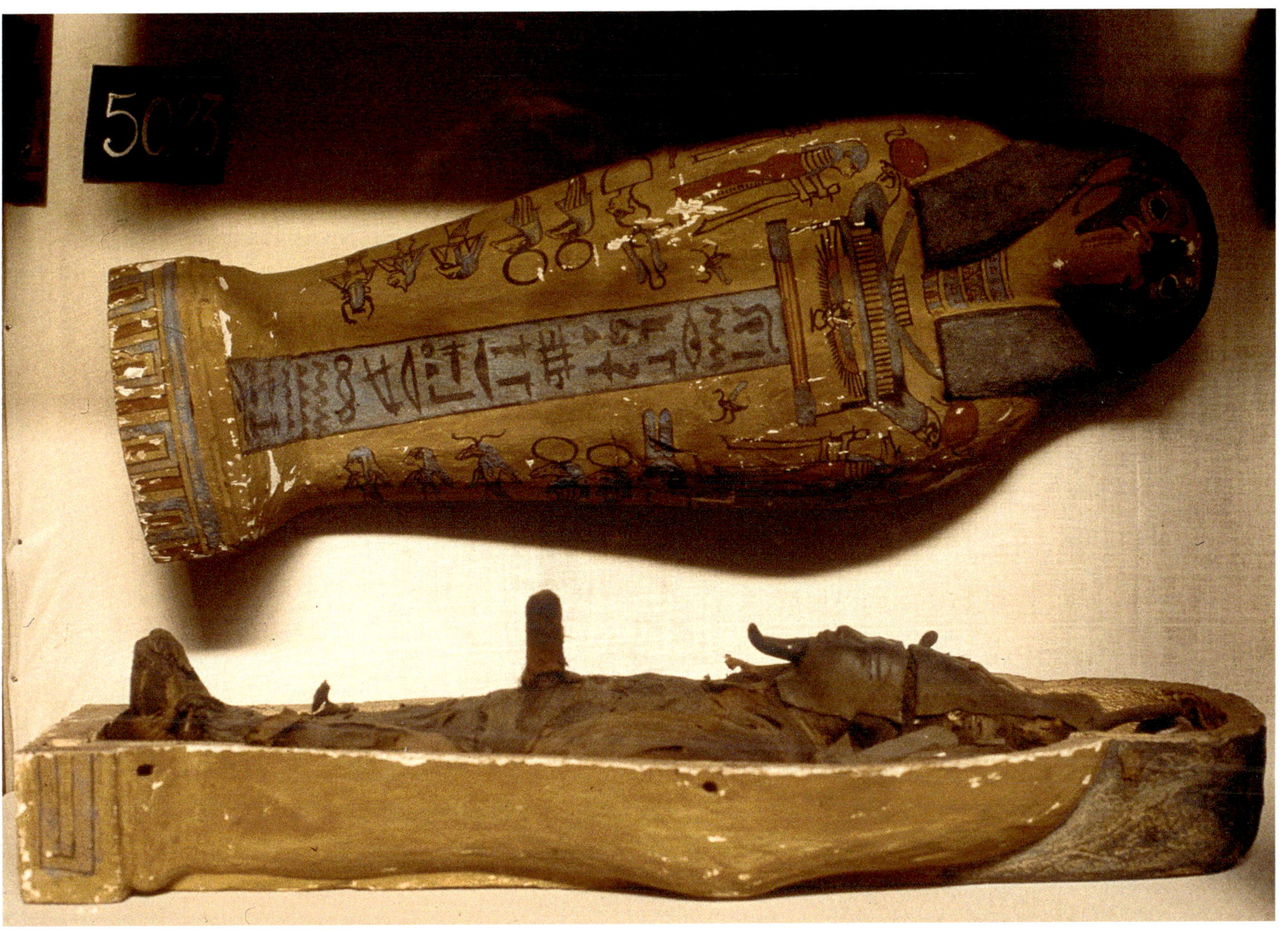

Plate 3. Small ritual sarcophagus made of stucco and painted wood, probably a funerary offering, deposited in a tomb. The coffin has the shape of a mummified falcon, representing the god Sokaris-Osiris. On the lid, a blue central column, evoking the *djed*-pillar, is inscribed with the god's name and titles. The capital is topped with the image of the Sokaris barque, flanked by two of the four sons of Horus: Imset on the left and Hapy on the right of the onlooker. All four of the sons of Horus are represented, among other deities such as Khepri and Atum, placed two by two alongside the column. The base of the coffin completes the bodily appearance of the falcon mummy. It contains an ithyphallic figure of Osiris awakening to a new, creative life. Late period. Egyptian Museum, Cairo.

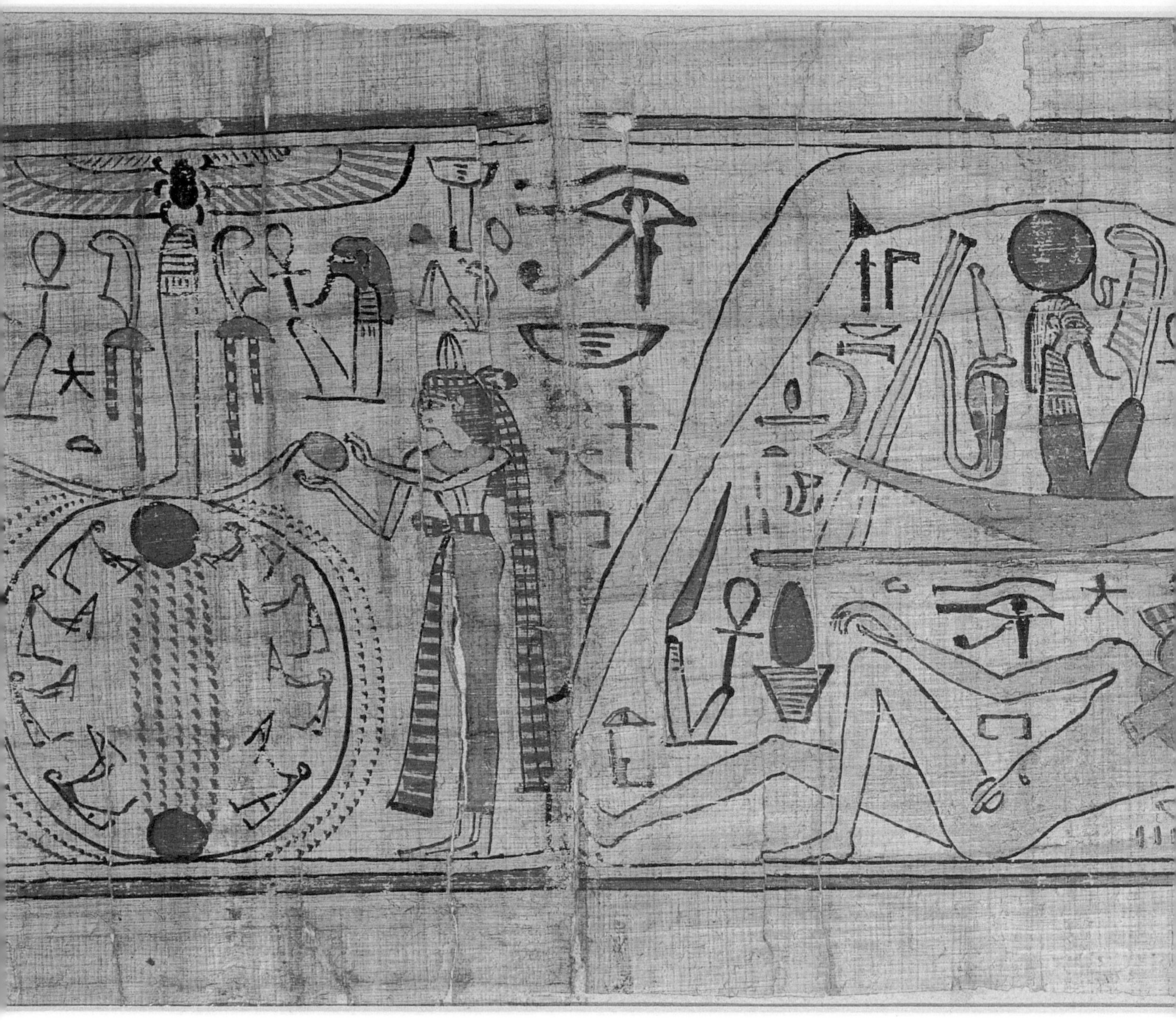

Plate 4. Mythological papyrus of the lady Nespakashuty showing the allegory of the cosmos. In the center, the famous separation of Nut, the sky goddess, from her husband Geb, god of the Earth, by their common father Shu who is seated in his barge. On the right, Shu is facing the "lake of flames" guarded by four baboons, the permanent adorers of the sun. In chapter 126 of *The Book of the Dead* they help the deceased to purify his mind and accede to a cosmic state. The image on the left is an allegory of the universal (be)coming of life. 21st Dynasty. Louvre Museum, Paris (see also figs. 1.13, 1.14).

Plate 5. Painted wood statue of a dancing Bes. The genie hits a tambourine to the rhythm of his joyous leaps. The accelerated beat is gradually leading to a state of modified consciousness, suggested by the presence of the intoxicating lotus flower. New Kingdom. British Museum, London.

Plate 6. The naos-shaped sistrum sekhem primary held by Ihy, the "musician," who rattles symbolically this instrument to call Hathor, his mother, to help him out of the darkness to life and light. The curved sistrum, *sesheshet,* is a sonorous ritual instrument. Its sound recalls the rustling of the papyrus thicket where Isis raised her son Horus. Both instruments are linked to the notion of birth, but the *sesheshet* experienced wide use throughout the Roman Empire. The sistrum shown here is purely votive and inscribed with the name of a ptolemaic king. Egyptian Museum, Cairo.

Plate 7. Image from the Tomb of Thutmes IV of the goddess Hathor maternally touching the deceased king's shoulders and extending the life-giving *ankh* to the nostrils of Thutmes IV. He is identified by the cartouches containing his birth- and throne-name. New Kingdom, 18th Dynasty. Valley of the Kings, Thebes-West.

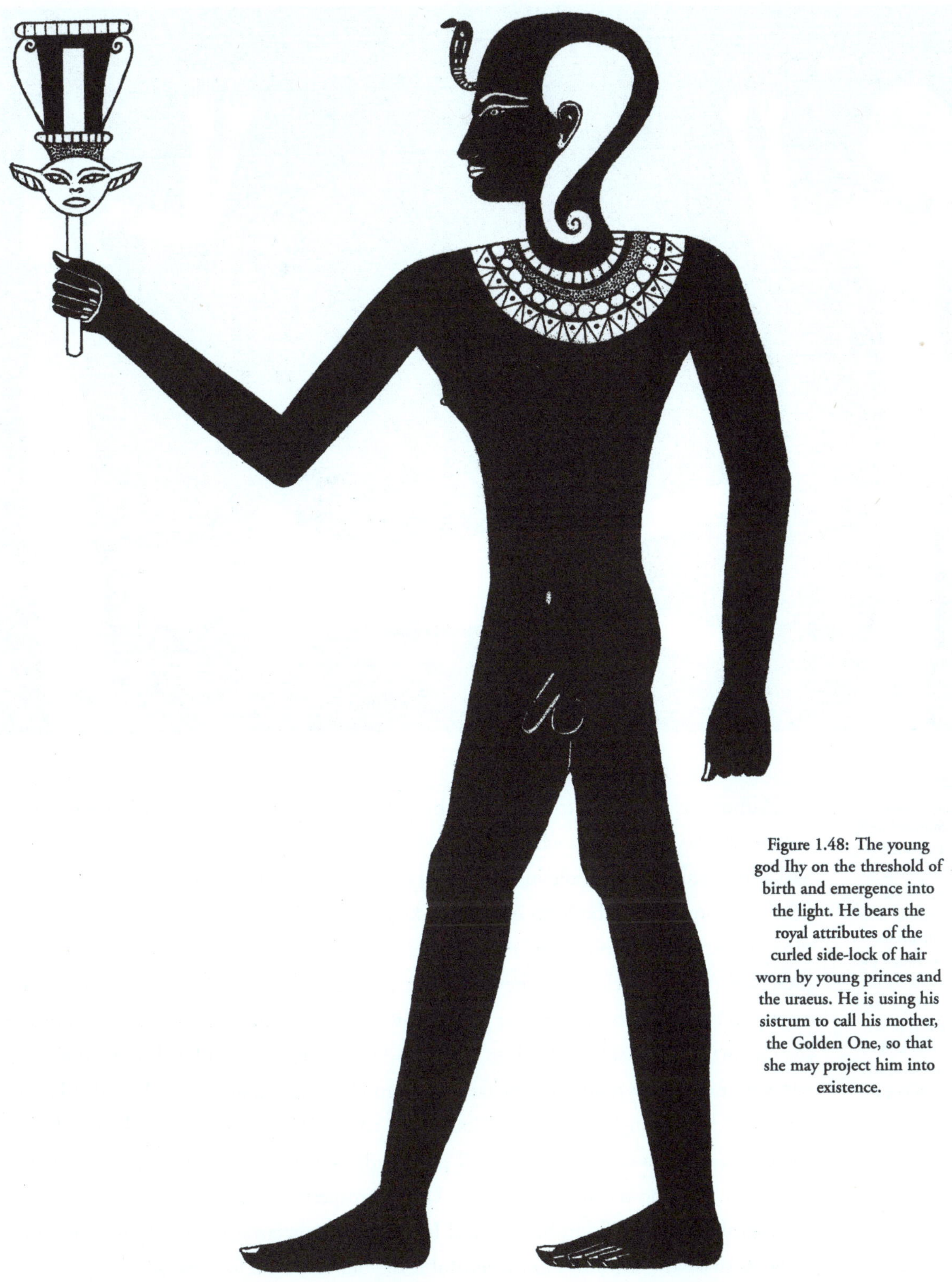

Figure 1.48: The young god Ihy on the threshold of birth and emergence into the light. He bears the royal attributes of the curled side-lock of hair worn by young princes and the uraeus. He is using his sistrum to call his mother, the Golden One, so that she may project him into existence.

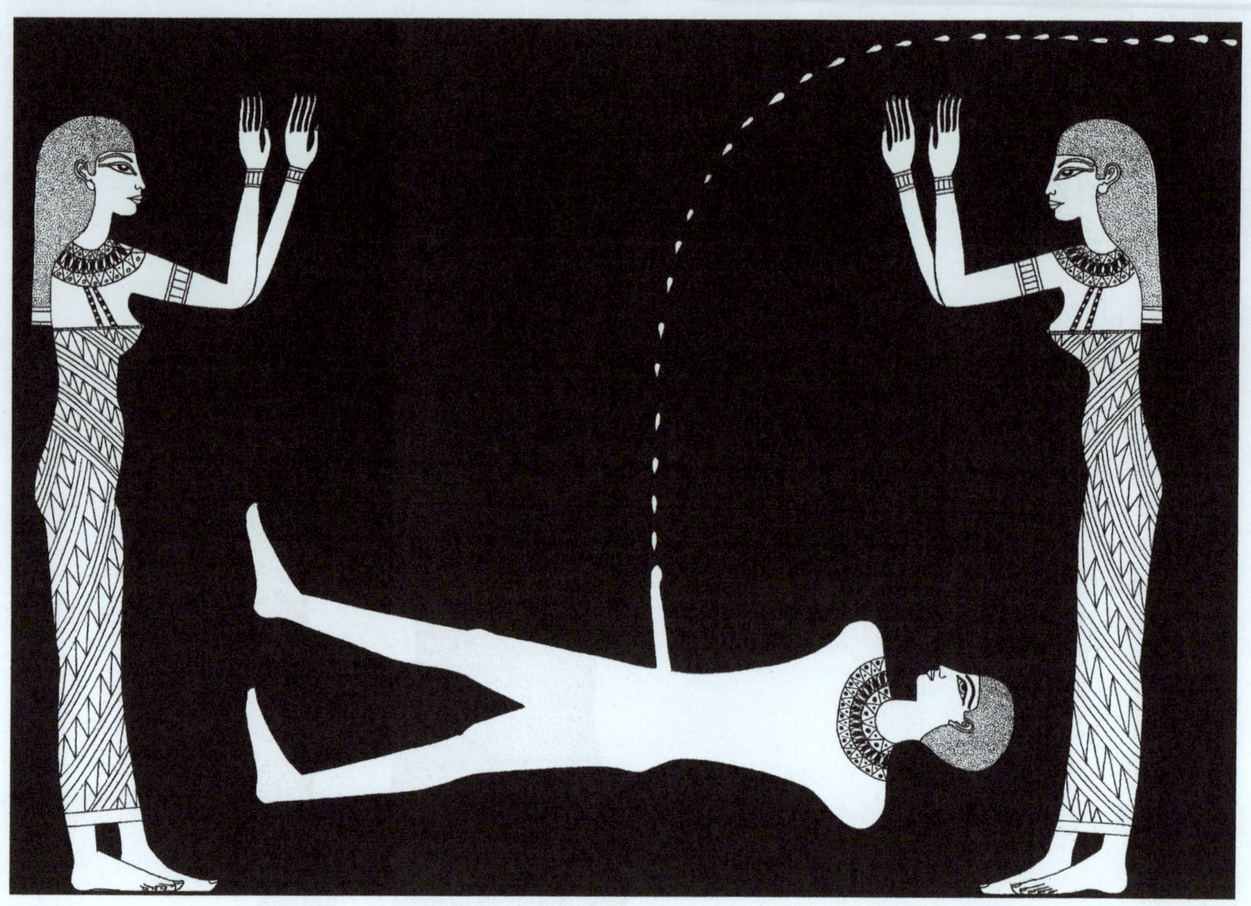

Figure 1.49: Isis and Nephthys, forever loyally joined and devoted to Osiris, are greeting the stream of divine semen in a pose of adoration. The image confirms the interaction between the two sisters and Osiris, between the indispensable feminine element that triggers creation and the active response of its masculine counterpart.

Hathor was presumed to have given birth to the king, the solar child. From this perspective the Seven Hathors, who happen to be in their human form and without their bull, and also because of their role in the funerary cult, became the seven benevolent fairies of fate.[20] The mystery of the birth of the god-king was the object of a secret worship taking place in the houses of birth, the *mammisi,* of the temples. These monuments are the best preserved on the precincts of the Ptolemaic temples, whose architectural elements and inscriptions are equally informative about Hathor's role at this later date. The columns of the sanctuaries dedicated to Hathor, or the goddesses, are crowned by almost cubic capitals, whose four sides reproduce the face of the goddess, coiffed in her emblem, the sistrum (fig. 1.50). Accordingly, we can read carved on the walls of the temple of the goddess in Dendara a formula of royal offering: "I present the sistrum to soothe you, luminous Bat (fig. 1.51), more powerful than the gods, Uto of prosperity, who makes Egypt green, rapid in magical action, skillful in her charms! It is Useret, protectress of her Horus, for whom the gods shake the sistrum. How beautiful it is, your face with four faces!"[21]

Figure 1.50: The capitals of the temples consecrated to Hathor or other goddesses are generally, during the later era, decorated with four faces of the goddess, often surmounted with the image of the naos-shaped sistrum (in this drawing, the faces are suggested according to the principle of two-demensional Egyptian perspective, making it so that the fourth face cannot be depicted). This evocation of Hathor quadrifrons is symbolic of the universality of the goddess who governed the four cardinal directions of the world.

Figure 1.51: Hathor, as a seductive young woman, brandishes the naos-shaped sistrum, which recalls the ancient idol Bat, emblem of the seventh nome of Upper Egypt. This idol has been confused with Hathor from the greatest antiquity (see figs. 2.1 and 2.4) and seems to have been connected to protection of the king. Here the goddess is also holding the *menat,* her other principal attribute.

The festivals in honor of Hathor took place throughout the entire year. The most important were "the Good Reunion," the mystic betrothals of Hathor of Dendara with Horus of Edfu; the rite of "touching the Aten" at New Year's, intended to recharge the *ba* of the goddess with solar energy, her initial essence; and the "Feast of Drunkenness" and the "Renewal of Drunkenness": [. . .] Hathor [. . .] Uto [. . .] Lady of Drunkenness who repeats drunkenness, beautiful sovereign of the four faces."[22] In the temple of Horus at Edfu there is a text echoing the one found in

Dendara: "I offer you drunkenness, Gold, Lady of Drunkenness, I soothe your *ka* by offering it 'the green eye of Horus' [. . .] rejoice in these four faces, which *Ra* loves to look upon."[23] Still in Edfu, Hathor unveiled her dangerous aspect, for she is compared there to the Memphis lioness Sekhmet: "O! Sekhmet, Lady of Misfortune by the evil she has brought, when you turn your face toward the south, north, east, west, it brings terror [. . .]."[24] The four cardinal directions allude to the four faces of Hathor, which symbolize the universal power of the goddess. Finally, the attributive title "She who coils on the head of her father,"[25] compares Hathor to the uraeus that adorns the brow of the demiurge—and the king. The uraeus is the protective serpent goddess as well as symbol of fecundity, plenitude, and aggressiveness in every domain, an aggressiveness that must be soothed.

Hathor can also be likened to the sky goddess, Nut, and appears in that celestial guise when fulfilling this role (see fig.1.32).

We have only listed here the principal possibilities of the incoporation of other goddesses into Hathor, but practically speaking there is no goddess who cannot be likened to Hathor, who is worshiped, under her different aspects, in virtually all the sanctuaries of Egypt, if only as "resident" or secondary deity. She is, of course, the center of worship at her main temple in Dendara.

The sacred objects of the goddess are symbolic of her activities. The most widespread were the two sistrums: the naos-shaped sistrum, *sekhem* (fig. 1.52), primarily held by Ihy (whose name means "musician"), and the curved sistrum, *sesheshet* (fig. 1.53), the sonorous ritual instrument that later experienced wide use throughout the entire Roman Empire. It was shaken by the priestesses and musicians connected to her cult and often used at the same time as another sacred object of Hathor's, the *menat* (fig. 1.54, 1.55, 1.56, 1.57). Both attribute and jewel, the *menat* represents in a very stylized manner the erotic attractions of the female: long hair, breasts, and sex; its name brings to mind the wet nurse. Following this same line of thought the bowl of milk was consecrated to the Lady of Life, as well as the *menu* jug, recalling sacred intoxication.

The mysteries, in the sense of religious performances or initiatory rituals, took place in her sanctuaries. We have precious little information about these rituals. Herodotus and Diodorus Siculus have only left descriptions of the popular celebration in honor of Hathor-Tefnut at the time of the annual flooding of the Nile. These celebrations prefigured the bacchanals, to which the ancient authors incidentally compared them, while explicitly stating that the women were the most unbridled participants of this joyful voyage over the immense lake that Egypt had momentarily become. When the boats, containing both men and women, sailed by a town, they would draw close to the shores and challenge the inhabitants in fairly rude terms, the women exposing their nudity. During

Figure 1.52: The naos-shaped sistrum, *sekhem* (also see fig. 1.51), depicting the narrow gate through which the child must pass in order to be born, is an image of the birth canal. *Sekhem* is also the name of the scepter used to consecrate offerings; it is the "powerful one," implying transformation and the liberation of vital substances.

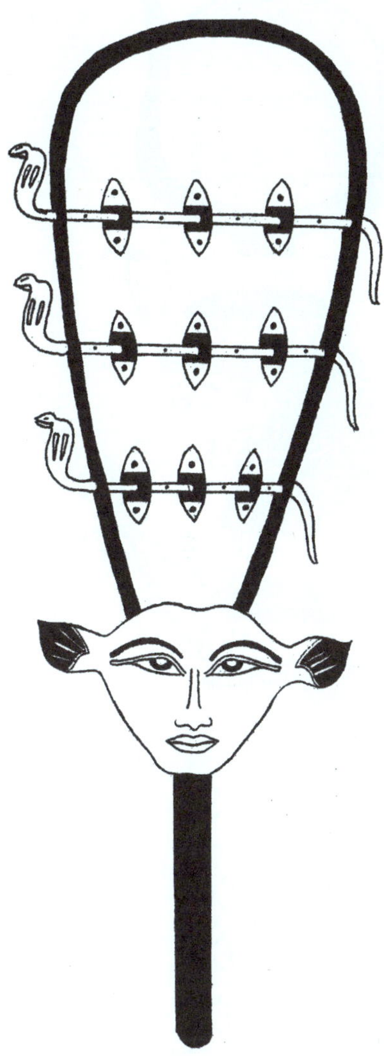

Figure 1.53: The curved sistrum, or *sesheshet,* which was an actual musical instrument, comparable to the rattle. Small metal plates were threaded on the rods that gave off a rustling and tinkling that must have sounded like the wind blowing through a thicket of papyrus.

the processions in honor of her return from far away (Hathor-Bastet), the women promenaded through the streets shaking enormous imitation penises. Wine and beer flowed freely during these festivals that lasted several days (fig. 1.58)!

The goddess of countless shapes, attributes, and activities is truly universal. She radiates

Figure 1.54: Hathor transmitting vital energy to the king by presenting him with the *menat,* symbol of the female element necessary to his rebirth. This is how she proves her love to the deceased king, who is mysteriously joined to the goddess by the touch of the *menat* and their interlaced hands (see fig. 4.14 for more on these gestures). (From a relief in the tomb of Seti I, Nineteenth Dynasty, Louvre Museum, Paris.)

Figure 1.55: Synthesized image from the late Ptolemaic Period (first century B.C., temple of Dendara) illustrating the complementary relationship between the *sekhem* sistrum and the *menat.* The strip of pearls of the *menat* is replaced by the *usekh* necklace, used here as the hieroglyph for "gold"—one of the attributive titles for Hathor. It is joined to the counterweight by four *sekhem* sistrums, attached by pearls and treated like amulets. The necks of the sistrums are unusually long and set up like columns; are they meant to recall the traditional supports of heaven or the two horizons? The barque of the sun seems to be sailing between two of these sistrums. The *menat,* identified with the Golden One, is thereby symbolically diffusing solar energy into the universe and putting the divine forces into operation.

Figure 1.56: Hathor, lady of the *menat,* is commingled here with her magical attribute, whose inscription states that she is the "mistress of heaven, lady of all the gods." It is necessary to understand that she is the female element that puts into motion the intrinsic forces of all manifestations of the divine. The goddess is lying upon a small edifice shaped like a naos, which in this context is her house, whether *mammisi* or tomb—for birth and rebirth can be prepared for in one as readily as in the other.

Figure 1.57: The mystery of rebirth is insistently expressed on a relief in the goddess's temple in Dendara in which she is also depicted in her *menat* form lying on the *mammisi.* In order for the ritual to achieve its goal—the birth of the royal and divine child—Hathor holds an *ankh,* symbol of life, in each hand, and her son Ihy has already taken position (we are outside space and time here) on his mother's forearm. This magical icon is preceeded by a depiction of Hathor as sovereign of Egypt, coiffed in the *pschent* flanked by the Osirian feather and seated upon the archaic throne of the divine ancestors who once ruled over the Two Lands. She is wearing a dress adorned with feathers, no doubt from the falcon—does her name not mean "dwelling of Horus"? In one hand she is holding a *sekhem* sistrum and with the other she is holding up an enormous *menat* necklace in the direction of Ihy, who has not yet emerged from the shadows. A prophylactic frieze of the signs of life and power runs along the throne's pedestal. The two scenes are accompanied by inscriptions listing the principal titles of Hathor. The ancient texts also designated the Temple of Dendara under the name of *h(u)t-menat,* "dwelling of the *menat,*" which is to say, Hathor.

Figure 1.58 (left): Bastet, the divine cat, is none other than Hathor in her tame form, the Distant One upon her return to Egypt from far away. She is holding the ritual sistrum of the worship devoted to her in Bubastis, located in the Nile delta, which was richly studded with papyrus thickets whose rustling was evoked by this instrument. In her other hand she is holding the lion-headed aegis, reminiscent of the goddess's origins. Would her housewife's shopping basket be intended to hold the numerous fruits of the flood, which has become as slack and serene as Tefnut, once she became a cat?

Figure 1.59: The Egyptian word for phoenix is *bennu.* This wonderful bird is often depicted in the tombs, painted in a delicate ashen blue that fits the legend perfectly. In the legend the bird is reborn from its ashes every five hundred, or even ten thousand, years, depending on which version you read. It was one of the ways used by the Ancients to express the duration of cosmic cycles.

the fire of Creation, whose power sweeps aside any and all obstacles. As Maat she watches over the cosmic order, as Hathor she maintains the engine of the world, with both violence and tenderness, surrounding gods and men, and infuses the living with her heat as well as those her flame has left so they might be reborn, like the phoenix, to live a new cycle (fig. 1.59).

CHAPTER TWO

The Sexuality of the Human World

THE SOCIO-LEGAL FRAMEWORK

Customs and Laws

Customs, laws, the familial and hierarchical structures of a society, as well as its moral literature, all combine to form the framework that conditions the evolution of individual erotic behavior.

The amorous relations between the sexes, before or outside of marriage, were possible and even tolerated to a certain extent, on the condition that those concerned were free and conducted themselves discreetly. This is not enough reason to conclude that these kinds of relations were the rule; the full weight of custom weighed upon the two partners, but there was no law imposing restrictions upon them. Nevertheless, they had to resort to subterfuges to maintain appearances—a widespread tactic throughout the world both yesterday and today. The love literature makes reference to these clandestine encounters, often arranged with the aid of servants—the lovers' secret thereby being a fairly relative one. They could only act within the limits established by familial and public tolerance, varying according to the spirit of the times and social classes. An incontestable promiscuity reigned at the bottom of the social ladder, and the higher the class the two partners belonged to, the stricter the criteria for behavior of both sexes. It is obvious, however, that men enjoyed a much greater freedom than women; in the domain of sexuality there was no equality between men and women. A bachelor could keep a mistress in his home, but it was viewed poorly, and public opinion was (and still is) a powerful restraint. It was not imaginable for a member of a respectable family to follow divine example and behave like Seth or the ram-god Khnum, "the Handsome Copulater." And it was totally out of the question for a young girl to mimic the goddess Anat or keep a lover in her home.

Marriage

We shall see that marriage was a private matter between families and had no legal structure, properly speaking. Contracts only appeared at a much later date and then only concerned the material modalities of the union. The essential was governed by custom: the request for marriage, the consent of the families concerned, the establishment of the young couple's household, and so forth.

The God King and the Great Royal Wife: Theogamy

In pharaonic society starting from the time of the Old Kingdom there was a direct link—one could say a fusion—between the divine world and the king who was a ceaselessly reincarnating god, with all the consequences resulting from this status. The king held absolute power, but by this token all responsibility for his country devolved on him as well. From the earliest periods of Egyptian history the sovereign enjoyed the protection of Hathor. The famous palette of King Narmer, a ritual object, is decorated on each side with two heads of the goddess. She dominates the warlike scenes portrayed thereon, in which the king is wearing the crown of Upper Egypt on one side, and the crown of Lower Egypt on the other. It does not fall within the framework of this study to examine the reasons for this quadruple depiction—which is quite archaic—of the divine face. Nevertheless, it may be suggested that the two pairs could correspond to the fundamental duality without which nothing would exist, symbolized by, among other things, the duality of Egypt, the "Two Lands," and the two crowns. The number 4 traditionally evokes the four elements and the four cardinal directions, all universal symbols claimed by the goddess.[1] On this palette, the divine cow's head is shown four times on the royal loincloth. So it appears that even at this time the generative organs of the pharaoh were protected by Hathorian magic (fig. 2.1). Is the sovereign wearing a phallic sheath (fig. 2.2) beneath his loincloth, like the *karnatas* that were widespread throughout the first Middle Eastern civilizations? The central flap of the ritual *shendjit*, an archaic remnant (fig. 2.3), could be a reminder of it.[2]

Figure 2.1: The skirt of King Narmer, decorated with a quadruple representation of the idol Bat, deity and symbol of the seventh nome of Upper Egypt, who was soon absorbed by Hathor, for whom Bat is an archaic form. Her quadruple representation attests that the concept of universality was connected to the goddess, Ra's daughter, even at this very remote period. This representation endured up to the Greco-Roman era as shown by the capitals of the temples to female deities. The image of the goddess of love seems to confer some sort of magical protection to the king's generative center.

The very stylized evocation of the Hathorian head on a vase dating approximately from the same period betrays her celestial origin (fig. 2.4). Her composite appearance as a bovine-headed woman (fig. 2.5) is a transitional form toward the entirely gynomorphic Hathor.

Seen from this angle we can better grasp why the king offers Maat during divine worship. Maat is another emanantion of the Sun, symbol of balance and the cosmic plan, of which he is the guardian on earth. The "heretical" pharaoh, Amenhotep IV (Akhenaten), expressed this interaction even more forcefully. He had himself represented as stamped with the seal of Aten, the ancient solar demiurge who he made the one god, and, in the company of his wife and often their daughters, celebrated his worship by raising the cartouches of the divine name toward the creator, the Sun that gives life to the sovereigns. The prerogative of the gods to give life to the sovereign is symbolized by

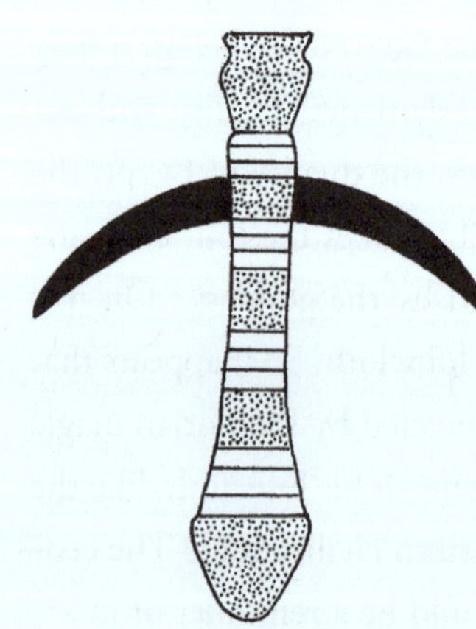

Figure 2.2: A phallic sheath, as depicted in the tomb of a high official of the Middle Kingdom. It may have been made of leather and possibly attached at the waist by a ribbon or belt that was inserted through lateral slots.

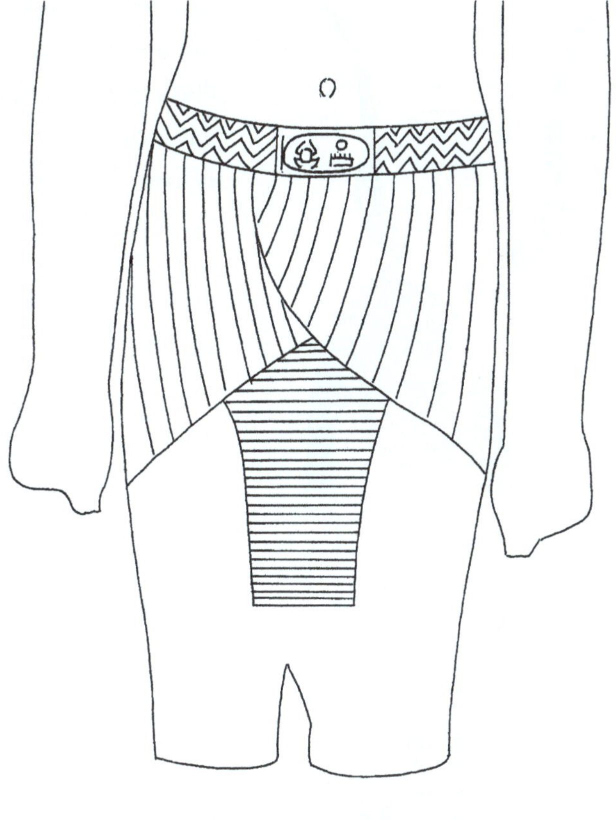

Figure 2.3: The ritual skirt of Tuthmosis III, depicted on one of his statues (Cairo Museum). The clothes of a king, during the Eighteenth Dynasty, were more sumptuous than this simple skirt, which remained intentionally archaic, as did everything connected to worship. The central flap between the two panels crossing over it could conceal a phallic sheath, or serve to conceal the sex organs.

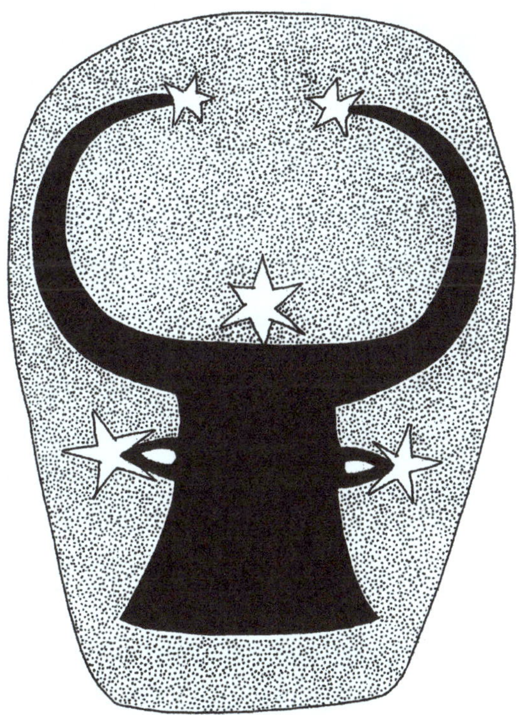

Figure 2.4: The idol Bat, prototype of the Hathorian image, surrounded by stars. It is an early depiction of the celestial goddess in her bovine aspect. Sirius-Sothis, the Dog Star, is another form of Isis-Hathor who appears in the famous zodiac of Dendara as a cow lying in the solar barque with an immense star between her horns. In addition, in the constellation of Taurus, the animal's head is suggested by three stars arranged in a triangle as seen from the earth. One of these, Aldebaran, is also called the "bull's eye." Let's note that the period known as the Age of Taurus in astrology covers part of Egyptian prehistory and the Old Kingdom.

Figure 2.5: Hathor, here a woman with a cow's head dressed in the magnificent tripartite wig of the deities. The solar disk appears between her horns, the floral scepter and ankh are in her hands, but she does not display her two typical attributes of the sistrum and the *menat*, which, as a rule, are not usually missing from her entirely human image.

the *ankh,* extended by solar rays to the royal nostrils. The "heretic" illustrated his reform with astonishing images, in the center of which figures the royal couple, receiving the life of Aten and transmitting it throughout the land through the vibrations of their quasi-divine sexuality (fig. 2.6).

We are far from the hieratic depictions of a strict chastity that present the nuptial bond of the demiurge (in this instance, the god Amun) and the queen, merely suggesting the divine conception of the heir to the throne (fig. 2.7). If it is necessary to decode this image, in which only the affectionate gesture of the arms and the interlaced legs of the couple evoke carnal union; the text of the theogamy, on the other hand, is unequivocally clear. Here are the essential passages. Thoth is leading Amun who has taken on the appearance of Tuthmosis I into the company of the queen Ahmose, wife of this pharaoh. "He found her sleeping within the intimacy of her palace. The aroma of the god awakened her; she smiled at the sight of his majesty. He immediately went to her. He lusted for her, and his desire carried him to her. He allowed her to see him as a god [. . .] and she rejoiced in gazing upon his perfection. His desire coursed throughout his body, while the palace was flooded with the perfume of the god, all his scents were those of Punt. The god's majesty did all he could wish to this subject.

Figure 2.6: Amenhotep IV (Akhenaten) and Nefertiti in their chariot beneath the Aten, which gives them life through the ankh symbol placed by their nostrils, drawing near each other in a transcendent kiss. The couple was no doubt clad in diaphanous robes, which makes these two individuals appear to be naked. In any event, this is a ritual composition that was not intended for public viewing. Nevertheless, it maintains a sense of humor: the little princess is teasing the horses with a pointed wand. This detail aside, the scene seems to prefigure the solar chariot of Apollo. (From the tomb of Ahmose, el-Amarna.)

She allowed him to take his pleasure of her. She kissed him [. . .]." Then the queen told the god Amun: "How potent your power is, my master! It is most gratifying to gaze upon your face, after you have joined my majesty to your luminosity, your dew runs over my entire body." After which, the majesty of this god "did all he could wish" with her. At the end of their encounter, Amun announced to the queen that "the daughter he had put into her belly" would be pharaoh and rule over Egypt. In spite of its religious content and its simultaneously poetic and straightforward form, this text is obviously of a political nature.[3] Its intention is to legitimize the ascension of Queen Hatshepsut to the throne. Legally, the daughters born of the king and the queen, the Great Royal Wife (which indicates there were other wives), could attain the throne, and several princesses, one of which was the great Hatsepshut, did indeed become pharaohs.[4]

Monogamy and Polygamy

The sexual inequality of the partners comes out in marriage, whether it be a marriage of royalty or of commoners. While monogamy was the rule, it did not automatically rule out polygamy, which was even institutionalized within the royal household for political motives,

Figure 2.7: Theogamy scene. The god Amun joining with Queen Ahmose, mother of Hatshepsut. Their marriage takes place within the celestial spheres, suggested by the starry hieroglyph of the sky that serves the couple as a nuptial bed, supported by the goddesses Selket and Neith. The carnal act is very modestly suggested according to a definite gestural code: their interlaced legs, the affectionate gestures of the arms and hands, and the presentation by the god of the life symbol to the queen's face. The *tet,* or knot of Isis, which hangs from the middle of Amun's belt and covers, on top of his apron, his sexual organ, belongs to the figurative code (see figs. 1.20 and 1.26) as an allusion to the androgynous creative power of divine entities. (Relief in Hatshepsut's temple, Deir el-Behari.)

though relatively rare among the upper nobility. On the other hand, up to the present time not a single trace of institutional polyandry has been found as a counterpart of polygamy, but the reality, especially among the lower orders, may have been something else entirely.[5]

The Royal Harem

The king maintained a large harem consisting of both noble and non-noble women. Did not the Asian king Tushratta send 270 women to Amenhotep III? (Let's not overlook the title introducing the first name of royal protocol: "Powerful Bull," underlining the sovereign's sexual role.) Among others, this same king wed a Mitannian princess, Gilukhepa, whose retinue included 317 beauties—and that's not all.[6] The number of residents in this impressive economical and social complex, placed under the queen's authority, could go as high as several hundred, at least, if not several thousand, because different harems were scattered throughout the country. All of these women (or almost all) had progeny, who were royal in theory. But given the fact that among the large male personnel of the harem—who performed administrative and service roles—there were no eunuchs and that there were limits to the generative ardor of the Son of the Sun (over whom the queen and royal wives kept watch), reservations are permissible as to the royal legitimacy of all these descendents. Furthermore, the children the king could have from his secondary wives were legally in the same position as the children of concubines in Egyptian society: they were excluded from the path of succession to the throne. The impressive number of children—both boys and girls—recognized by Ramses II, proves that this king had simultaneously and successively several great royal wives, in addition to his royal wives, not to mention concubines.[7] There was ferocious intrigue among the harem women to find the best possible positions for their respective offshoots. Several pharaohs had bitter experiences with harem conspiracy. It cost at least two of them—Pepi I and Amenemhet I—their lives. Ramses III seems to have escaped a similar plot.[8] While love could bind the king to his queen and perhaps also, on an ad hoc basis, to a very limited number of his secondary wives, in the case of the king's visits to his harem it was no doubt only a question of erotic satisfaction, whose ritual nature, during certain festivals, cannot be excluded (see chapter 4).

Fidelity and Adultery

The primary goal of marriage was, as it is today, to create a legitimate lineage. Consequently the woman was more tied down to conjugal faithfulness than the man, who could entertain sexual relations with his domestic staff without it being considered adulterous. But the children born of a concubine, servant, or slave were illegitimate and excluded from the succession: the situation was clear-cut. In contrast, the adulterous child of a wife posed a real judicial dilemma, because the child was officially considered to be the offspring of the husband, who had to prove the contrary, not an easy task at that time. In general—judging by the documents that have survived from the New Kingdom, but especially the Late Period—the woman could cleanse herself of all suspicion with a solemn oath that she had not committed adultery, which stopped any proceedings against her and could even, quite logically, earn her damages and interest, charged against the husband in payment for the wrong unjustly suffered by his wife.[9] It was an entirely different situation if the husband surprised the guilty parties or if he had witnesses of his wife's forbidden relationships. In this case, punishment was harsh, if we are to believe the Westcar Papyrus, which blends reality and magic.[10] In the case presented there, the deceived husband was a priest and magician. He trapped the lover with an enchanted crocodile and left the decision of the guilty ones' fate in the hands of the king. The sovereign condemned the lover to be handed over to the crocodile and the wife to be burned at the stake. Her ashes were then cast into the Nile. Two observations can be made from this story: on the one hand, the deceived husband must turn to a higher authority for punishment of the guilty and not render justice himself. There were exceptions to this custom such as that related in "The Story of the Two Brothers," in which the elder brother killed his faithless wife whereas the younger brother made his wife's fickleness the subject of judicial proceedings.[11] This text betrays an evolution in manners and custom. On the other hand, while the husband has almost total liberty within his own home, the same is not true if he "enters another house," as it is phrased in the old texts. Inciting a wife to commit adultery, and especially double adultery if the man himself was married, was a serious crime that could lay both partners open to punishment. The rediscovered records of a trial concerning the inhabitants of the village of Deir el-Medina where the artisans of the royal necropolis lived, are quite revelatory on this subject.[12] A husband, who surprised his wife in flagrante, dragged the lover before a judge. The lover was ordered to swear not to approach the woman in question again, on pain of having his ears and nose cut off (but not the *"corpus delicti,"* if we may be so bold to say so). Furthermore, he would be sentenced to exile in Nubia. Alas! The man in question went back on his sworn word (the woman was thus not punished) and had to again swear before the court never again—but really never!—to commit such an act. In the case of breaking his word, the punishment was stiffened; besides the mutilations he would be sentenced to forced labor in the granite quarries of Aswan.

According to Diodorus, the adulterous woman generally risked the mutilation of her nose and her lover the bastinado—which often caused irreparably broken bones.[13] Aside from the matter of the legal relationship, Egyptian society possessed a tolerant understanding of the amorous passions of the two sexes. Yet it was possible for a betrayed and deceived wife to accuse her husband in court of adultery committed with another married woman.

Rape

The rape of a woman—virgin, married, or widow—was severely punished. A fickle wife could escape all prosecution by declaring under oath that her seducer had raped her, with the hope that the court would not have the bad taste to order a fact-finding inquest.

Transmission of the Inheritance

Marriage set firm boundaries to the two partners' sexual activity and enjoyed the protection of the state, although it had been contracted by mutual agreement as a private matter, as we have already said, without recourse to any sort of legislation or religious benediction. The famous marriage contracts, which are known to date from the Twenty-second Dynasty and after, only specify the material conditions of the marital estate and the parties' ability to contract such a union—namely, the two partners had to be free and not slaves. Ethnic and social differences could constitute a check but not an obstacle. These contracts also regulated the obligations of the two partners, the rights of their children, the transmission of the patrimony and/or matrimony (both partners could leave wills), the conditions for divorce, and so on.

Divorce and Remarriage

Separation was possible and could be established unilaterally on demand of the man or the woman for various reasons: adultery, sterility (always presumed to be the woman's fault!), discord (sexual or otherwise), physical repulsion or aversion for a specific reason, desire to contract a marriage with another partner, and so forth. Generally, divorce prompted by the husband's demand (risk-free in the case of the woman's adultery) entailed heavy material obligations on his part, the prospect of which contributed in large part to the stability of the union. Trial marriages (which could be changed) or those of a predetermined duration also existed. It was possible for the couple to move into the husband's or the wife's family's home under specified terms, but generally the young couple set up their own home. In short, everything was governed by custom, the realistic and humane principles of which seem astonishingly modern to us.[14]

Incestuous Marriages and Intermarriages

Lovers and wedded couples often called each other "brother" and "sister," which brings to mind intermarriage, even incestuous marriage. While the divine model may have been followed by the royal family in this regard, the same was not the case with the general population. Marriage between close relatives has been confirmed, but these were arrangements generally contracted between first cousins, and also, but more rarely, between half brothers and half sisters. Finally, even among the lower orders, unions between brothers and sisters of the same parents must be presumed.[15] The Egyptians had an acute sense of family unity and a clearly endogamous bent that persists into our own time.

Incest between father and daughter—perhaps even between mother and son—must have existed, but the parties concerned were discreet and we have no documents on this subject at our disposal. On the other hand, marriage between brother and sister was frequent and official in the royal family during the time Egyptian civilization was at its peak—and not only in Egypt, but also in the royal households of the Middle East.[16] The most famous Egyptian example, confirmed by the couple in question themselves on a stele, is the marriage between King Ahmose, founder of the Eighteenth Dynasty, and his sister-wife, Ahmose-Nefertari—not to mention the Ptolemaic era, where family relations have turned into a veritable brainteaser for the historian. Obviously, in the absence of a male heir to the throne, a princess who was issue of the royal couple could either succeed her father or marry a half brother born of the king and one of his secondary wives, because the right to the throne was transmitted through the females of the line by virtue of the dogma of the theogamy. The same concept prompted sovereigns to marry one or more of their daughters, so as to pass on the divine spark with which they had been invested by their mother, who the demiurge had visited and known (in the biblical sense). These marriages between father and daughter have been alleged for Amenhotep II, Akhenaten, Ramses II, and Ramses III of the New Kingdom, but even half a millennium earlier, Amenemhet III wed his daughter, Neferuptah. Amenhotep III and Akhenaten each took their own daughters as brides, and the same was true for Ramses II and III. The reality of these marriages had long been contested by Egyptologists, but skeptics have necessarily been forced to bow to the evidence that Ramses II had at least one descendant from his marriage with his eldest daughter, Bintanath.[17] There is no doubt concerning the marriage of Akhenaten (husband of the beautiful and renowned Queen Nefertiti) with his first three daughters, Merytaten, Maketaten, and Ankhesenpaaten (the future queen of Tutankhamun). Each of these daughters gave their father and king a child; only in the case of the very young Maketaten did the event seem to turn to tragedy. The royal couple can be seen on an Amarnian tomb relief as parents grieving before the inanimate body of their daughter while a woman is carrying the newborn infant out of the room (fig. 2.8). The very unusual relations of the "heretic" king with his progeny are illustrated in striking fashion by a stele depicting the Amarnian family (fig.2.9).

For certain rulers the application of the dogma of divine royalty, with all its attendant consequences, facilitated the satisfaction of their unbridled sexual appetites and their obvious taste for a changing variety of sexual partners, already encouraged by numerous

Figure 2.8: The sorrow of the Amarnian royal couple before the lifeless body of one of their daughters, the little Maketaten, who had been married to her father. The scene suggests that the princess died giving birth to the child she had conceived with her father. The sorrow and mourning are also expressed in accordance with a traditional code. (From the royal tomb, el-Amarna.)

political marriages and constantly available harems, even during their military campaigns (note 6).

Added to this are even more refined erotic pleasures. We will only cite the famous rowers of Snefru as an illustration of this. The king was bored and ordered that the magician Djadja-em-ankh be sought out to amuse him. Once found, the magician advised the pharaoh to choose from his harem beautiful girls "whose belly had not yet been opened by childbirth, and to have them clothed in fishnets after their dresses had been removed" and that boats be readied for which they would be the rowers. His Majesty rejoiced in the sight of the supple and rhythmic movements of the beautiful rowers sailing over the palace lake. The story ends with a miracle performed by the magician, who separates the waters of the lake so that one of the rowers can recover her "brand-new turquoise amulet" that fell into the water.[18]

Love between Husband and Wife

The Egyptians were quite modest, though some of the illustrations in this book could make one presume the opposite. There are relatively few documents testifying to the love

Figure 2.9: This composition carved on a stele is often labeled as an image of affectionate family harmony. But on closer analysis, it can be seen that the way the king is holding his daughter and her gesture caressing her father's neck derive from the code of love. The princess sitting on her mother's knees seems to be drawing the queen's attention to a particular aspect of what she is looking at. The last princess, still very young, is innocently playing with her mother's earring, without taking any notice of what is going on around her. The queen's attitude is marked by calm maternal affection. Aten pours his rays upon the family and transmits life to the nostrils of the sovereigns. Another detail: the king is seated on a neutral "civil" stool, whereas the queen's stool bears the *sema-tawy*, the royal emblem, probably to highlight the importance accorded by the heretic to the female element. (From the Egyptian Museum, Berlin.)

shared by husband and wife, who are always depicted, especially on their tombs, as very dignified, serene, and ageless (fig. 2.10). Their gestures, coded but vivid, betray the profound affection that united them beyond their earthly existence. The simple fact they are always depicted together—though they no doubt did not die simultaneously—is indicative of their desire to continue together on the path to another world and that, with the help of the rituals, they will again have need of each other. It is interesting to note that the bond between the living and the dead was considered to be an active reality, which reveals the extent to which the term "the living," as a designation of the deceased, corresponds to the convictions of the ancient Egyptians. In their mind, the departed could act on one's behalf, protect one, and help one, but also cause one harm. This belief is revealed in the letters to the dead, of which a dozen have come down to us.[19] They contain requests for aid in judicial matters, mainly concerning inheritance, but also requests from sterile women to their fathers for their help in conceiving a child. In another letter, a widower reminds his deceased wife of all the good he has done for her and specifies that in the three years since she left him he has not "entered into another house," has not remarried in memory of her, and has not frequented prostitutes. So much virtue deserves her

Figure 2.10: The vizier Rekhmire and his wife depicted in their tomb. She is embracing the shoulders of her husband, who holds the *sekhem* scepter (the same word is used for both scepter and sistrum), and both of them, adorned for the big journey, seem to be confidently heading toward eternity.

help. The request that follows this is not very clear, because it refers to family matters that are unknown to us.

The sexual practice of married couples seems to have taken place as naturally as possible (fig. 2.11) with no constraints or taboos—the man did not generally assume the position of Osiris during his "reawakening" by Isis! The woman was not a passive partner though, and even the tale of the theogamy alludes to the attitude of the queen honored by Amun: "She allowed him to take his pleasure of her." Obviously, she took her pleasure with him as well.

SEXUALITY AND RITUAL PURITY

From the religious point of view, everything touching upon the functions of the sexual organs, which are excretory as well, does not conform with the rules of ritual purity.

For this reason, congress with a woman, whether his wife or not, was forbidden to a priest before undertaking his duties in the temple and during the length (ten days on average) of his watch. A modest diet was recommended at the same time. We do not know if the female personnel of the sanctuaries—the "recluses of the god" (his harem),

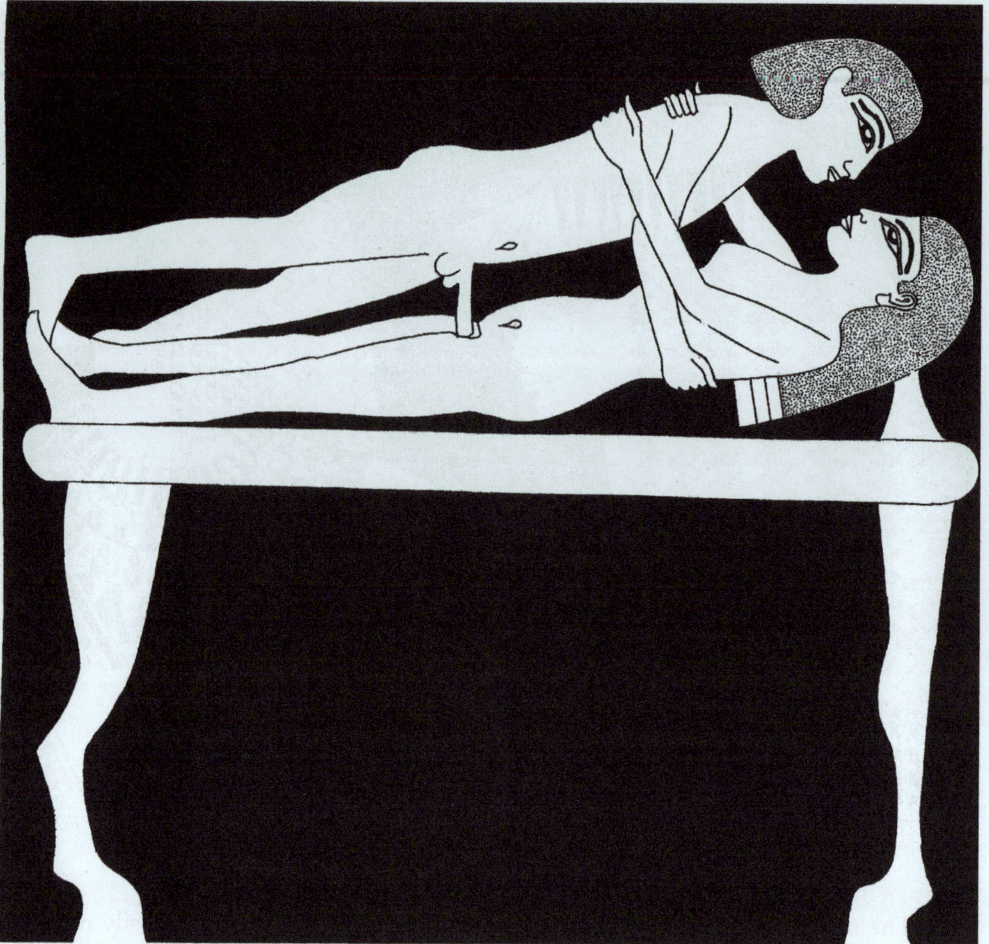

Figure 2.11: A couple joining together in the "classic" style on a bed-vehicle, because this drawing, at once free-form and ritual, is tomb art. The woman's head is resting on a very uncomfortable bedhead and the bed-vehicle itself has feet that are facing inward! We are therefore dealing with a composition inspired by ritual scenes that have been freely interpreted.

singers, musicians, and above all, the divine worshiper—were subject to specific restrictions concerning themselves as women.

Sexual relations and menstruation were considered by the Egyptians, like most peoples, as incompatible with ritual purity. The attendance records of the workers and artisans of the royal necropolis attest to a rather unexpected application of these principles. In fact, the absence of a worker from the work site because of his wife or daughter's menstruation was accepted and considered justified. Was he not working on the construction of the house of eternity for the god-king, that nothing should soil, not even the emanations transmitted by a third party?

On the subject of the royal necropoli, consisting of those established during the New Kingdom, in the Theban mountains (as well as those in the Valley of the Kings and the Valley of the Queens) there is one feature that leaps out: the sepulchers of the pharaohs were dug very deep and straight down into the rock (save for a few exceptions), throughout a very hard to reach and narrow valley. The layout of these tombs earned them the name of *syringes* (sing. *syrinx*). This form could also be labeled phallic, like the natural pyramid of the Holy Summit, another well-known phallic symbol that dominates the necropolis, although it is invisible from the Valley of the Queens. This latter is formed by a large wadi, which opens like a womb at the foot the mountain. It was probably hollowed out by the waters of the rare but torrential rains that, spilling off the high plateau, created a large basin at the foot of the cliff. This view brings to mind the waters of birth escaping from the universal matrix of the celestial cow. The tomb plans of the princesses and royal wives—among which is the exceptional tomb of Ramses II's favorite queen, Nefertari—emphasize a more spread-out design, larger than that of the syringes; a very steep stairway leads toward two or more interconnecting large rooms, flanked by annexes. The myths of creation and rebirth incontestably presided over the selection of these two sites.[20]

THE EARTHLY HAREM OF THE DEMIURGE

Was there ritual prostitution in Egypt of women connected with the worship of a god representing generative powers? The question remains unanswered. What should we think of sacerdotal titles such as "superior of the recluses of Min," which often devolved on women from high society, or "singer of Amun" (or Min)? For lack of any proof to the contrary, these women rendered a purely ritual service to divine entities whose sexual potential was represented by their erect phalluses. But it is possible that, during a later era, this "harem" performed more tangible duties. There is nothing attesting to any official status in this sense, however, as is the case for the Greek *pallacidiae,* for example. But Strabo reports that "the Egyptians consecrated to Zeus (Amun) one of the most beautiful girls, born of an illustrious family. . . . She became a prostitute and could have relations with whoever she chose until the moment of the purification of her body (menstruation) took place. After this purification, she would be given in marriage to a man, but before this, a ceremony of mourning would be held in her honor."[21]

The role of the "divine worshiper" or "god's wife" is different from the first, as is made explicit by Herodotus: "A woman sleeps in the temple of the Theban Zeus (Amun), and it is said these women have no sexual relations with any man."[22] Let's not forget that a half millennium separates these two authors.

These priestesses occupied the highest sacerdotal rank that women of ancient Egypt could attain. They represented the incarnation, in the company of the demiurge, of the goddess Nebet-Hetepet-Iusaas, and also Mut, Tefnut, or Maat.[23] They must therefore maintain the creative excitement of the god during his daily worship. This cosmic responsibility was entrusted to women of high lineage, queens, and princesses. In any event, these queens were doctrinally considered as the spouses of the god incarnate, the king. From the New Kingdom onward, all who were selected for this honor were accompanied by a significant amount of material belongings—necessary for the establishment and upkeep of these numerous recluses of god—thereby forming veritable courts and economic units in their own right. Starting around 1000 B.C., when Egypt was governed by parallel dynasties in Upper and Lower Egypt, the god's wife took on an increased importance. The responsibility was reserved for princesses, generally the daughters of the reigning king. They exercised the rights of royalty and eventually came to dominate the priest-kings of Upper Egypt. They had to devote themselves exclusively to the service of the demiurge (the Theban Amun) whose mystic brides they were, and they had to be virgins and remain celibate. These conditions seem to have been respected. The role was passed on through adoption, according to the political fluctuations of the time. The best known of these priestess-queens of the Twenty-second through Twenty-sixth Dynasties are Karomama, the Amenirdis, and the Shapenipet.[24] As we can see, these powerful princesses lived in an atmosphere permeated by mystical eroticism and sexuality.

PROSTITUTION

There is no doubt that female prostitution has existed since ancient times, but it was during the New Kingdom that it seems to have been very widespread in the large cities, notably in Thebes. Numerous direct testimonies (trial records) and indirect testimony (drawings, sketches on ostraca, see fig. 2.12) have been preserved in museums and private collections. They are also echoed fairly frequently and insistently in wisdom texts. Listen to what Ani has to say to his disciple:

You sit in taverns
Surrounded by loose women (. . .)
You consort with a girl
drowning in perfume,
a garland of flowers around her neck,
who drums her fingers on your belly.
You stagger and topple to the ground
and you are covered with filth.[25]

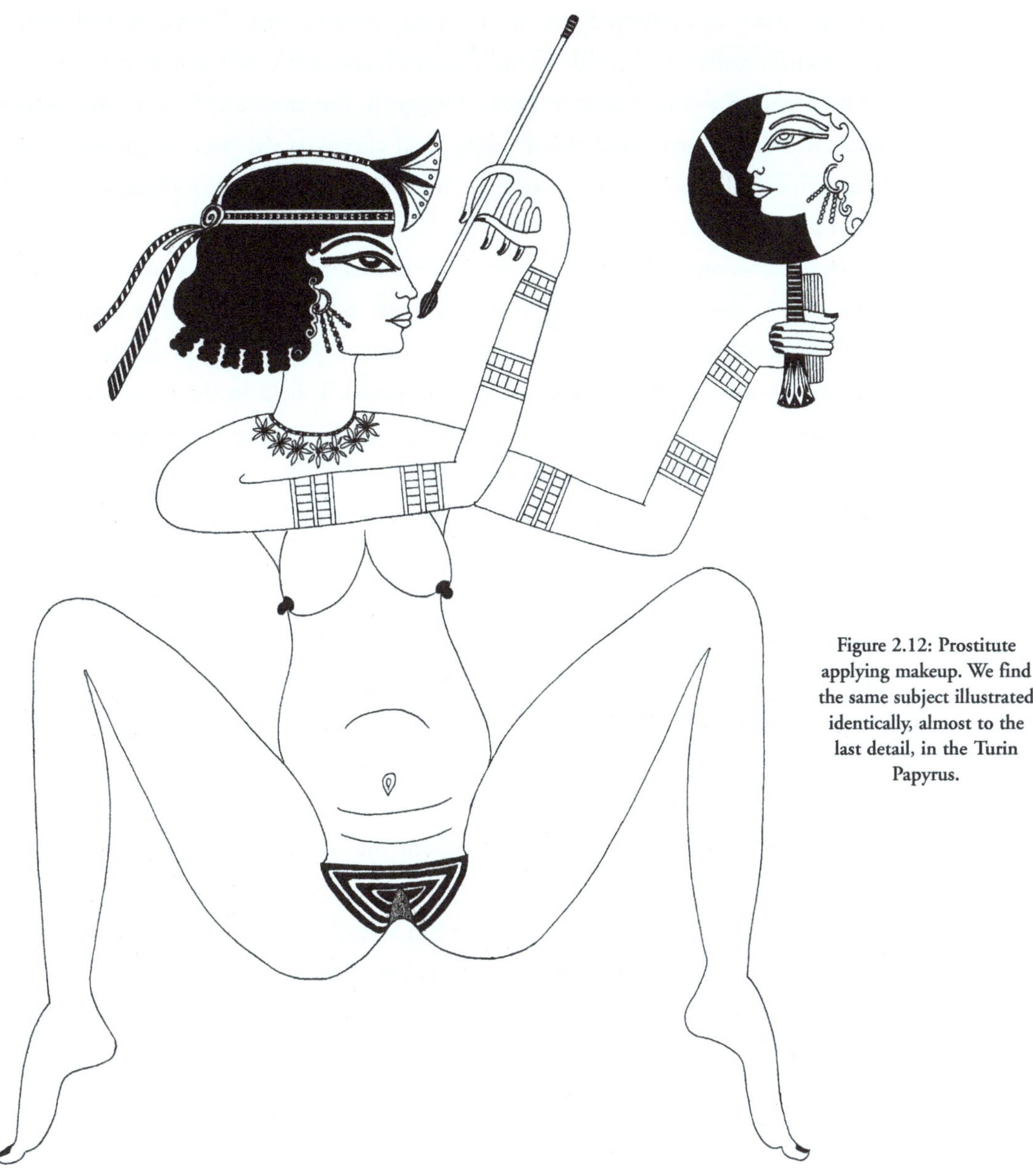

Figure 2.12: Prostitute applying makeup. We find the same subject illustrated identically, almost to the last detail, in the Turin Papyrus.

The detailed description of this scene allows one to presume it was based on several personal experiences lived by Ani before he became a "sage" who could give lessons in good conduct.

Prostitution was organized in antiquity similarly to the present, having at its disposal veritable recruitment networks where the transfer and sale of beautiful slaves took place.

They primarily came from Syria, but the trade went in both directions, and many beauties from the banks of the Nile found themselves on those of the Euphrates.

Prostitution was practiced in ancient Egypt in the same way it still is throughout the entire world. Women could either solicit their clients in the street or perform their profession in establishments such as taverns, beer houses, cabarets, brothels, and even be "on call" for private clients.

The profession of the musician was close to this milieu. These young women traveled quite a bit as they were required to enliven with their art festivals that often ended on a fairly exuberant note. The British Museum owns a painted wood statuette depicting a female harp player. The instrument, a small model, is held in the hands of the standing musician, who, to better stabilize it against her body, is clasping the pointed end of the neck between her thighs where it touches her sex.[26]

Musicians often wore tattoos, depicting the god Bes, guardian of the gynaeceum, as Champollion rightfully labeled him early on. Bes was always near women, and his presence, in two- and three-dimensional images, is confirmed in places devoted to physical love. Archaeological excavations at the beginning of the twentieth century uncovered the remains of a house, whose walls still bore large depictions of this deity. Several phallic figurines have also been extracted from this dwelling located on the Saqqara plateau.

Dancers, if they were not specialists in ritual dance, also lived on the fringe of professional erotic entertainment.

Male prostitution probably existed, given the tolerance shown toward homosexual practices, but the texts are mute in this regard before the Ptolemaic era.[27] One can readily presume that such practice had its roots in an earlier era. The assumption of power by Lagides and the establishment of a Greek ruling class in the country also modified custom in this regard (see chapter 6).

CHAPTER THREE

Love, Eroticism, and Sexuality in Literature

The people of the Nile had a great love of writing. They wrote on many different mediums and in diverse styles appropriate to the given subject. The most costly medium was papyrus, the fabrication of which was a royal monopoly. It was used for all important, administrative, religious, judicial, epistolary, and belletristic writing. Lapidary inscriptions were displayed on very precious and, fortunately, more durable mediums. Intermediate mediums were leather, which could be rolled like papyrus, and smooth, flat, plaster-coated wooden tablets on which a text could easily be erased and then started over. This operation was more difficult and often not completely successful on papyrus, which, when scratched out and reinscribed, retained a weak trace of the first text—to the joy of papyrologists, because modern techniques have made it possible to partially read these palimpsests. Remaining, finally, are the fragments of earthenware vessels and limestone shards, used for writing of lesser importance. Student scribes learned their art on these cheap, throwaway shards, known as ostraca. Neglected by the Ancients, they are valuable for the modern philologist, as these writings were copies of classic literary texts assigned to students by their teachers thanks to which it is sometimes possible to partially complete a papyrus full of gaps. One should proceed with caution though—these ancient schoolboy exercises are loaded with errors.

SARCASM, INSULTS, AND BLASPHEMY

Insults, some consisting of the crudest kinds of sexual innuendo, have been a factor in all times and all places. During the pharaonic era, the upper classes of society probably did not make use of them, but among the common folk—as among the residents of the divine world—the most unseemly remarks were thrown in people's faces, and this was already in evidence during the time of the pyramids. Such insults can be found in the sacrosanct Pyramid Texts, as well as in the "word balloons" surmounting the scenes decorating tombs. These hieroglyphic "balloons" reproduce the remarks made by the laborers and peasants hard at work (fig. 3.1). This literary genre—we may consider it as such because it is written—is another facet of Egyptian civilization. We insert it here, because half oral and half written, it finds its place between marginal forms of erotic behavior and the harsh and moralizing instructional texts.

Figure 3.1: Workers pulling on the drawstring of a birdcatching net. Here their remarks are strictly professional: "So pull! You've almost got the birds," but often these words of encouragement degenerate into insults.

Freud truly perceived the cultural role of the psychic safety valve formed by the insult when he said that the first man who hurled a curse at his adversary in the place of a stone was the true founder of civilization.[1] The Ancients took a more subtle position and disdainfully regarded those who could not hold their tongue or who used shocking and vulgar language. They were certainly staunch traditionalists, but what is nowadays labeled as "evolution" poorly conceals a debasement and impoverishment of language, which, with the exception of vulgarities, loses its colorfulness. This is not the case for time-honored swear-words, as we shall see.

We find the most widely used terms in the domain of sexuality: *nek, nekiu* ("to copulate"), for which the word and meaning have entered certain Western languages unchanged (among which is French) by way of Arabic. A *hemety,* literally a "man-woman," is a homosexual, a "gay" or a "fairy"; a cowardly man or one who suffers from impotence is called a "eunuch" or "castrated" (*sekhety* in Egyptian). This is almost the entire repertoire—relatively moderate in length—of insulting sexual allusions to men, to which "fornicator" should be added.

The scornful expressions directed against women and the blasphemies cast against the goddesses are clearly more cutting and obscene, something that is a deplorable tendency on the part of men in general. In this instance the men in question are the gods.

Isis is forced to hear (Pyramid Texts, 1272) that she is a "used up, stretched out bag" and she is to be sent back to a place where she was "crushed" or "beaten" (Pyramid Texts, 201)! Nephthys is treated even more poorly, being called a "pseudo-woman with no vagina" and she is encouraged to go to the place "where her behind was staved in" (Pyramid Texts, 1273 b). Attacking powerful sorceresses in this way borders on a complete lack of awareness, even on the part of the gods (who in some instances had occasion to regret it). But neither did they possess the verbal discretion recommended in the wisdom texts when insulting each other. Thoth is "he who had no mother" (Pyramid Texts, 1271). The god Bebou, a veritable Egyptian Priapus, insinuates that the naos, or reservoir, of Ra is empty. The demiurge, incensed by this attack on his generative powers, avenged himself by retorting that Bebou was a "failure," and an impotent god, and Thoth teased him by saying "your testicles are far away!" (Jumilhac Papyrus).

A similar talent for rude invective was shown in the world of men. To wish bad luck on an enemy, one uttered the wish that he or she would be raped by a donkey. This animal is the substitute for Seth, and we are well aware of the unbridled sexuality of this god who never hesitated to resort to bestiality; the curse is intensified by inverting the roles of the partners. A good-for-nothing is considered to be "unfinished," and even now, such people are crudely encouraged to "go back up their mothers' vagina." The ancient insult "old tube" addressed to thin, old, shrewish women corresponds to the current popular Egyptian insult "old clothesline." Vulgar meanness seems to be more durable than civilizations and even the gods!

THE MORAL LITERATURE

Instructional texts date primarily from the Middle Kingdom, but also from later eras (often only copies have survived into the present). These texts are written in the form of teachings, whether of a father to his son, a tutor, or even a king, to his successor, or to his disciple. The best known of these codes of good behavior for men and women (but which look at life from the male point of view—especially in the domain that concerns us here) are the teachings of Ani (Ramesside era), whose contents display similarities with the teachings attributed to Ptahhotep (dating from the Middle Kingdom); those for Merykare and for Kagemni; and, in a later era, the teachings of Sheshonq.[2] These writings examine religious, political, civil, and family issues. Their other common objective is to codify and demonstrate the moral basis of relations between the two sexes, and even sexuality in general. This was no doubt necessary, if one compares them to the exuberant sensual verve of the love literature, without going back to the divine model, which was hardly suitable for mere mortals: *quod licet Iovis, non licet bovis!*

A father's concern for setting his son's feet on the right road has existed throughout history. Figuring among the most ancient testimonies are the recommendations of the heir to the throne, Prince Djedefhor, to his son Au-ib-re. Only fragments survive of this Old Kingdom text, from which we have extracted a significant passage:

Be clean before your own eyes,
Else, others will cleanse you.
When you have prospered, found your household,
Take a woman who governs her heart,
She will give you a son.
You will build a house for your son,
As I have built for you the one you are living in.

As you can see, this is very wise and down-to-earth advice.

Several copies of the extremely long exposition of the maxims of Ptahhotep, vizier during the reign of Izezi, Sixth Dynasty, have survived.[3] The following passages concern our study.

If you wish that amity (for you) endure
Within the house where you have entered
as master, brother, or friend,
and wherever this may be (there) where you are invited,
refrain from approaching the women!
Misfortune waits in the place where this is done,
Unwelcome is he who intrudes in this way.
Thousands of men are turned away from doing good:
a short moment, like a dream
Then death arrives for having known them.

Following this demonstration of "what not to do" comes the counterpart—advice on what one should do.

When you have prospered and founded your house,
and ardently love your wife,
fill her belly, cover her back [with clothes],
[give her] ointments [that] soothe her body.
Give delight to her heart for as long as you live,
for she is a fertile field for her master.
Do not seek to oppose her in court,
but give her no power, restrain her.
Her eyes are her tempest, when she gazes. . . .
In this way, you will keep her in your house.

We will close our look at these texts with several quotes taken from the "Educational Instructions"—the title given them by their author. They date from the New Kingdom and offer an original conclusion: instead of humbly accepting the paternal advice, the son retorts that they are too difficult to understand and, especially, to apply.[4] A discussion ensues that ends to the elder's advantage insofar as he has the authority and more experience, and thus the better arguments; but the worm is in the fruit.

Take a wife when you are young,
so that she may give you a son;
she should bear children for you, when you are [still] young,
[for] that is the time indicated for making men.

Happy the man who has many,
He is hailed for his [numerous] progeny.
(. . .)
Beware of any foreign woman,
one who is not known in her city;
do not look at her when she passes,
do not know her carnally.
A woman far from her husband
is deep water, whose currents are not known. . . .

The same wavering attitude is true for the husband far from his wife, but that does not seem to have been a concern for the moralizing Ani. This passage also reflects the endogamous tendency of the Egyptians, which persists into the present in certain milieus, especially the countryside.

Spy not on your wife in her house,
if you know she is efficient [and virtuous].
Do not say to her, "Where is that thing? Bring it here!"
when you know she has put it in its proper place.
Let your eyes observe her silently,
in this way you will know her capabilities.
It is a joy when your hand is in hers:
many are those who know not [to do] that.
If a man abstains from quarreling in the home,
he will not [even] encounter its beginning.
Any man who sets up a household,
should restrain the hastiness of his heart.
Do not run after another woman,
do not let her steal your heart.

It is not surprising that the young man found these paternal precepts a little too austere. We maintain that these maxims only concern young men, not young women, but this was not because they were angels. But yesterday as today in this land, they were more tightly supervised. Another interesting fact: the wife was considered the property of her "master," a "fertile field," intended especially for producing children. A marriage agreement clearly says that in exchange for her maintenance and the goods she receives, "she gives her vagina"! There is not very much amorous poetry in these maxims. Furthermore, they describe the woman as a potential danger for the husband's reputation and peace of mind. He should watch over her closely and not let slip the bridle from the neck of his better half. The opposite was probably the more frequent case.

A young husband is advised, however, to show proof of his equity and affection for his wife, especially if she is virtuous and scrupulously fulfills her obligations: "Do not be brutal, you will obtain more from her with esteem than with violence (. . .) Open your arms to her, summon her [to your side] and declare your love to her"—a love that should be exclusive, he is advised! In any event, "one does not learn how to understand the heart of a woman, no more than anyone can understand the heavens" (fig. 3.2).

Figure 3.2: Hieroglyph of the heart that is read as *ib*.

This counsel shows the extent to which the instinct of male domination is alarmed by the eternal feminine.

LOVE POETRY AND EROTIC LITERATURE

When reading these texts, one cannot help but regret that they form merely a small portion of what must have existed before time, climate, and the relentless destruction of men took their toll. Fortunately, several superb papyri escaped destruction, such as the Chester Beatty Papyrus, which belonged, during the Ramessides era, to the archives of a family of scribes in Deir-el-Medina.[5] Other papyri, the ostraca previously mentioned, and a piece of pottery[6] complete our sources, which are more than three thousand years old. The writings are grouped in collections or thematic cycles. Among the themes evoked, that of lovers in nature may be compared to the Song of Songs.

The poems are written in verses that do not rhyme but follow a metrical scheme (which is difficult to reproduce in translation). They are organized into couplets with a rhythm that should guide the recital of these texts. The reading was perhaps even preferred by two people, for example a man and a woman in alternation. The modern reader may experience some difficulties in perceiving these subtleties, as well as the play on Egyptian words and underlying meanings that emerge, but will be nonetheless charmed by the colorful turns of phrase.

These writings are addressed to all classes of society and assume the context of high society as their model: poetry is a dream. The lovers thus live in luxurious dwellings, have servants, and travel by chariots drawn by spirited horses.

The environment, habits, and activities they describe provide the reader with a "Hathorian mirror" of ancient Egypt.

Physical attraction is the trigger of amorous feelings of young girls and young men equally—how could it be otherwise? Listen to their voices coming to us from over the millennia, heaving sighs one after the other and calling each other "brother" and "sister."[7] This is how one such love-struck "brother" describes in great detail the charms of his young woman:

The One, the "sister" who has no equal,
More beautiful than all the rest,
To look on her is to see the star that rises
At the beginning of a good year.[8]
She of the radiant perfection,
Of the resplendent complexion,
She who gazes from such lovely eyes.
Sweet are her lips when she speaks:
She never says a word too many.
She of the delicate long neck over breasts in full bloom.
Her hair is veritable lapis lazuli.[9]
Her arms surpass any gold
And her fingers are like lotus buds.
She whose back is so lithesome, her waist so narrow,
And whose beauty her hips still stress.
Her bearing turns the heads of every man who sees her
Happy is the man who embraces her,
He is first among all lovers
When she is seen emerging from [her house]
It is like [the appearance] of the One.[10]

Let's now take a look at how the young woman perceives her "brother" with a lover's eyes and ears.

My brother so moves my heart with his voice,
that an illness takes hold of me.
He is a neighbor of my mother's house
[but] I cannot go to him.

Figure 3.3: Hieroglyphs of the word "love," *merut*. The man depicted as a determinative sign (that is not pronounced) is bringing his hand to his mouth. This is a codified gesture for all expressions relating to eating, drinking, speaking, and expressing sensations.

My mother in vain advises me:
"Do not see him anymore!"
My heart refuses and when it dwells upon him,
Love takes hold of me [see fig. 3.3]
I encountered the "brother" at the entry to the pool,
His foot resting in the water,
His skin was rippling along his body as he stretched,
His stature outshining his broad shoulders.

Although completely smitten, she does not compare the young man to a god. She has set her sights further:

As I went by to see him at his home
I found his door open,
And the brother standing next to his mother,
all of his brothers and sisters with him.
He turned his eyes upon me when I passed.
I was alone to exult,
My heart was exhilarated,
"Brother," when I saw you!
Oh, if my mother knew how I felt,
She would accept [it] immediately!
Oh, Golden One, put it in her heart!
Then will I go to the "brother,"

And I will kiss him in front of his companions,
I will not care what people think,
[but] rejoice at their understanding
that you know me (. . .)

The constant mention of the mother and the house of the mother highlights the important role of the mistress of the house, who young girls dream of becoming. She also waits for her heart's chosen one to send a letter to her mother to ask for the hand in marriage of his "sister." Apparently the mother is the one who makes all decisions concerning marriage; at no time is the father involved.

The Golden One is one of the popular titles of the goddess Hathor who the young woman ardently invokes. The young man also entrusts his hopes with the divine mistress of love:

I worship the Golden One, I praise her majesty,
I exalt the mistress of heaven,
I make salutations to Hathor,
And glorifications to the mistress.
I made my entreaties to her, and she listened to my pleas
And the mistress sent my "sister" to me.
She has come to see me of her own free will.
What great wonder has happened to me!
I was joyful, exultant, elated,
When [I] was told: "Look, here she is!"

And the young man counts the days.

It was three days, yesterday, that I made my pleas
But it has been five days since she has left me!

The beloved's absence even causes him to fall ill—a true love sickness! He knows that neither the doctors nor the exorcist priests can cure it, for they "cannot identify his illness."

Nothing but the fact of telling me "There she is!" will cure me.
Only her name can soothe me.
Only the visits of her messengers can heal my heart.

My salvation would be that she comes (. . .)
But it has been seven days that she has left me [alone].

Jealousy begins to work its way into his mind, but the "sister" is in a similar state, as her heart is no longer in its rightful place:

It is prompt to steal away, my heart,
When I think of the love I bear for you.
It no longer lets me walk like everyone else:
It has leaped from its place!

She is disturbed to the point of neglecting her personal appearance, in spite of its essential role.

I no longer put on my shawl,
I no longer make up my eyes.
I no longer even perfume myself . . .

Her mind fills with dark thoughts.

My reason is troubled.
It has dispatched a messenger to me (. . .)
Who comes and goes, saying he has deceived me.
So he has found another (. . .)
(. . .) the suffering caused by another works its way within me.
My mind is at the mercy of the love I bear for you;
But half of my head is combed,
Yet I came running to you (. . .)
So I may be ready at any time.

All these tensions lead to quarrels between the two lovers and the depressed young woman reproaches her friend for only coming to see her "when he wants to eat," and asks him the question: "Are you a man who is slave to his stomach?" Does he wish for clothing? She has sheets. The invitation is quite clear, as is the following proposition: "Have you come here for beer? I will let you take my breasts, they have an abundance of riches for you." She calls him "my little jackal who arouses pleasure." The jackal and the wolf in Egyptian literature are metaphors for constant sexual desire.

Figure 3.4: Young woman dreaming of her beloved, her "brother" of love. Here the lotus is not a funeral accessory, but rather a psychotropic element of an intoxicating perfume.

She dreams of sleeping in the pergola of her "brother" (fig. 3.4), hoping "to achieve her desire of seeing his beauty," meaning the ardent body of her lover. Then she is brought back to reality by the call of a swallow that is comparable to the voice of another bird that was just as cruel for Romeo and Juliet as for the Egyptian lover: "It is dawn! What road will you take?"

Both lovers aspire to be together and the following text could readily fall from the mouth of either of them: "I long to take for myself your crowns of flowers," with which they are adorned, "while you are stretched out within your room, while I am massaging your feet, while (. . .)." Failing to conquer his belle, the "brother" wishes to become her Nubian slave, so that at least the anger of his mistress will fall upon him, or the servant who does her hair (fig. 3.5), or even her laundry man, so that he may "rub himself with the linens that have touched her body and are permeated with her perfumed balm." Nor does he find the role of porter displeasing, as he can then open the door for her and observe her comings and goings.

Lovers, as we all know, live in another world, and anything that opposes their passion should be eliminated, even if it earns them the worst kinds of punishment. The "brother" braves the powerful social conventions; the "sister" is ready to be kicked out of her house, provided her passions may be assuaged. In response to a love letter from his girlfriend, the lover hastens to her taking himself for the pharaoh's courier in his chariot (fig. 3.6), terrifying the wild animals who spring away in headlong flight before his team (fig. 3.7a, b, and c). He meets the "sister" in the country, while she is setting bird traps. This is a metaphor because she is the snare, and the captured bird is the young man—unless it is her own heart that has been ensnared (fig. 3.8).

I am returning from the country, "Brother," my beloved.
My thoughts are turned toward your love,
I wish to tell you of all you have involved.
Here is what happened:
I came to set my snare,
Equipped with my cage and my reed mat (. . .)
A bird anointed with olibanum arrived first,
And took hold of my bait.
His perfume was imported from Punt,
His claws were covered with gum:
My thoughts turn toward you, so that we may let it go
its way together,
While I would be with you, alone (. . .)
Your love turns me upside down.
I do not know how to let it go.[11]

The "sister," who wants to bathe in front of and even with her "brother," catches a red fish, symbol of the heart transformed by love and suggestively phallic; she offers it to the young man.

It is my desire is to come down and bathe in your presence,
That you may see my beauty [see fig. 3.9],
In a robe of the finest royal linen,
That will be imbued with unguent (. . .)
I will go down into the water with you.
I wish to pull forth from the water a red tilapia fish for you
[see fig. 3.10],
I wish to place it before you on (. . .)
"Brother"! Come look upon me![12]

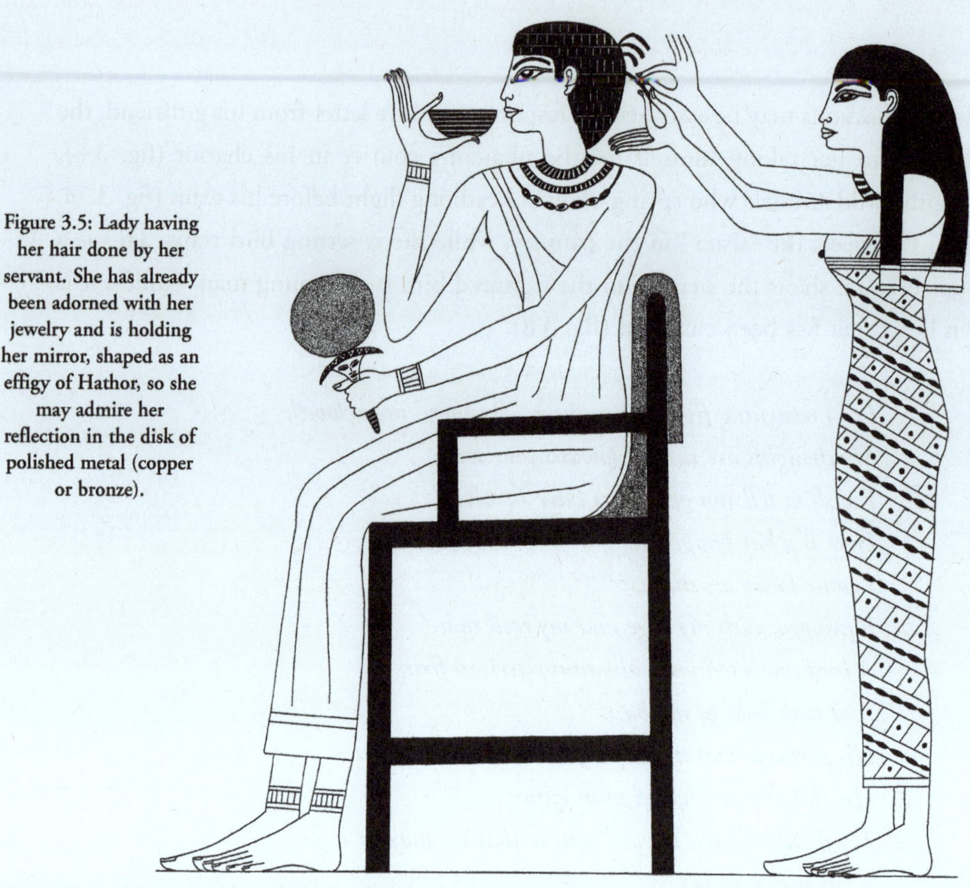

Figure 3.5: Lady having her hair done by her servant. She has already been adorned with her jewelry and is holding her mirror, shaped as an effigy of Hathor, so she may admire her reflection in the disk of polished metal (copper or bronze).

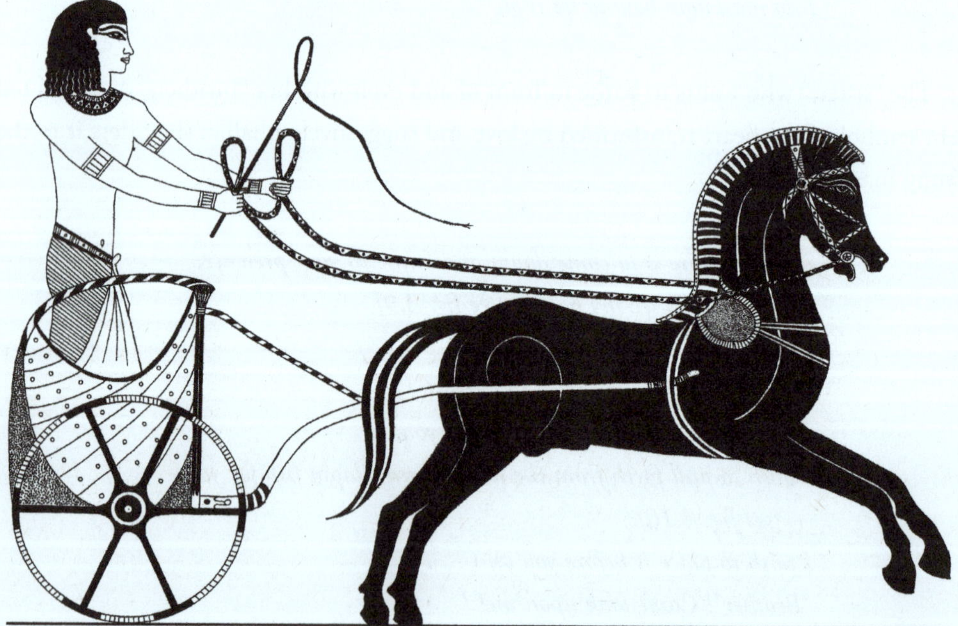

Figure 3.6: The pharaoh's courier in his chariot pulled by a spirited charger.

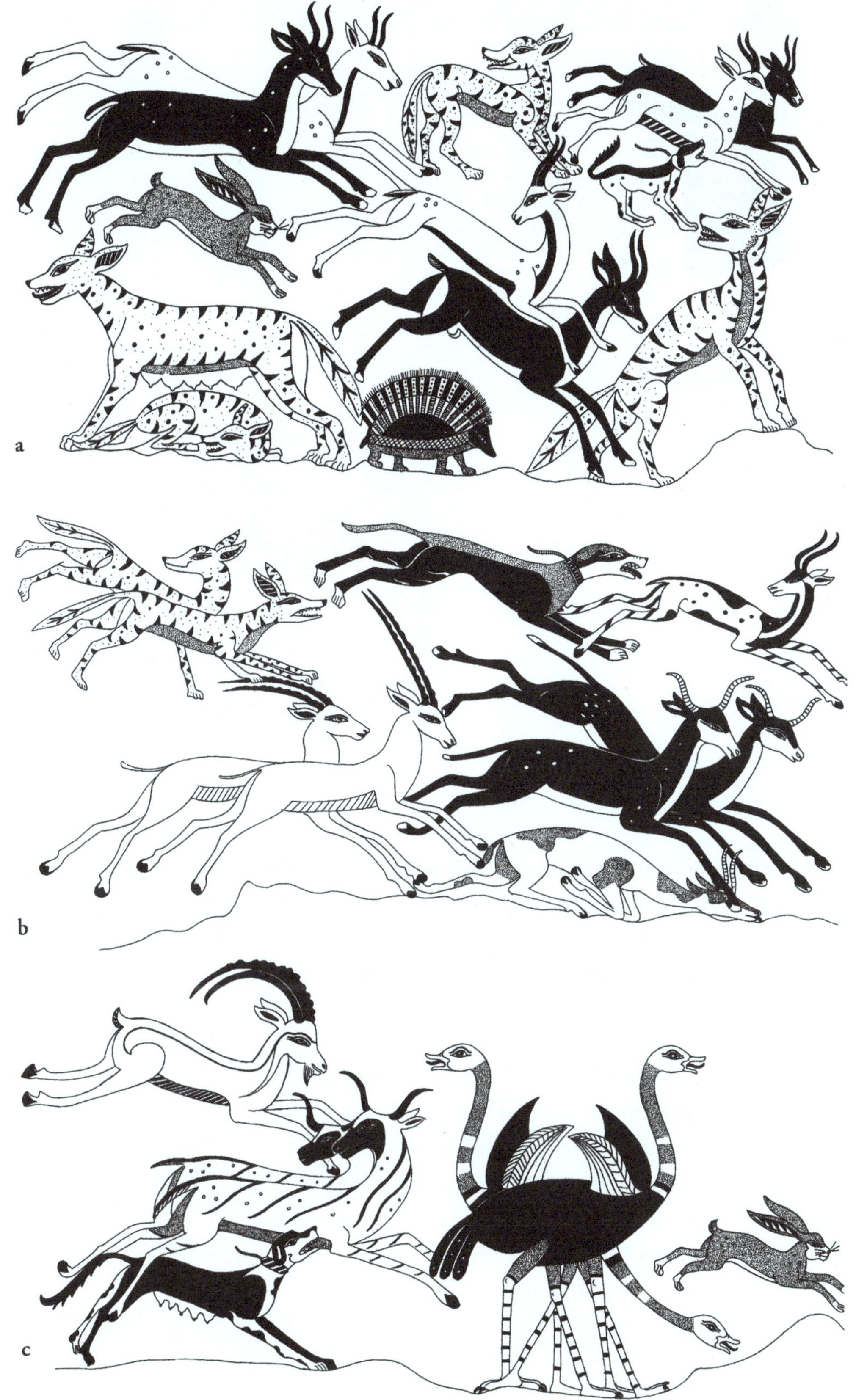

Figure 3.7 (a, b, and c): The headlong flight of animals before the speeding chariot. These scenes are extracted from ritual depictions, the wild animals being likened to the demons pursued by the pharaoh with the aid of his dogs. Here they represent the obstacles that may prevent the lover from rejoining his belle.

Figure 3.8: A young girl who has trapped a duck, an erotic allegory based on a scene out of everyday life.

Their love transports them to mythical marshes, where they devote themselves to the hunt—the young woman holding a nestling tightly to her breast. The young bird is an image of female sexuality (fig. 3.11). On another outing, the two lovers find themselves facing each other separated by a large expanse of water, but the young man braves the crocodiles in order to rejoin the one his heart desires.

The love of the "sister" is over there, facing me:
The river could flood my body,
[because] the Nun is powerful in this season.
A crocodile lies in wait on the banks [see fig. 3.12],
[but] going down into the water, I wish to cross over
through the waves
by showing great courage in the canal.

Figure 3.9: A beautiful swimmer gliding between the aquatic plants and fish. A startled baby bird (duck? flamingo?) flies off in great haste. This scene can be read on several levels. It is probably a reproduction of circumstances from rustic life (though it is debatable that young women bathed like this) but, beyond its erotic connotation, it also reveals a substratum of funerary magic: the fish is the temporary container of the soul of the deceased in the process of transformation, and the departure of the fowl, chased away by the female element, clears the path to rebirth.

Figure 3.10: The *Tilapia nilotica* and the lotus of rebirth correspond to the lover's desire: the red fish, the color of love, becomes the image of his heart.

Figure 3.11: The young woman is clasping a young bird to her heart as if she wished to spare it from her father's boomerang (not shown). This is both a cliché of funerary magic and a symbol of female eroticism.

Figure 3.12: The sacred animal of the god Seth represents the untamed dangers of nature. He is here a worthy adversary of another uncontrolled force, love. The young man has no hesitation in confronting the Typhonian beast.

The bucolic parties within these oneiric countrysides are charming, but where could they find a real, well-protected refuge? The house is closely watched, and, even if the porter is asleep, the door remains obstinately shut, for it is inhabited, as is the house, by vigilant spirits and the offerings promised by the young man do not succeed in making them relax their guard. The lovers' world being enchanted, they feel as if they are in step with nature. The large, shady, flower-filled garden of the villa is an ideal meeting place—it's therefore the place where we shall find our two turtledoves, within the shelter of magic trees who have a few words to say (fig. 3.13)![13] The pomegranate tree speaks first, showering compliments upon the young woman (the beginning of this text is lost):

(. . .) her voice,
my seeds are like her teeth,
my fruits like her breasts (. . .)
I remain constant in all seasons:
when the "sister" acts with the "brother"! (. . .)
While they are intoxicated upon wines and liquors,
And liberally sprinkled with oil and balm (. . .)
Though I still stand upright, shedding my flowers,
Those of next year are (already) in me.
I am the first of my companions,
[but] I have been treated like the second!
In future, if they again begin to act this way
I will not keep my silence on their behalf!

The young woman's lack of attention for the pomegranate has irritated this enchanted tree. In order to soothe its feelings, the young man promises to take steps to prompt the "sister" to look after it immediately. Next, the fig tree speaks through the rustling of its leaves, and it too has grievances toward the lover.

(. . .) is there another as noble as I?
But because no slave is present,
I am the servant (. . .)
as captive of the beloved.
She has had me placed within her orchard,
she gives me no water
at those times I wish to drink,

Figure 3.13 (a and b): A young ape savoring a nut he picked up from beneath a doom palm. Some trees are shown growing around a pool in the Eden-like setting of the garden. Pictured here are the doom palm, the sycamore, and the date palm.

she fills not my body
with water of the well
but comes seeking me for her amusement!

There is obviously a need to calm this complainant by promising it water in abundance—with a first "installment" poured right away.

Finally, the sycamore, gifted with a mouth, takes the stage: is the tree not a manifestation of the goddess Hathor (fig. 3.14)? The tree can boast of having been planted, at a very young age, by the very hand of the "sister" who has cared for it so well, because it has grown in such wondrous fashion. Without inhibition, the tree lists its own distinguishing qualities and describes its beauty. The tree "has placed a message in the hand of a servant, the daughter of the gardener, and sent her running after the beloved."

Come spend a moment (. . .)
I have a pavilion, a tent beneath me.
My gardeners rejoice,
and exult at the sight of me (. . .)
Dispatch your slaves to me with all haste.
To run toward me is cause for intoxication
before even having had a drink.
Obey me (. . .) make them come (. . .)
so they go in search of beer of all sorts (. . .)

We easily recognize here the "advice of the Lady of Drunkenness, who repeats drunkenness!" The obliging Mistress of Love also arranges the contribution of various breads, fruits, and vegetables and speaks through the tree:

Come spend a pleasant time,
without interruption for three days,
remaining seated in my shadow.
Your companion is on your right
whilst you make him drunk,
being attentive to what he says (. . .)
(. . .) in the frenzy of drunkeness (. . .)
She is going to remain with her "brother."
The "sister" carries a secret
in her strolls,

Figure 3.14: Another image of funerary and amorous iconography, for the two have been blended since the beginning of Creation. The goddess of the sycamore is none other than Hathor refreshing the deceased, and, on this occasion, quenching amorous passion.

Figure 3.15: The coupling of these two goats (from two different breeds) is an erotic metaphor that requires no further commentary.

Figure 3.16: The blind harper is a typical character in gatherings that include musicians in ancient Egypt. He was renowned for the subtlety of his fingers and his often melancholy chants. The famous "song of the harper" tells of a disillusioned musician inviting the listener to live his life one day at a time, for none have returned from the land of the shadows. Not everyone appears to have been persuaded by the official belief in the "Happy West."

[but] I am discreet enough not to reveal
by my words what I see [see fig. 3.15].

The discretion of the blind harper, summoned to make their intimate meeting yet more languorous with his music and his lament (fig. 3.16), is something they fully take for granted.

At this point they are ready to meet and make love clandestinely. They make appeal to messengers, generally domestics, but also sometimes they rely on fellow citizens whose appearance is so different (fig. 3.17) that it draws attention away from those who empty them.

Figure 3.17: The dwarf monkey-keeper was often a member of a great lord's domestic staff in imitation of the pharaoh. Dwarves could play an important role in the royal entourage and ascend to high posts within the administration.

The following text is coded with metaphors and innuendoes, whose meaning was obvious to the ancient Egyptians. It is still easy for us to decode. A benevolent deity—if it is not Hathor herself—whispers to the suitor some advice that we have extracted from a larger work and rearranged:

You must present yourself at the house of your "sister,"
alone, with no one else.
Go up to her door (. . .)
It is up to you to master her lock (. . .)
Like one unlocks a reception room.
How splendid is her pergola!
She is provided with song and dance,
wines and beers of ceremony are beneath her shadow,
while the colonnade is open to the breeze.
It is through the wind that the sky displays itself,
it will bring her aroma [that of the "sister"];
her perfume spreads, intoxicating those who breathe it.
It is up to you to agitate your "sister's" senses,
and bring them to a pinnacle during the night!

Figure 3.18: This tender tête-à-tête also comes from a tomb. The plant that surrounds the young couple is still associated with love, birth, and maternity. It climbs along the supports of the birth pavilion and surrounds the figurines of "death's concubines." In the present instance, it symbolizes the hopes for the fruits of love. (Tomb of Rekhemire, Theban necropolis, Eighteenth Dynasty.)

Then she will say to you: "Take me in your arms!
Dawn will find us in the same position."
It is the Golden One who has presently appointed her for you,
so that you may put the finishing touches upon your life.[14]

With this delightful and poetic evocation of the first night of love for the young couple, we will close the shutter on the literature of pharaonic Egypt (fig. 3.18).

CHAPTER FOUR

The Code of Love

THE CODE OF LOVE IN FIGURATIVE ART

Royal Art

We need to turn again toward the divine and royal domain to decode this particular iconography. We have already analyzed the scenes of royal and divine love having to do with theogamy (fig. 2.7) and the new version provided of it by the heretical pharaoh (fig. 2.6). Ramses III, in his temple of "millions of years" at Medinet Habu, was probably inspired by that of Ramses II's "Ramesseum" (also located on the west bank, the funerary side of Thebes), which had fashioned a synthesis of these two conceptions of the role of the pharaoh as a link between the cosmic creational power of the demiurge and that of mere mortals, insofar as he participates, through his divine essence and his human body, in both spheres, which interpenetrate within his person.[1] In the temple's entry tower (the *migdol*) illustrations in relief on the theme of mystic and ordinary sexuality unfold from right to left, like a film. The images spring from classic iconography, but their details betray the liberating influence of the revolutionary representations of the heretic king.

At the entry, the king is depicted seated on a comfortably padded throne. He adopts a nonchalant pose facing three young woman who are naked but for their jewels and elaborate and ornamented hairstyles (the hair and high diadems) that identify them as "ornaments of his majesty," meaning his favorites (fig. 4.1). Two of them are approaching the

Figure 4.1: Royal favorites who happen to be princesses and daughters of the pharaoh bearing symbolic fruits of love to their king and father who is visiting the harem.

king, carrying cups filled with pomegranates and figs, two fruits with symbolic meaning. Because of their form and fleshy color pomegranates were compared to women's breasts, and their numerous sparkling seeds were likened to the teeth of youth. In Greco-Roman Egypt, the pomegranate was synonymous with fertility. Because of their shape and appearance figs were symbols for testicles. They were used in the pharmacopoeia as medicine against heart disease. The two favorites are also holding something that is either a flabellum (which is not a flyswatter but an insignia of rank) or a fan for refreshing the king. The latter is also caressing the chin of the third beauty with one hand and grasping her wrist with the other at the level of her navel (fig. 4.2). She is supporting the extended arm of the king whose hand is touching her chin. The next image shows the king playing *senet* with two young women who have taken off their diadems (fig. 4.3). The one who has already approached the king remains at his side, representative of the ritual feminine element. The sovereign drapes one arm over her torso grazing her navel. She responds to this gesture by delicately touching the nipple of her partner, who seems to be

Figure 4.2: Pharaoh and one of his favorites engaged in foreplay.

Figure 4.3: The king's love play in his harem borrows elements from the funerary magic of passage. The pharaoh is preparing to enter into a trance, aided by the feminine element—doubly present.

concentrating on his game and is picking up a pawn. But his friendly adversary is picking up two with an expression of delight. The board is placed on a stool, decorated with the Ruty lions leaning against a floral *wadj* column.

Finally, in figure 4.4, the favorite is standing so close to the king that her lower belly is almost touching the pharaoh's knees. He is meanwhile caressing his partner's sex with a hand gesture that can also be seen in certain rituals. The ruler is holding his other hand between his loincloth (flush with his sex organ) and his navel, in the same position. The young woman is raising her arms in a gesture of worship or ecstasy that can only be amorous here.

The above description of these scenes may appear overly fastidious, but it is necessary for the interpretation, as each detail counts. A clear-cut progression of the erotic intensity of the images can be observed: the young women, although nude, soon strip off the emblem of their rank in the harem, the tall headdresses. One of them approaches the king and begins exchanging gestures of love with him, which intensify in the scene of the *senet* game, during which the king, although still devoting his attention to his gaming partner, draws the other favorite to him and caresses her belly. By caressing his chest, the young woman shows him that she shares his mood. This touching of the erogenous zones of the body has its effect: the king remains alone with the young disciple of Hathor, and stimulates her sexual organ with a delicate gesture. The king's sexual excitement is not shown,

Figure 4.4: The chosen one of the moment and the king touching. This is a coded image of the carnal act, whose meaning derives from the ritual of preservation and the continuity of the powers of creation, as well as the transmission of the divine essence to the pharaoh's descendants. This interpretation is suggested by the fact that these harem scenes decorate the walls of Ramses III's temple of "millions of years."

but there is no doubt as to what is to follow. The scene of the *senet* game is a key to the code. Normally, as it is primarily depicted on the tombs, the deceased (man or woman) plays *senet* alone against an invisible partner—destiny—in order to obtain his or her passage to the beyond and ascend to the transformations necessary for rebirth.[2]

If the dead individual were a man, his wife would be next to him, as invocation of the feminine principle; single deceased women are not accompanied by a masculine principle in these circumstances, they appear to have been sufficient on their own. Here we have a variation on this classic scene. The king is in the company of an active feminine element, but he seems to be playing against another representative of this element, who seems to be winning by the triumphant lifting of two pawns. We are in the world of the living and inside a temple, the ritual content of the depictions is indicated by the details:

the stool supporting the game board is decorated by the Ruty lions between whom the sun rises for its reappearance, suggested by the lotus-shaped *wadj* columns, "the green," the "vigorous." The gesture of the *senet* player seems to indicate that the operation has succeeded and the king has recovered all his divine and earthly potential, which he has apparently decided to immediately put to the test forthwith.

A question arises concerning the identity of these friendly young women: their finery and especially their coiffures with the long flowing locks suggest they are the king's own daughters, which is confirmed by the inscription accompanying the scene. Their presence therefore conforms to the theory of the transmission of divine royalty discussed in chapter 2.

Following in the footsteps of Ramses II, Ramses III also utilized the forms of classic iconography. We have already noted that the same cannot be said of one of his predecessors, the "heretic" pharaoh, Akhenaten, who revolutionized the depiction of the king and his family on the basis of his Atonian dogma, which inspired Ramses II in his reinforcement of the concept of divine royalty.

The heretic had himself depicted with an almost androgynous body, as we have seen, and it is no longer the "Son of the Sun" who transmits the divine vital spark, but the royal couple, who seem to have no hesitation about publicly displaying (but always in ritual fashion) their amorous couplings. For the Ancients, these images acted as mirrors reflecting the energies at work in the Great Work back toward the cosmic creator. The king is always accompanied by his feminine counterpart, the queen, and often his daughters, living proof of the vital flux. Their official activities together (fig. 4.5, and the cult of Aten notably), and their public embraces, caresses, and kisses (fig. 4.6) are only a demonstration of the divine sexual unity rediscovered. From this dogma stems the importance of women in this reign, to whom Pharaoh constructed sanctuaries known as *shut-re,* meaning "wind of the sun," a term referring to the beginning of the cosmos, but also containing the ideas of "solar light," *Shu,* and "shadow" *shu(y)t.* We suggest that this play on words may allude to the activity of the Sun demiurge who overshadows the human feminine element—a notion found again in several religions, which do not escape the equation: "divine cosmic creation = sexuality, whatever mystical screen they erect between the creator and his earthly livestock.

Official Civil Art

Official ritual civil art, but not royal art, as we have seen, applies the same code with lesser and more discreet emphasis. This changes nothing of the profound meaning of these statues, reliefs, and paintings. Among the scenes adorning the most elaborately decorated

Figure 4.5: Akhenaten and Nefertiti, accompanied by two of their daughters, show themselves at the "window of appearances" in their palace for the ceremony of the distribution of "the gold of reward." This was an important official act because these valuable necklaces, which were tossed to high officials, were the sign of royal satisfaction for services rendered. With all due consideration to respective cultural difference this corresponds to the awarding of medals of honor in our time by modern leaders—who as a rule do not allow their wives to share in their distribution! In contrast, this detail highlights the importance of the Amarnian queen, the king's indispensable complement. Naturally this scene takes place with the blessing of Aten.

"dwellings for eternity," some amusing details can be picked out anyway, such as the lady or guest who, quite unconstrained, vomits the excess of her wine consumption, while demanding her cup be refilled! During funeral banquets—where one did not eat but drank generous libations in honor of Hathor and of the *ka* of the deceased (his energetic double)—only the couple who are owners of the site are depicted seated side by side. The other guests are placed according to gender, the women being more numerous, indicative of their Hathorian role in benefit of the deceased; the new Osiris promised rebirth. Above one of the gateway passageways of the tomb, the game of *senet* is depicted, the mystical implication of which has already been mentioned. Another theme parallels that of the royal harem: the deceased is supported by his feminine alter ego. The role of the two divine weepers with Osiris is suggested by a "hieroglyph" in a civil tomb (fig. 4.7), a depiction that already smacks of the freer style, albeit moderately.

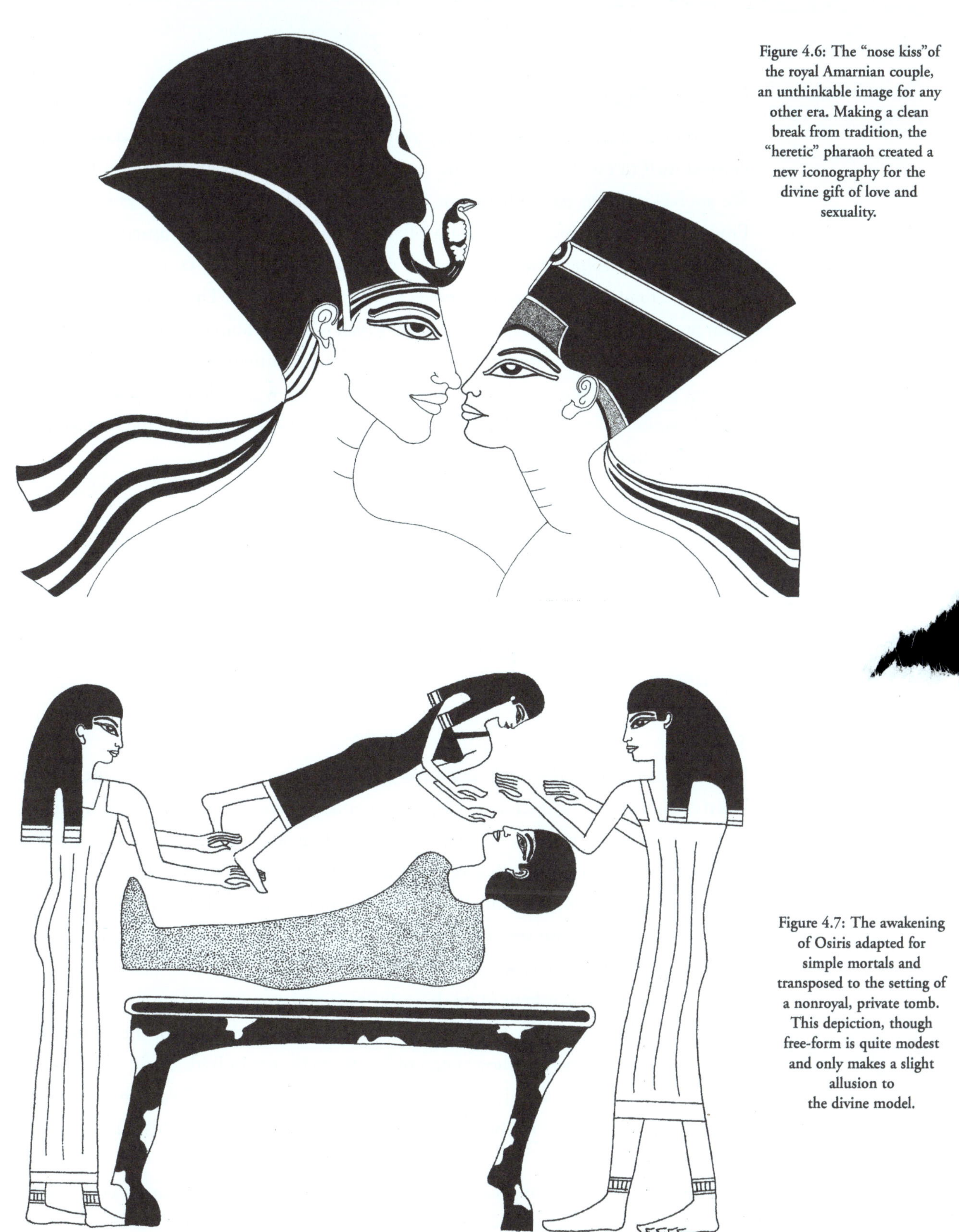

Figure 4.6: The "nose kiss"of the royal Amarnian couple, an unthinkable image for any other era. Making a clean break from tradition, the "heretic" pharaoh created a new iconography for the divine gift of love and sexuality.

Figure 4.7: The awakening of Osiris adapted for simple mortals and transposed to the setting of a nonroyal, private tomb. This depiction, though free-form is quite modest and only makes a slight allusion to the divine model.

Freestyle Figurative Art

In contrast to ritual art, freestyle art, in general a form of popular expression, wholeheartedly devoted itself to the illustration of the sexual and erotic fantasies of the ancient Egyptians. We are making a necessary distinction here, even if its limits are not always very precise. Erotic art obeyed an amorous sensibility often lacking in purely sexual illustrations. This free art has primarily come down to us by way of ostraca, and also thanks to the graffiti inside homes and tombs. We will provide several samples here (fig.4.8). These themes can be seen again in the famous Erotic Papyrus of Turin, which is also an object of study in this book.

Archaeological excavation at the beginning of the twentieth century on the plateau of Saqqara uncovered the remains of a house, whose walls were still adorned with human-sized depictions of the god Bes, the guardian of the gynaeceum as Champollion so rightfully called him.

COMPONENTS OF THE CODE OF LOVE

The Five Senses

The code of love makes its appeal through the five senses, vehicles of our perceptions and emanations.

Sight

The first element of this code concerns the sight that transmits erotic signals to us, whether consciously or unconsciously, from a potential partner. Elegant clothing or suggestive garments such as the transparent dresses of ancient Egypt, as well as jewels (fig. 4.9) and adornments, for both sexes, and cosmetics (fig. 4.10[3]) enter into this category of objects of seduction, with which the gods also adorned themselves. Coiffures and especially wigs (fig. 4.11) also served a similar purpose. A woman's luxurious head of hair has always been viewed as an erotic trump. Now, for reasons of hygiene in this extremely hot climate, natural hair was kept quite short, for men and women, and covered by sophisticated wigs, which also served as an exterior sign of the social status of the wearer. This invitation from the man to the woman of his desire occurs in both erotic and romantic literature: "Put on your wig and let's spend a happy time together."[4] Beautiful women also require a mirror, with a Hathorian handle preferably, the better to keep tabs on their appearance (fig. 4.12)!

The expression "I cannot stand the sight of this person" indicates, on the contrary, the importance of this first visual contact in human relations in general.

Figure 4.8: Scenes depicted on ostraca that are typical of popular erotic expression. The same motifs are used in the Papyrus of Turin. (a) From an ostracon in the British Museum, no. 50.714, New Kingdom. (b) From a sketch on wood from a Theban New Kingdom tomb. The object is now lost, published by Manniche, *Sexual Life,* p. 66, ill, 55. (c) From a piece of graffiti in a Middle Kingdom tomb, Beni Hassan.

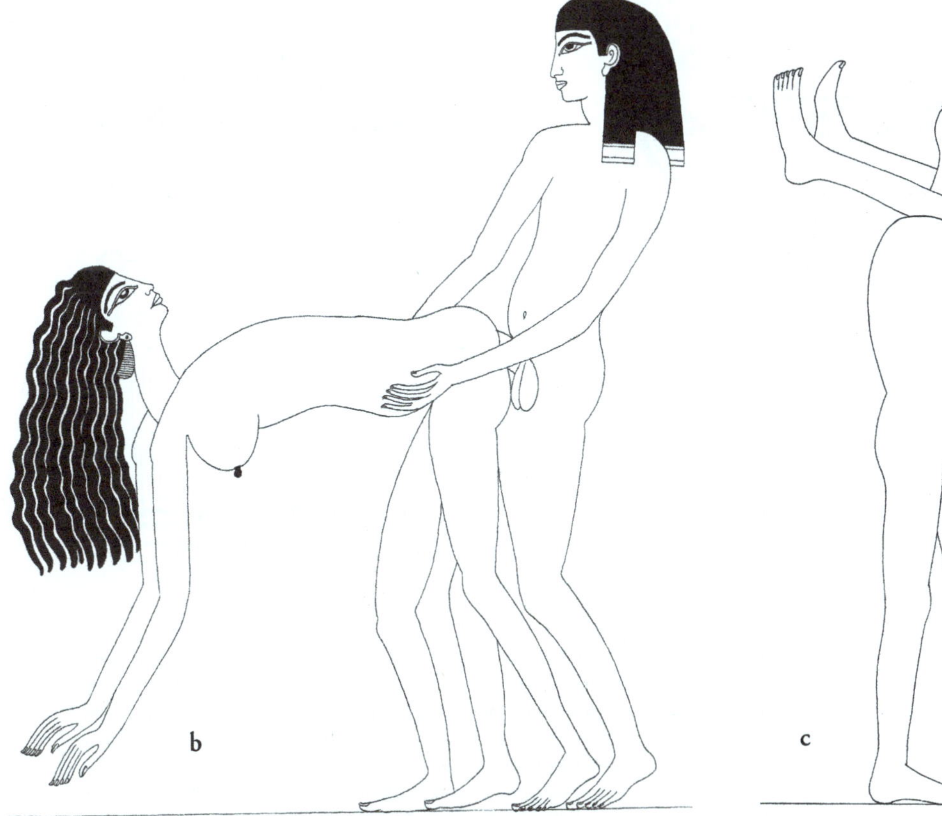

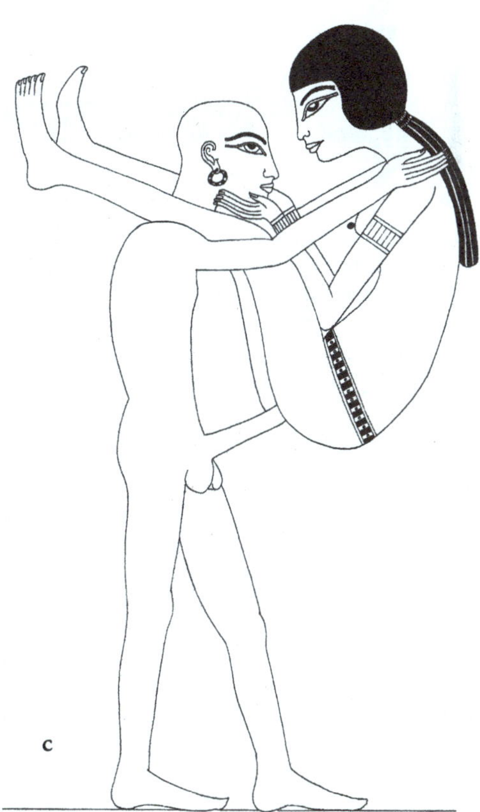

Figure 4.9: Jewels, earrings, pendant, and necklace in the image of the goddess of love. The icon of Hathor is always shown facing forward, as on the sistrums. It is otherwise when it comes to depicting the goddess as an individual in her own right.

Figure 4.10: Cosmetic spoon. These ravishing objects, which were elaborate creations during the New Kingdom, were not tools of everyday life, but intended as offerings, often in the context of funerary magic. The meeting of all the symbols of rebirth on the example depicted here confirms their meaning and puts into play their erotic elements, necessary for the creation of life: the young female musician, the premier feminine element, beating the rhythm with her drum, imitating the beats of the heart and inducing a trance state; the mandrake, the fruits of love, and the blue lotus with its intoxicating perfume, a true psychotropic; finally, in conclusion, the cupule flanked by two umbels of papyrus forming the symbol of life. (Wood, New Kingdom, from I. Wallert, "Der Verzierter Löffel," *Ägyptologische Abhandlungen* 16 [Wiesbaden, 1967]).

Plate 8. The "Two Sisters," Isis and Nephthys, are also called the "Two Women with Braids" in the ritual celebrated to revive Ihy-Osiris by stimulating his sexual ardor. Ramesside era.

Plate 9. Painted earthenware erotic oil lamp representing a man who, apparently completely exhausted, is resting in a crouched position on his overly large phallus, out of which flames would rise. The theme of the scene can be compared to sequences 6 and 7 of the Turin Papyrus. Ny-Carlsberg Museum, Copenhagen.

Plate 10. Bes as a harpist, dancing to his own music. Ptolemaic era. Temple of Hathor, Philae.

Plate 11. Tomb painting of Nut, goddess of the sky.

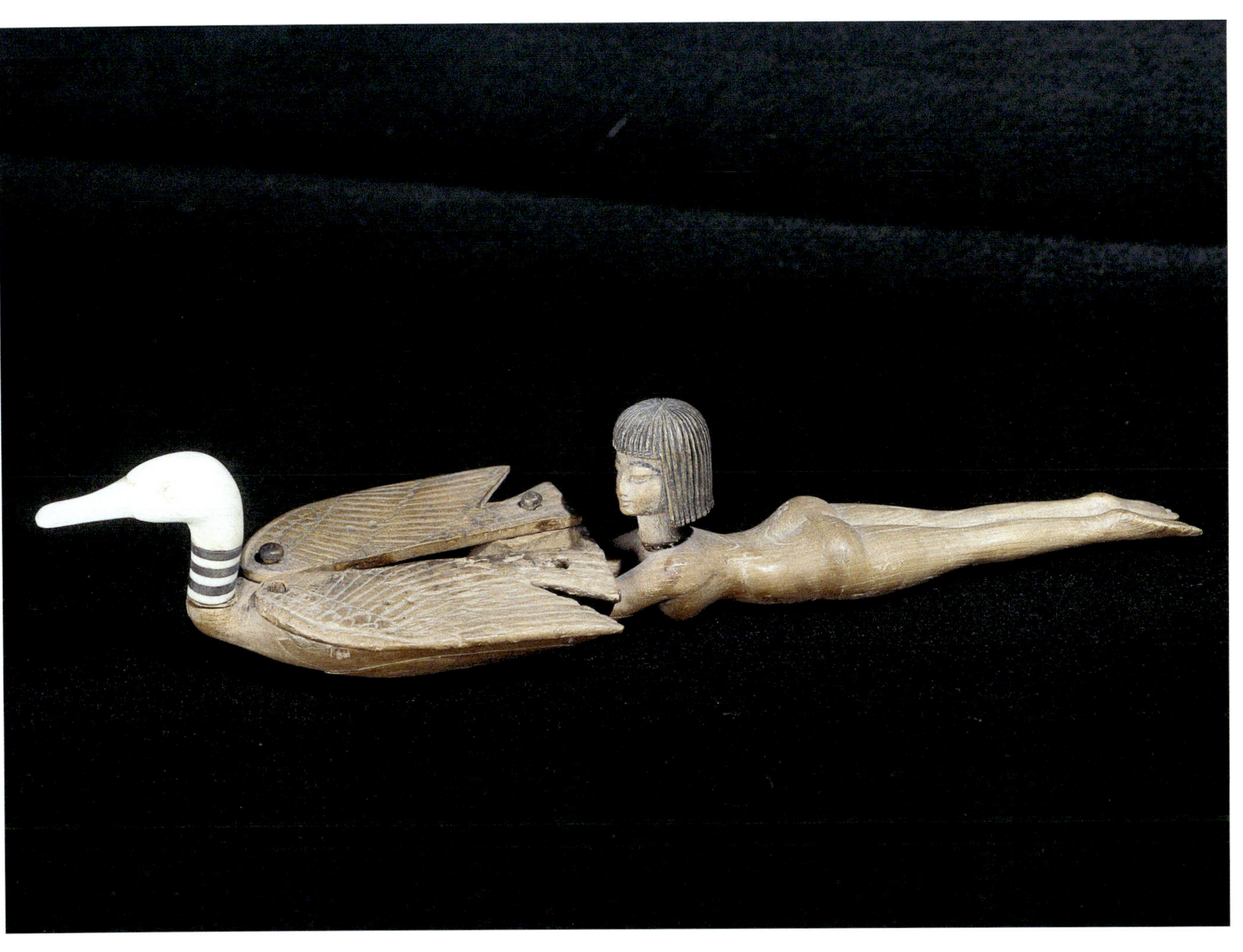

Plate 12. Wood and ivory cosmetic container in the shape of a duck held by a swimming girl. Ducklings are symbols of feminine sexuality. The bird's wings are the movable lids of the receptacle containing an ointment or a solid perfume. This object perfectly represents the refined aesthetics of the 18th Dynasty. New Kingdom. Louvre Museum, Paris.

Plate 13. Detail of the central scene depicted on Tutankhamun's ritual throne. The image shows queen Ankhsenamun anointing her husband, which means (here in this funerary context) that she prepares him for his afterlife. The rite is accomplished under the beneficial radiations of Aton, the god of the heretic pharaoh Akhenaten, despite of the official return to the Amonian dogma under Tutankhamun's reign. The scene is composed of wood, plated with gold and electrum, and the figures are engraved or embossed and inlaid with semi-precious stones and colored glass. New Kingdom, 18th Dynasty. Tutankhamun's treasure, Egyptian Museum, Cairo.

Plate 14. Wooden ornamental cosmetic spoon inlaid with "Egyptian blue." The cupule is shaped like the big loop of the life-sign *ankh.* The elaborate handle represents a young princess, her social rank being indicated by her elaborate braid. She is surrounded by and holds lotus flowers, the inebriating perfume of which she is steadily inhaling. The charming object is not only an evocation of bucolic surroundings but has also significance pertaining to magic and rebirth, as suggested by the poppies (?) and the dead adult ducks. The latter are supposed to be demoniac incarnations, living in the papyrus thicket where Isis raised her son Horus. New Kingdom, 18th Dynasty. Louvre Museum, Paris.

Plate 15. Limestone detail of the torso of a fragmentary statue, representing a queen presumed to be the daughter and Great Royal Wife of Ramses II, Meritamun. The royal lady is depicted holding a *menat,* the counterpoise of which is topped by a feminine head which could be her portrait. She wears a heavy ceremonial wig and is adorned with bracelets and a large necklace, the *usekh.* Her tight linen dress is embroidered with marguerites enhancing her feminine form. New Kingdom, 19th Dynasty. Egyptian Museum, Cairo.

Figure 4.11: A charming beauty skillfully made up and sporting a voluminous wig—an erotic signal, as are the jewels she is wearing, notably the large necklace, whose pearls are shaped in imitation of mandrake, lotus, and papyrus. These motifs are repeated on the headband of the wig, which is crowned by a cone of perfumed fat.

Figure 4.12: Mirror with the Hathorian icon. The metallic reflecting disk does not describe a perfect circle but a slightly flattened-out ellipse, conforming to the general representation of the celestial luminary bodies.

Hearing

The second element is hearing. The lover in the Chester Beatty Papyrus is deeply moved by the voice of her "brother," which causes her heart to turn upside down. The resonance and subtle modulations of a smooth voice and the scale of laughter, are often underestimated elements of attraction and understanding. A disagreeable voice that is either strident or harsh is incompatible with the harmony of the couple. Music and songs are the traditional complements of this scale, topped off with dances, which make an equal appeal to touch. A paragraph will be devoted to that specifically.

Smell

Smell deserves the third position. The particular smell of a person can be either pleasant or unpleasant; it's a question of individual perception. If, from the onset, someone

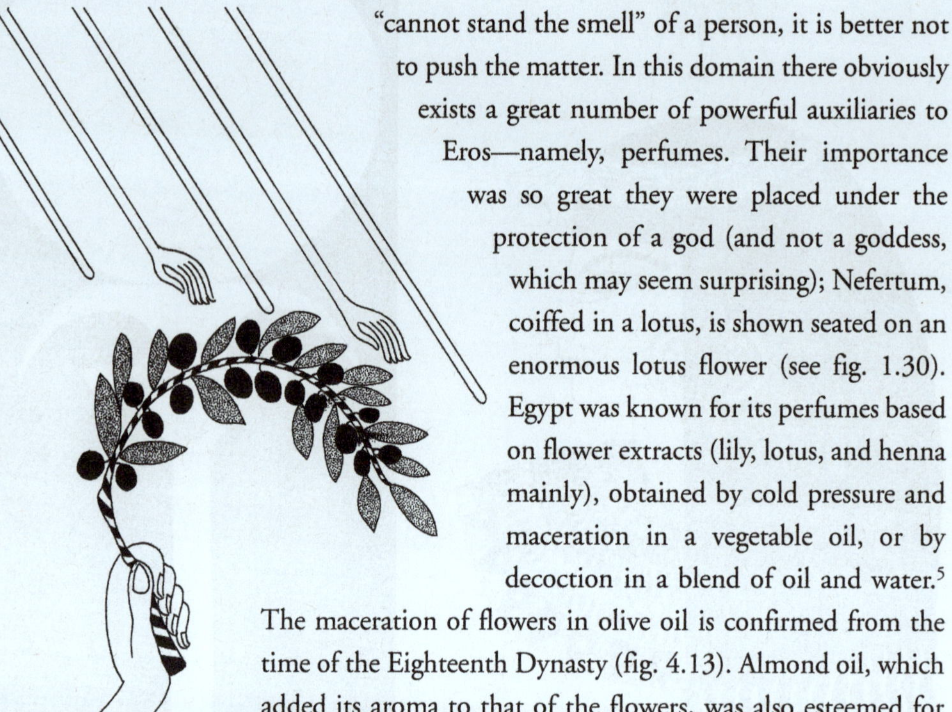

Figure 4.13: An olive branch beneath the rays of Aten. This depiction dates from the plant's first appearance in Egypt by importation and acclimatization during the New Kingdom. The oil of its fruit was used chiefly in Egypt's pharmacopoeia.

"cannot stand the smell" of a person, it is better not to push the matter. In this domain there obviously exists a great number of powerful auxiliaries to Eros—namely, perfumes. Their importance was so great they were placed under the protection of a god (and not a goddess, which may seem surprising); Nefertum, coiffed in a lotus, is shown seated on an enormous lotus flower (see fig. 1.30). Egypt was known for its perfumes based on flower extracts (lily, lotus, and henna mainly), obtained by cold pressure and maceration in a vegetable oil, or by decoction in a blend of oil and water.[5] The maceration of flowers in olive oil is confirmed from the time of the Eighteenth Dynasty (fig. 4.13). Almond oil, which added its aroma to that of the flowers, was also esteemed for its soothing properties. Perfumes also existed in solid form, with the addition of wax, gums, and plant resins. Solid perfume is still manufactured in Egypt using ancient traditions, and it is still, as it was in antiquity, an article of exportation.[6] In fact, the perfumes manufactured in Mendes were so famous throughout the Middle East that they became synonymous with "perfume."

The inscriptions on the walls of the temples of Edfu and Philae have preserved several recipes for making perfumes that not only serve as toiletries, but were also used as medicine—among which is the famous Kyphi[7]—and were manufactured by the temple's "pharmacists."

Balms and ointments were obtained by the incorporation of aromatic or medicinal extracts into fatty substances formed into various shapes: the perfume cones worn on the heads of the guests at feasts and banquets are the best known (figs. 4.11 and 4.27), The amorous "brother" of erotic poetry longs to be his beloved's laundress so he can wrap himself in her sheets that give off the odor of her body and her perfumes. Cosmetics and perfumes were indispensable ingredients of the rituals—and to the professionals of the art of love. Other mellow fragrances are the incense from the land of Punt, myrrh (consecrated to Venus and perhaps earlier to Hathor, and still worn by brides in certain countries today), and the olibanum (frankincense) that accompanied the worship of the gods, soothed the body, and accented life.[8]

Taste

In the fourth position we mention the adjunct to smell, taste, which it is necessary to know how to share with one's partner. Amorous poetry details the delicacies of the palate: all sorts of breads, cakes, delicious fruits, and vegetables. It suffices to examine the offering tables, loaded with an abundance of foodstuffs, to get an idea of the variety of comestibles available. Beer, of which there were several kinds, was obtained from the fermentation of barley grain in water.[9] Neither the beer that had already tamed the Distant One, nor wine, the prominent beverage of the Lady of Drunkenness, could be missing from festival tables. The precious liquid was kept in large jars bearing the date it was set down, the name of the vineyard, and sometimes even that of the vintner—veritable *appelations contrôlées* on these sealed containers.[10] Wine was an offering to the gods, which Pharaoh presented them on New Year's Day, symbol of the return of life and the demiurge with the silt-reddened waters of the flooding Nile. The people were generally satisfied to get drunk on beer in honor of the Mistress of Love. They found ample occasion to do so during various aquatic pilgrimages and unrestrained festivals, the most exuberant of which seem to have taken place in Bubastis, the city and temple dedicated to the cat goddess Bastet, the tamed form of the Distant One (see chapter 1).

Touch

The final element of this code, but not the least important, is touch. We have at our disposal an entire repertoire of gestures that we have already had occasion to note: the oblique interlacing of the arms of two partners, mutually holding up each other's elbow or grasping the wrist, is an erotic approach. On the other hand, the interlaced legs (see fig. 2.7) is the modest icon of coitus. The progressive touching and caressing of the sensitive parts of the body are essentially erotic and do not necessarily lead—although in the majority of cases they do—to the carnal joining of the partners. These gestures are applied along the front and back acupuncture meridians, transporting the energy, and also involve the seven *chakras,* energy centers of Eastern medicoreligious traditions. The Egyptians had empirically discovered and codified these zones that reacted to touch.[11] The hand is the universal subtle and crude tool of this game (fig. 4.14) into which the feet may also enter—the "foot of Hathor" is mentioned in funeral rituals and keeping in mind respective cultural differences, we say "to play footsie with someone" in a broader sense, but the phrase is probably of erotic origin and still unmistakably translates a coded request.

Music and Dance

It is not within the scope of the present work to study musical instruments, how the musician's profession was organized, or how the dancers' trade was arranged.[12] We have

Figure 4.14: These images of hands, classically hieratic or voluptuously supple, are perfect illustrations of the code of touch.

also stayed away from military music, as it does not enter into the field of our study. We are simply planning to present in a succinct fashion the principal forms of these closely connected arts.

Music and dance are the traditional accomplices of lovers, so be it! We are forced to note, however, that here again we find a ritual face and a profane face.

Ritual dances are accompanied by music, or, at least by rhythm instruments, the clapping of hands, and the snapping of fingers. Among the older manifestations of music from this category figure those performed by the *muu* dancers (fig. 4.15), recognizable by their perforated plant crowns (?), and the characteristic gesture they make with one hand. The exact meaning of the service they provide has not yet been completely explained, but it seems that this procession by large strides represents the coming of the royal ancestors, who race to welcome the recently deceased king. This dance forms part of a royal ritual in Buto.

The dancers depicted on a relief from an Old Kingdom tomb belong to the same category of ritual performers. Their uncustomary clothing (male loincloth and crossed scarves over an otherwise naked torso), their hair cut short like a man's, the masculine musculature of their bodies confer upon them a very crude, mannish appearance.[13] Only their definitely feminine breasts permit us to identify them as women (fig. 4.16). They

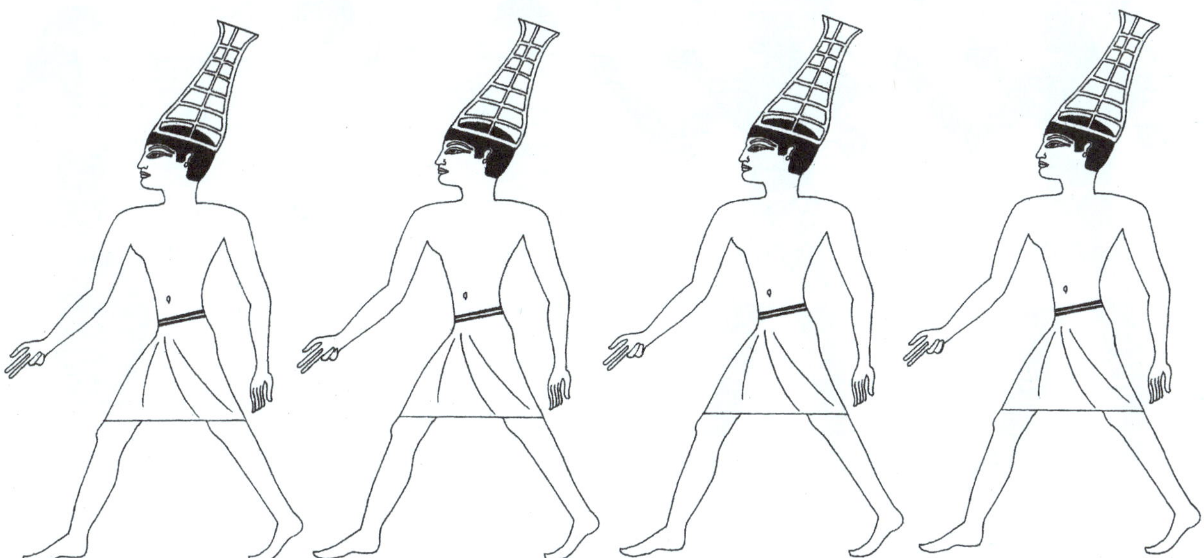

Figure 4.15: A line of marching *muu* dancers. Many of the elements of the ritual, which they perform at double speed clothed in an unusual loincloth-skirt and wearing odd perforated crowns, have not been fully explained, such as, for example, the gesture of their right hands, which remains a mystery. The dancers possibly represent the shades of the royal ancestors. (Thebes, Twelfth Dynasty; from N. de G. Davies and A. H. Gardiner, *The Tomb of Antefoker, Vizier of Sesostris I, and of his Wife Senet* [London, 1920]).

Figure 4.16: Ritual choreography depicted on an Old Kingdom tomb relief. This odd dance is performed by young women with male musculature that clashes with their sizable breasts. They wear their hair like men and their torsos are naked save for some skillfully knotted scarves. Four are wearing a loincloth-skirt and the other three just loincloths. These latter are snapping their fingers while gracefully looking over their shoulders, while their four companions are brandishing their sistrums like weapons (these sistrums are the oldest known variety). A dwarf, who is also holding the archaic form of the sistrum, marches in step with them while singing. There is no doubt that this is a Hathorian dance, perhaps evoking both her male and female elements, but for lack of any supporting documentation a complete analysis of the scene cannot be made at the present time. A comparison with certain dances from the royal jubilee can be suggested. (Relief from the tomb of Nuneter, Giza, Fourth or Fifth Dynasty, housed in the Kunsthistorisches Museum, Vienna, ÄS 8028, published in the exhibition catalog, *L'art égyptien au temps des pyramides* [Paris, 1999], no. 93, p. 254 [C.

Figure 4.17: A Hathorian dance involving first, two men with exceptional attributes—*menat* necklaces with double counterweights and castanets ending in male heads—then a man clothed in a short dress, a young male dancer leaping, and finally, a woman wearing a long clinging dress. All of them are stressing the rhythm—two with castanets, one clapping his hands, and the woman snapping her fingers—for the dancer, whose gesture indicates he is beginning to get dizzy and is entering into a trance. (From Davis and Gardiner, *Tomb of Antefoker.*)

are performing a gyrating dance around a dwarf while shaking archaic versions of Hathorian sistrums. Music and a rhythm section consisting of four assistants clapping their hands accompany their dance.

A dance of an ancient Hathorian ritual, depicted on a tomb painting, features dancers shaking some very unique-looking castanets and wearing necklaces reminiscent of the Hathor *menat* as well as a man and a woman who clap out the rhythm with their hands for a young dancer who is jumping to their beat. This should allow him to attain a trance state, similar to the one induced by whirling dervishes (fig. 4.17).[14]

The ritual (fig. 4.18) and acrobatic dancers (fig. 4.19) perform movements related to the powers of Hathor, for these dances form part of the jubilee ceremony—the *sed* festival—of the king Amenhotep III, depicted in the Theban tomb of Kheruef. The jubilee is meant magically to renew the sovereign's vital forces; he undergoes a phase simulating death in this ritual and another celebrating his mystical resurrection. The participation of Hathor, goddess of death, love, and rebirth, is obvious insofar as the pharaoh in this tomb is seated next to Hathor, and behind this divine couple stands the queen Tiyi, coiffed as Sothis, the star goddess of the new year and renewal. Above the dancers a song is inscribed that takes away any remaining hesitations we may have about the meaning of this scene:

> Jubilation for the Golden One and sweet pleasure for the Mistress of the Two Lands, so that she may grant to Nebmaatre [Amenhotep III], endowed with life, a long lifespan. Come! Appear! so that I may praise you at dawn and make music for you in the evening. O Hathor, you are exulted in the hair of Ra, for to you have been given the sky, the deep night, and the stars (. . .) to you belongs everything. O, my mistress, come and protect the king Nebmaatre, endowed with life. Give him the health of the eastern side of the sky, so he may be happy, prosperous, and glorious on the horizon. If you desire that he

Figure 4.18: Dancers performing ritual movements intended to inspire the Lady of Love to renew the king's vital forces. We find here the same naked torsos, adorned with scarves similar to the Old Kingdom dancers, as well as the same short skirts. But the gestures of the two dancer couples are different here and unquestionably more erotic, as are their abundant heads of hair.

Figure 4.19: An acrobatic dancer making a bridge, depicted on an ostracon. This is probably a preparatory sketch for a more official depiction. One will note the completely naked torso, the miniscule knotted loincloth, the earring, and the magnificent hair of this young woman. All these details, and especially the figure being performed, combine to form a very erotic image. (Nineteenth Dynasty, Turin Museum.)

Figure 4.20: (a) Two dancers moving in opposite directions but both making welcoming gestures, and (b) a third who is gracefully kneeling, looking down at a mandrake bush. All three suggest an invitation to love, emphasized by their nudity, sophisticated hairstyles, and their jewels.

Figure 4.21: The genie Bes, whom the Distant One seems to have brought back from the heart of Africa, shows up here as a musician in her honor.

lives, make him live for millions of years, always. Pray, so that this may be (his) protection.[15]

These charming dancers are located on another level of the wall, still in honor of Hathor, but here they are depicted naked and adorned with jewels (fig. 4.20).

In this context we should not overlook the god Bes, here a dancer, singer, and harper, roles he assumes both for amusing and soothing his divine mistress (fig. 4.21).

The dancers and lyre- and double-flute-playing musicians could belong to the retinue of the gynaeceum guardian, because they have placed garlands of convolvulus (fig. 4.22), or rather a clematis, on their floating, transparent tunics.[16]

On another scale—but still ritual—is the digni-

Figure 4.22: Two dancers preceding two musicians, a lyre and a flute player, probably to celebrate a happy birth. Their odd necklaces and long ample tunics decorated with the plant associated with giving birth bring such an occasion to mind.
(Tomb of Kynebu, Theban tomb no. 113, Twentieth Dynasty.)

fied parade of sistrum players who are probably attached to the divine worship as "singers to Amun" (fig. 4.23), stimulating the passions of the demiurge with the instrument of the Golden One. Figure 4.24 shows another, clearly less conventional, parade of female tambour players and figure 4.25 depicts female musicians treading a dance measure, carried away by their music. During a festival or banquet, musicians would set up with their instruments, like the flutist directed by the gestures of the chironome (fig. 4.26), or the player of the double flute accompanied by the rhythmic clapping of hands by the guests (fig. 4.27), or by young women—like these seated beneath a vine arbor (fig. 4.28)—or the harpist with her cumbersome instrument (fig. 4.29), whose undulating sounds are accompanied by those of the lute.

We have already mentioned that certain musicians lived close to the milieu of professional erotic entertainment, without belonging to it. This may well be the case for the tantalizing lutanist (fig. 4.30) with the tattoo of Bes on her thigh, accompanied by her pet monkey who is tickling her buttocks. And what can we say about this scene pictured in figure 4.31, in which an imperturbable harpist is watching a man dance who, having had too much to drink, has stripped off his clothes, but not his jewels, and whose sex organ is depicted in a very peculiar fashion.[17]

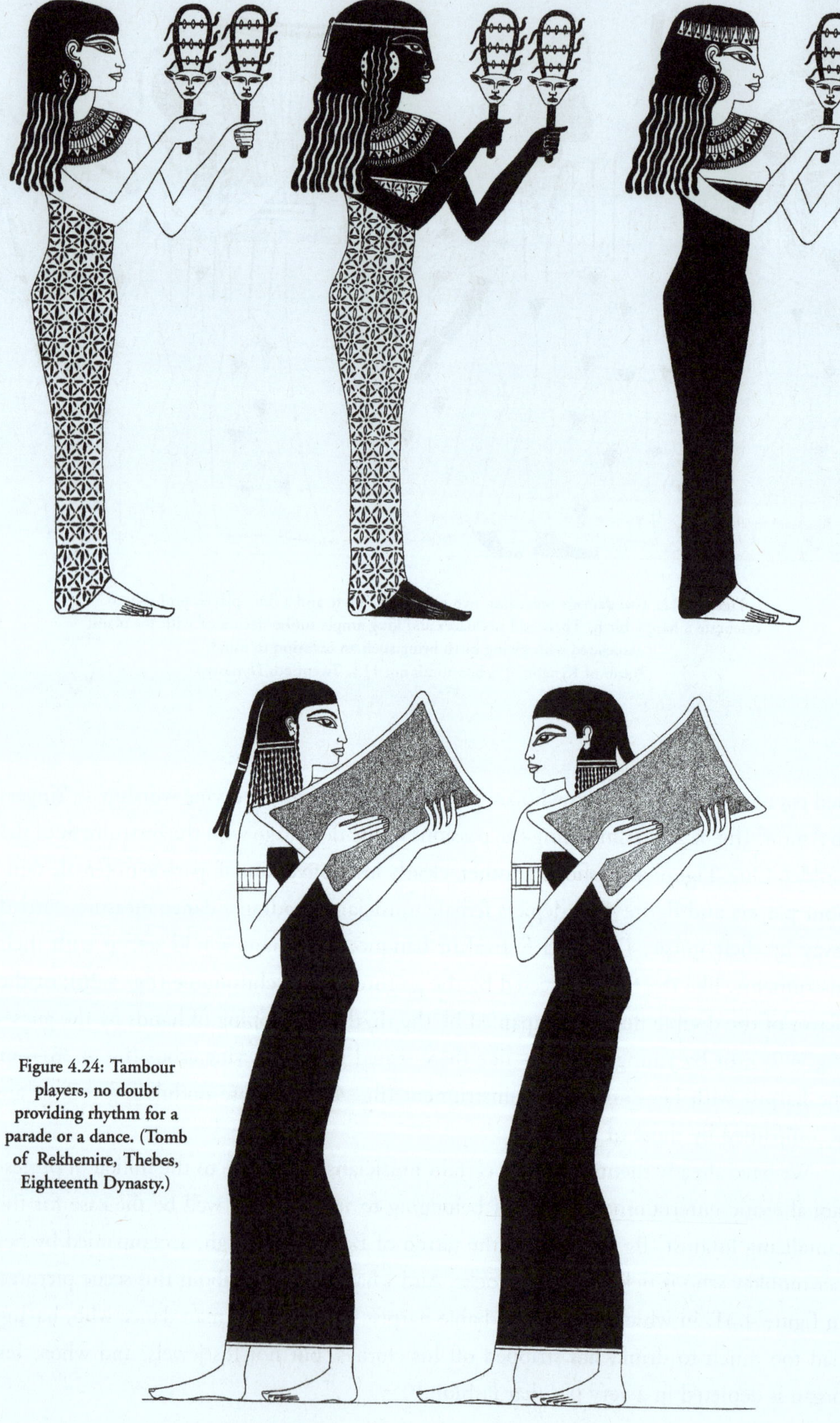

Figure 4.23: Three "singers"—or musicians—of Amun, concentrating on their ritual performance. They are part of the harem of their god and hold the rank of priestesses. They recruit their members from the higher (in principle) and middle classes of society and are under the orders of a "harem superior" who is a high-born lady. (From Chassinat, *Dendara* 4.)

Figure 4.24: Tambour players, no doubt providing rhythm for a parade or a dance. (Tomb of Rekhemire, Thebes, Eighteenth Dynasty.)

Figure 4.25: Musicians in a festival parade. A lute player and her small companion are both nude but covered with jewels and sport skillfully arranged hair. They appear oblivious to all but their own music, paying no attention to the musicians following them; a flutist (double flute) and a lyre player who, themselves, are harmonizing their own playing. These last two are wearing festival dresses. (Tomb of Djeserkareseneb, Theban tomb no. 38, Twenty-third Dynasty.)

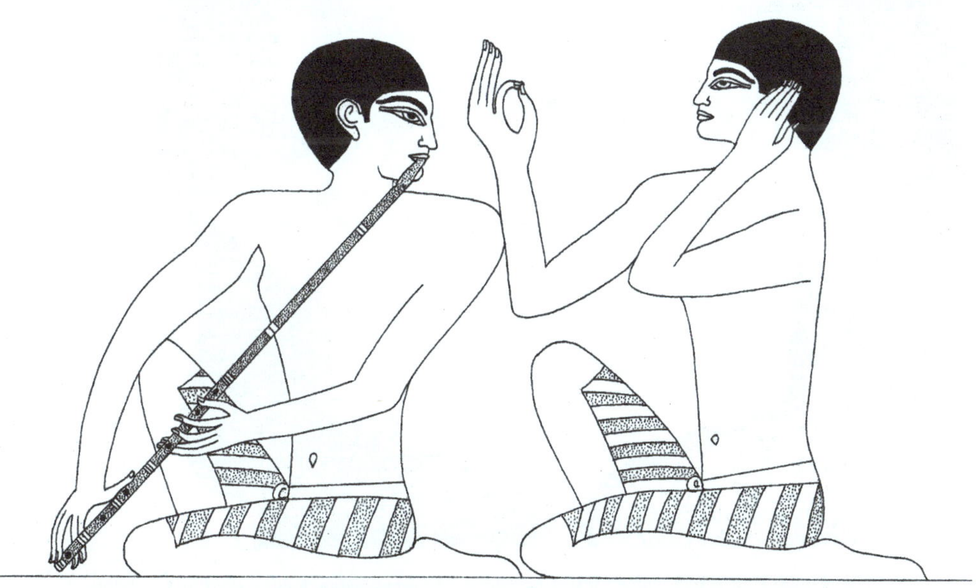

Figure 4.26: Flutist attentively following the gestures of the chironome directing his playing. This method is still used in popular Egyptian music. (Detail from a bas-relief, tomb of Niankhkhnum and Khnumhotep, Saqqara, Fifth Dynasty.)

Figure 4.27: Festival or funeral banquet? Whatever the case, the fact remains that these richly adorned young women are clapping the rhythm for the music played by a woman playing a double flute (or an oboe?).

Figure 4.28: Four young women seated beneath a vine arbor clapping out a rhythm, no doubt for a festival, judging by their beautiful dresses, their ceremonial wigs, and their numerous jewels. (Detail from scenes related to *sed* festival of Amenhotep III, bas-relief, tomb of Kheuef, Thebes, Eighteenth Dynasty.)

Figure 4.29: Two musicians conscientiously endeavoring to draw smooth and harmonious melodies from their stringed instruments, a large harp and a lute. (Tomb of Rekhemire, Thebes, Eighteenth Dynasty.)

Figure 4.30: Female small-lute player accompanied by her monkey familiar. She is seated upon a cushion, probably in a home where she is about to give a performance. Naked, but perfumed, adorned with jewels, and artfully coiffed, and with a tattoo of Bes on her thigh, she could easily fit into a milieu of those who delight in the good things of life. Yet, this scene is also ritual, because it is painted on an earthenware bowl of a prophylactic blue-turquoise color on which the young woman is depicted seated beneath an arbor of grape vines—the vine of Osiris—column-bouquets of lotus and papyrus. (New Kingdom, Eighteenth Dynasty, Museum of Antiquities, Leyden.)

To close this section, here are some verse extracts from the "word balloons" inserted between the characters of these genre scenes. The text is particularly interesting, for it clearly confirms the assimilation between Hathor and Maat, already discussed in chapter 1 in the section concerning cosmogony.

> *Is this Maat, on whose face can be read a desire to get drunk?*
> *The beauty of your face is radiant,*
> *You appear, you come in peace.*
> *O you, who are as beautiful as gold, O you, Hathor!*
> *One gets drunk merely by looking at you [see fig. 4.32].*

Psychotropic Agents

Psychotropic plants are not only the formidable accomplices of Eros but also of drunkenness, both sacred and profane, which through their effects, potentiate those of alcohol. They facilitate access to an altered state of consciousness, a term also employed in psychotherapy about the phenomena of the transition between life and death. Isn't the act of love called a little death *(la petite mort)?*

Figure 4.31: Harper strumming the strings of her instrument without appearing to take any notice of the strange dancer who is looking back at her in delight.

Figure 4.32: The Golden One, Lady of Drunkenness, whose strange face with its hypnotic gaze dominates the hieroglyph for "gold," which is also one of her names. Her head is crowned by a naos serving as the sound box of a *sekhem* sistrum that opens a way for the young musician, Ihy, who is approaching the light. (From Chassinat, *Dendara* 1.)

The spotlight here is on the mandrake *(Mandragora officinarum)* and on the blue lotus *(Nymphaea caerulea),* which has a more intoxicating perfume than the discreet scent of the white lotus *(Nymphaea alba).* In Europe, extracts from the latter have been employed to reduce the libido, whereas in ancient Egypt they were used for just the opposite reason, and no doubt successfully, as both lotus and mandrake had the reputation of being aphrodisiacs. In this category of plants, we need to include the silphium, probably used during the *sed* festival, and an unidentified plant, the *menhep,* which is noted in the Berlin dictionary (Wb. II 82, 18) as being a "useful drug for coïtus." *Cannabis sativa* was known, but not apparently for its effects. Lettuce was consecrated to the ithyphallic god, Min. Given that lettuce is a sedative, two hypothetical explanations can be proposed: either the whitish and viscous sap of the plant was compared to sperm, or this sedative was used to calm the passion of this god.

What do the experts who have wrestled with this question say? An American researcher examined the psychotropic effects of the blue lotus and the mandrake between 1979 and 1982.[18] He came to the conclusion that these two plants were powerful psychotropics and narcotics. They contained complex chemical substances that other researchers had isolated and called nupharine or nymphaealine, as well as nuciferine, because they were strongly concentrated within the flowers of the blue lotus. When inhaled, these molecules rapidly induce a trance state, even intoxication.

In Europe the mandrake was the center of colorful folklore and a superstitious, almost religious, veneration of its erogenous powers, which recent scientific studies have justified.

Furthermore, during the 1990s, molecular biology research on the tissue of Egyptian mummies (the dates of these were not specified)[19] revealed the presence of hashish and nicotine, discoveries confirmed by the cytological examinations of the mummy of Ramses II, during its restoration in Paris and Grenoble.[20]

a

b

These results hardly surprised the Egyptologists, who are quite familiar with the bucolic paintings that had been used to illustrate tombs since the time of the Old Kingdom. These represent the deceased, no matter his social status, hunting and fishing in the marshes, accompanied by the women of his house, but rarely any servant, or even a son. How can one not recall the scenes depicting Akhenaten, his queen, and his daughters (never a son!) in the varied performance of their ritual duties? The wife of our hunter takes a protective position behind him, like Isis at the side of Osiris. She is laden with blue lotuses and sports a cone of perfume on her head. The deceased and his family (but not the servant, a simple supernumerary who does not take part in the rituals) are adorned in their most handsome finery, hardly suitable for such expeditions in the papyrus thickets (fig. 4.33). These scenes bring to mind the story of Isis secretly raising her son Horus, which is a metophor for gestation. The deceased kills the aquatic birds, supposedly demons threatening his later life, while his wife and daughters are holding superb blue lotuses out to him. The fish (always two!) for which he is fishing represent his lives, his soul of yesterday and his soul of tomorrow.

In the depiction of funeral banquets, the guests are adorned in the same flower and offer small bouquets of water lilies and mandrake. They symbolically surround the deceased, shown in the process of breathing the magic flower, whose fragrance rapidly produces its effects, attended by the women who assist him (fig. 4.34). Psychotropics help the transformed one to traverse the "narrow gate" and reanimate the generative forces of the new Osiris, which fact is expressed by the *sekhem* scepter (fig. 4.35) that he holds upright in his hand, having always at his side the feminine element, sometimes two women, evidently playing the roles of Isis and Nephthys around Osiris on the occasion of his awakening. The deceased can also be represented drinking a liquid (or inhaling

Figure 4.33 (a and b): Two of the traditional scenes known as "hunting and fishing in the marshes," which are not reminders of the everyday life of a class in Egyptian society whose members could spend time in these leisure activities, but a reference to the magic of rebirth, which is erotic and sexual by definition, as we have explained in the discussion of these images in the text. Here before our eyes are all the symbols of the effort for rebirth and the code of ritual gestures that are needed to succeed, as well as the image—magically active for the Ancients—of an abundant growth of narcotic plants. We should note again that these rites are established from solely a male point of view; none of these scenes show a woman hunting in the man's place. Yet, in accordance with the dogma, the woman also becomes at death an androgynous "Osiris" who has need of his complement to live again. Certainly, in addition to the "dead person's concubines," numerous phallic figurines have been exhumed, as we have already said, but whether found in former sanctuaries or family tombs, we do not know for whom they were placed there. Furthermore, the majority of tombs were set up either for couples or entire families, each individual deriving a personal benefit from the rites of rebirth. The queens and highly ranked women of the crown were, however, given individual tombs and a ritual decor adapted to their person and rank, being—all things considered—very close to that of the king. For the sovereign and queen alike the sexual complement is located in the divine world. Mere mortal women make do with the fallout from the rituals intended for their husbands, in which they play an active and honored role, and thanks also—for the most fortunate—to the passport to the beyond, the Book of the Dead, which personalized its vignettes and by adding their names to the text preceded by the epithet "Osiris." (Tomb of Menna, Theban tomb no. 69, Eighteenth Dynasty, from the facsimile by Nina Davies, Metropolitan Museum of Art, New York.)

Figure 4.34: Three seductive young women and the wife aid the deceased so as to open to him, with the intoxicating blue lotus and the toasts made to his *ka,* the gate of the beyond where his transformation should be achieved. All the various erotic attributes are gathered together here: the nudity of the assistants whose only garb is an overabundance of jewelry setting their bodies in relief; carefully arranged hair held back by lotus headbands; the presentation of cups containing intoxicating beverages (wine in honor of Hathor or other psychotropic drinks); and a long narrow container next to a piece of linen that may serve for inhaling other substances inducing trance states. As for the wife, adorned with all the accessories of seduction, she is embracing her husband amorously, assisted by the servant holding the man's elbow (a gesture from the code of love, as we have already seen). Her prominent chest, swollen like that of a nursing mother, indicates that she is ready to receive the seed of her husband, his future child, so that he may be reborn of his works into a new life. (Tomb of Nebamon, Thebes, Eighteenth Dynasty.)

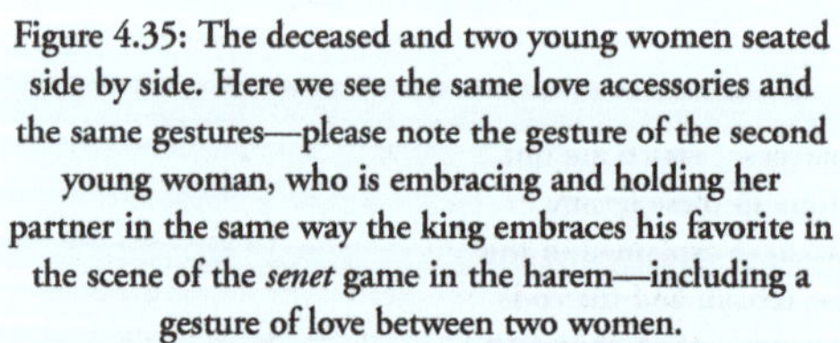

Figure 4.35: The deceased and two young women seated side by side. Here we see the same love accessories and the same gestures—please note the gesture of the second young woman, who is embracing and holding her partner in the same way the king embraces his favorite in the scene of the *senet* game in the harem—including a gesture of love between two women.

The deceased is holding the scepter of power, here a sexual attribute. The cat attacking a young bird is both a realistic sequence and a magical wink of the eye: Bastet-Tefnut extending her claws while spitting is a way of reminding the symbol of feminine sexuality of its proper place in the scheme of things. It is no doubt intentional that this group is depicted beneath the seat of the woman with homosexual tendencies who seems to be forgetting she should be playing the role of Nephthys in the company of Isis and Osiris. (Tomb of Ramose, Thebes, Eighteenth Dynasty.)

vapors?), no doubt of a narcotic substance, allowing him to attain the same goal (fig. 4.36). A similar liquid is probably poured for the women participating in the rite that is called "for your *ka,*" as the inscription in figure 4.37 specifies, and thus intended for the generative force of the deceased.

In the royal sphere, the queen offers her exhausted and weakened king, propped up by a cane, a lotus and a mandrake, the fruits of love (fig. 4.38). On the famous gold naos of Tutankhamun,

Figure 4.36: The deceased stretching his hand toward the table of offerings (not shown) placed before him, while drinking or inhaling an intoxicating substance. (Mastaba of Ptahhotep, Saqqara, Fifth Dynasty.)

Figure 4.37: Extract from a scene of a funeral banquet—during which one should only drink not eat. In (a), however, a servant is bearing a large cup filled with cakes, probably to prevent the wine from going too quickly to the guests' heads (see also fig. 4.34). The naked servant is pouring out a libation (of wine) to the *ka* of the deceased, while her companion (in b) is bending toward the kneeling guests to pour a stream of some liquid into the outstretched hands of the woman in front. No text explicitly states what is going on here, but a parallel can be established with a scene from the golden naos of Tutankhamun (fig. 4.39) and figure 4.36.

Figure 4.38: The queen is offering her tired partner a stimulating bouquet—in the texts, "the tired (ones)" are the deceased. It is also therefore a ritual erotic scene, a meaning explicitly suggested by the queen's skillfully highlighted naked abdomen. (Royal couple [Smenkhkare and Merytaten?], Eighteenth Dynasty; Berlin Staatl. Museum.)

Figure 4.39: A scene of a mystic nuptial chamber depicted on the outside of Tutankhamun's gold naos. Ankhesenamun is offering the narcotic lotus to her husband and is pouring him a drink, allegedly for altering his state of consciousness so as to begin a transformation culminating with his rebirth. Clothing, crowns, and furniture (chair with the *sema-tauy*) place this scene in the royal milieu. (Tomb of Tutankhamun, Eighteenth Dynasty; H. Carter and A. Mace, *The Tomb of Tut-Ankh-Amen,* 3 volumes [London-New York, 1923–33]; also C. Desroches-Noblecourt, *Vie et mort d'un pharaon—Toutankhamon,* [Paris, 1902], pls. 7 and 9a.)

Figure 4.40: From the same source as figure 4.39, this scene depicts the culmination of the rites of love, set within intimate surroundings. The queen is wearing the crown of Sothis, whose appearance coincides with the beginning of the annual flooding of the Nile and the New Year. The king also is going to return to life "with all the fathers and mothers of Egypt."

the queen is pouring a stimulating liquid for her husband, seated on a chair bearing the royal emblem of the *sema-tawy* (fig. 4.39). He responds to her, but in very private surroundings for this intimate scene. In figure 4.40 the king, holding lotus and mandrake, pours a long stream of a liquid from a small cruet into the queen's hand, which she is holding open like a cup. This is the coded, chaste, and poetic image of the culminating moment of the sex act.

During the Late Period, the soporific properties of the poppy (fig. 4.41) made this plant the symbol of eternal rest. Appearing on the Greco-Roman funerary masks held in the hands of the deceased are bouquets or crowns of poppies; these braided flowers are a reinterpretation of Osiris's crown of vindication, which survives even in our modern cemeteries.

These scenes are often adorned with illustrations of the tables of offerings laden with all the magical goods we have just described (fig. 4.42).

One final detail, of a botanical nature, should be mentioned. The white nymphaea blossoms over a three-day period, its corolla rising on a stem above an expanse of water. It opens around eight o'clock in the morning and closes when the sun is at its zenith. At the end of the three days, it disappears back into the waters where its fruit will ripen. When Ra is at the height of his revealed power, Osiris returns into the abyssal depths to recharge his latent energies, symbolized by the blue lotus that flowers at night—thus the cycle ends, to begin again, endlessly.

Magic and Amulets

How could we talk about love without bringing up—and not only in the case of antiquity—the appeal to magic? This art played a great role in all areas of life for the Ancients; appeals have always been made to divine or demonic forces throughout human history. The goddess Weuret-Hekat, whose name means "the Great (One) of Magic," can assume different forms. Isis has a natural right to this title, as does the hippopotamus goddess, Taweret the Great One, and among others, the perturbing Qadesh (fig. 4.43), who came from the nearby Asiatic lands as the goddess of love and its spells. These practices were primarily aimed at obtaining the love of a desired partner, either man or woman. They could also, and even frequently, be put to work with the intention of causing harm to a rival, or with the purpose of achieving revenge. Countless recipes for love potions, containing surprising and very unappetizing ingredients—such as the body parts of magical animals (black rooster, toad, insects, snakes, fish, bats, etc.), sacrificed under ritual circumstances (full moon, new moon, at a specific hour, etc.), macerated in extracts of hallucinogenic or narcotic plants (poppy, datura) then buried to conceal the beverage from the light of the sun—are proposed. We can only wonder how the apprentice sorcerer succeeded in making the object of his desire swallow such a horrific beverage—and we have just spoken of the role taste plays in love! According to the same methods, magical oils were prepared into which an oxyrhynchus fish could be included as an ingredient; this is the same fish that swallowed the phallus of Osiris. The lover would then anoint his penis with this oil.[21] For a woman to attract the man of her dreams, she needed to procure the uterus of Tefnut (we are not told how), but a bat could also get the job done! There is no need to keep citing examples; all the great deities of Creation—Ra and Shu

Figure 4.41: Poppy and mandrake, such as they are represented in Egyptian iconography, planted on the edge of a pool.

Figure 4.42: A table laden with a great offering of food that can also be symbolically depicted by the *wedjat* eye. Indeed it is similarly complete and contains all the products necessary for the effectiveness of the rites of survival and rebirth.

Figure 4.43: The disturbing Syrian goddess Qadesh, an unofficial but apprarently effective goddess of love, holding her active attributes of lotuses and serpents (phallic symbols?). Her vehicle is a male lion (Shu? Maï?), dociley advancing beneath her feet. Her role is clearly spelled out by the lunar crescent and disk, as well as her curly Hathorian hairstyle, her breasts adorned with daisies, like those that often decorate the lower part of the *menat* counterweight, and the clinging dress embroidered with a lotus at the location of the vulva. (Stele of Qadesh, Nineteenth to Twentieth Dynasties, Louvre Museum, Paris, C86.)

are frequently invoked also—are ready to make their contributions to help little earthlings in their erotic adventures.

For an act of revenge or an act meant to cause harm, the panoply of sorcerers and sorceresses had various charged objects at their disposal. In general these were representations of the targeted person in crudely fashioned figurines made of mud in which needles or thorns were stuck at strategic locations on the body. These would be forced deeply into the figurine accompanied by spells and magic passes with the hand. Sometimes the figurine would be wrapped in a piece of linen or small piece of papyrus inscribed with astounding spells. The customer had only to introduce this noxious product into the home of his potential victim, or bury it secretly beneath the threshold of his house.[22]

The custom of wearing amulets, talismans, and other good-luck charms is as old as humanity.[23] The ancient Egyptians had an impressive array of things of this nature to

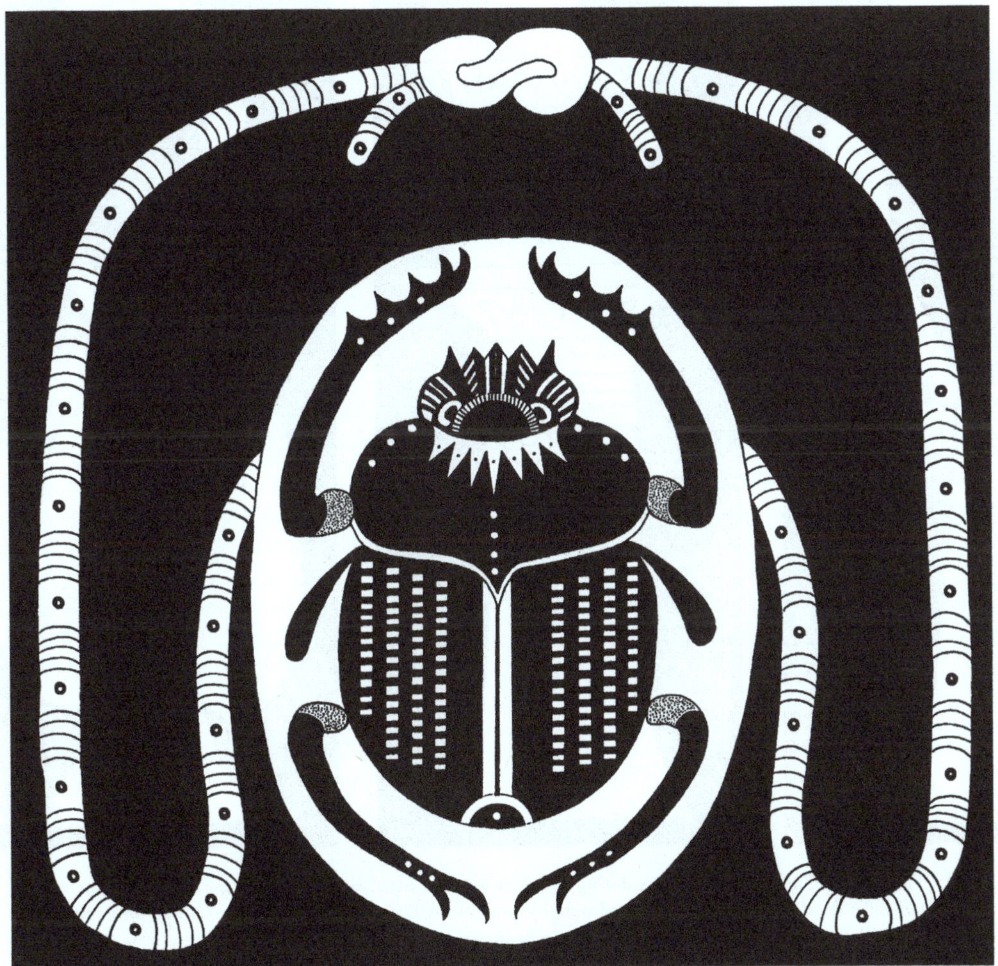

Figure 4.44: Scarab amulet and its necklace. The scarab is simultaneously the embodiment of the future, the god Khepri, and the hieroglyph for "becoming." This is probably the most widely used amulet.

Figure 4.45: The *wedjat* eye, a highly valued talisman. It represents physical integrity, food, luminous existence, magical protection by the sacred serpent, and the protection by the sign *sa*, added here.

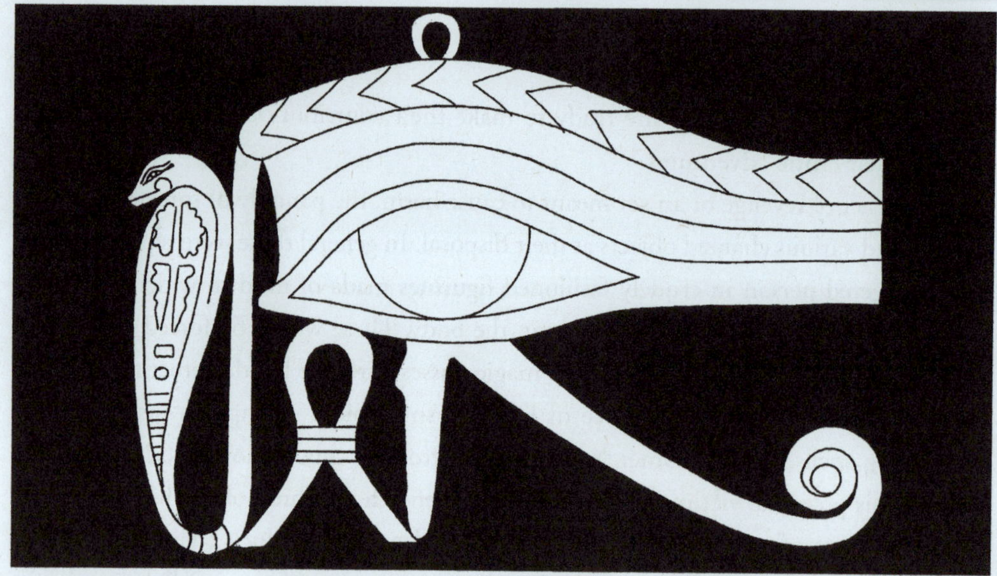

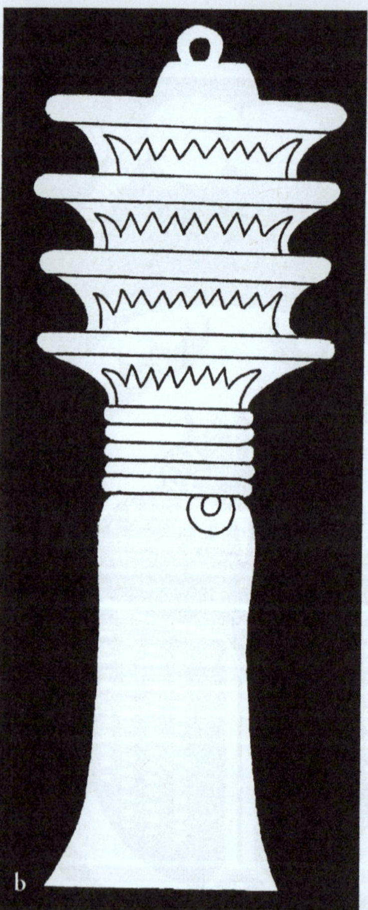

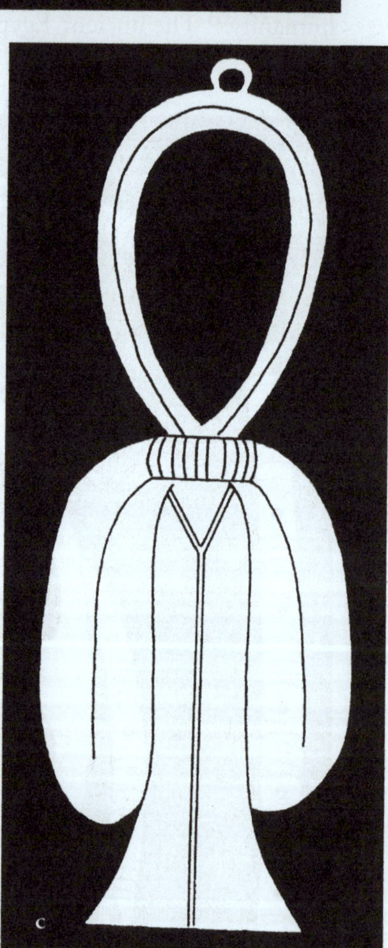

Figure 4.46: Three amulets known during antiquity for their beneficial efficacy: (a) the cross of life, or *ankh;* (b) the *djed* pillar of strength and stability; and (c) the knot of Isis, the *tet.* The Osirian *djed* and the Isis *tet* are complementary. A parallel can be drawn between the ankh, *djed,* and *was* during the Late Period, with Shu, Osiris, and Tefnut.

choose from, among which are the scarab (fig. 4.44), the *wadj* column, the *wedjat* eye (fig. 4.45), the *djed* pillar, and the Isis knot, as well as the symbol for life, the *ankh* (fig. 4.46), but the main spotlight was definitely on the small figurines of the gods.[24] These objects, enjoying a new lease on life thanks to tourism, are still quite popular. But no one in ancient times would have dared to sport the cartouche, the divine and royal emblem bearing the name of its humble owner. What a sacrilege! In the eyes of the Ancients this would have transformed the amulet into a bad-luck charm.

CHAPTER FIVE

Medicine and Sexuality

THE PRIMARY SOURCES

This subject is so vast that all we can attempt here is a rapid overview, necessarily limited to the subject of the present study. Pharaonic civilization has left, in spite of the fragile nature of the media, a great number of medical texts, such as the famous Edwin Smith Papyrus (on surgery), the Ebers Papyrus (on general medicine, gynecology, gastrology, and urology), as well as the gynecological papyri of Kahun and Berlin.[1] There is even a treatise on the veterinary art, because everything forms part of the "livestock of God." These didactic texts, meant for teaching future physicians the necessary knowledge, are called *shesau,* which specifically means "teachings." Diagnosis is called "seeing" *(maa)* or "observing"—especially if the treatment has failed; it is necessary to give future disciples and their patients the benefit of the masters' experience, even if it is negative. Ancient medicine was closely tied to religious and magical ideas. The doctor placed his patient under the protection of a particular healing god, but it is Sekhmet, the patroness of priests specializing in medicine, who was head of the profession, assisted by her son Nefertum, responsible for ointments. The Old Kingdom architect and great scholar Imhotep was deified during the Greek era. The Ebers Papyrus stipulates that "medication is effective by virtue of magic, magic is effective by virtue of medication"; you cannot have one without the other. The Ancients already understood the body-mind relationship.

GYNECOLOGY AND OBSTETRICS

The main concerns of gynecology, a domain falling under the protection of the goddess Taweret (fig. 5.1), were with medications encouraging fertility, such as those based on plants, milk, beer, and fruits (dates), or, on the contrary, contraception, for which a sort of cloth pessary coated with honey and/or resins were used; crocodile excrement was recommended for the same purpose. Results were never reported. On the other hand, modern medicine has confirmed the spermicidal action of the acid contained in gum arabic and acacia sap, both used for contraception in ancient times.[2] Male contraception does not seem to have existed.

Figure 5.1: Taweret, the hippopotamus goddess, protectress of mothers. The Hathorian horns crowning her head refer her to certain aspects of the goddess of love.

Advanced readings of a pregnancy, especially concerning prediction of the child's gender with the aid of urine's action on cereal grains, were quite important. These techniques, with their haphazard results, are still practiced in the rural areas.

Obstetrics was rudimentary and practiced by midwives (cutting of the umbilical cord, small incisions); there is no confirmation for true obstetrical interventions, and it is believed they did not exist. Cases of birth complications, such as the death of the mother and sometimes that of the child, were not rare, as the examination of female mummies, as well as certain writings, have shown. Premature births and fetuses had the right to a sepulchre, at least in certain milieus—we have in mind the two mummified fetuses found in the tomb of Tutankhamun.

Birth (fig. 5.2) took place in a spot that was also reserved for women during their menses. The young mother passed her time until her purification in a kind of pavilion (fig. 5.3) decorated with the southern clematis for easing birth, an effect verified by mod-

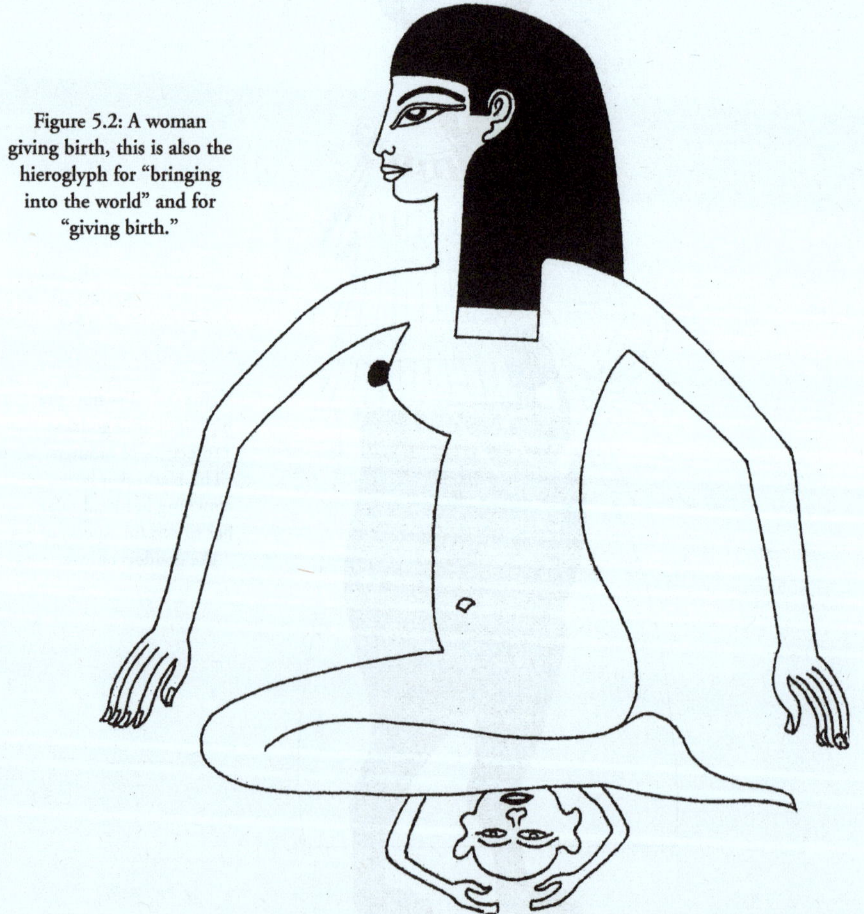

Figure 5.2: A woman giving birth, this is also the hieroglyph for "bringing into the world" and for "giving birth."

Figure 5.3: The young new mother, nursing her baby in the area reserved for the period just following delivery. The pavilion was ventilated for the comfort of mother and baby and surrounded by the southern clematis, associated with labor. Coquetry still asserts its rights even here: a servant is holding up a mirror and cosmetics container with a stiletto to the young woman, in order that she can restore her beauty and inspect her elaborate hairstyle, which seems to be mandatory under these circumstances. The whole of this scene is a Hathorian allegory. (Ostracon from Deir el-Medina, British Museum, no. 8506.)

ern science.[3] The mother nursed her child for a period of around three years (fig. 5.4), a practice that also works as a contraceptive, to a certain extent. But as a rule, births followed one another in rapid succession, and a number of women suffered from ills incurred by their repeated pregnancies. The medical treatises list consequences such as cases of prolapse, infections, and so on, while indicating the appropriate remedies, which had limited effectiveness.

Figure 5.4: The goddess Anuket nursing the child-king. The image is purely symbolic in the divine world, for nursing corresponds, in this iconography, to the gestation period, thus prenatal existence, during which the being in becoming is fed with "divine milk," essentially, the blood of the mother.

VENEREAL DISEASES

Sexually transmitted diseases were known during the pharaonic era. They are only mentioned occasionally. Gonorrhea is the only one known to have existed for certain.

SEXUAL MUTILATIONS

Male circumcision, curiously enough, was not mentioned in the surgical treatises, but its practice is confirmed by several illustrations from the Old Kingdom. This procedure, performed at adolescence, was probably not considered a medical activity but a rite of initiation (fig. 5.5); it was widespread in Africa and the Near East, and mentioned in reference to the Jewish population in the Old Testament.[4] Circumcision involves removing part of the foreskin of the penis. The operation is painful but has no detrimental effects on a

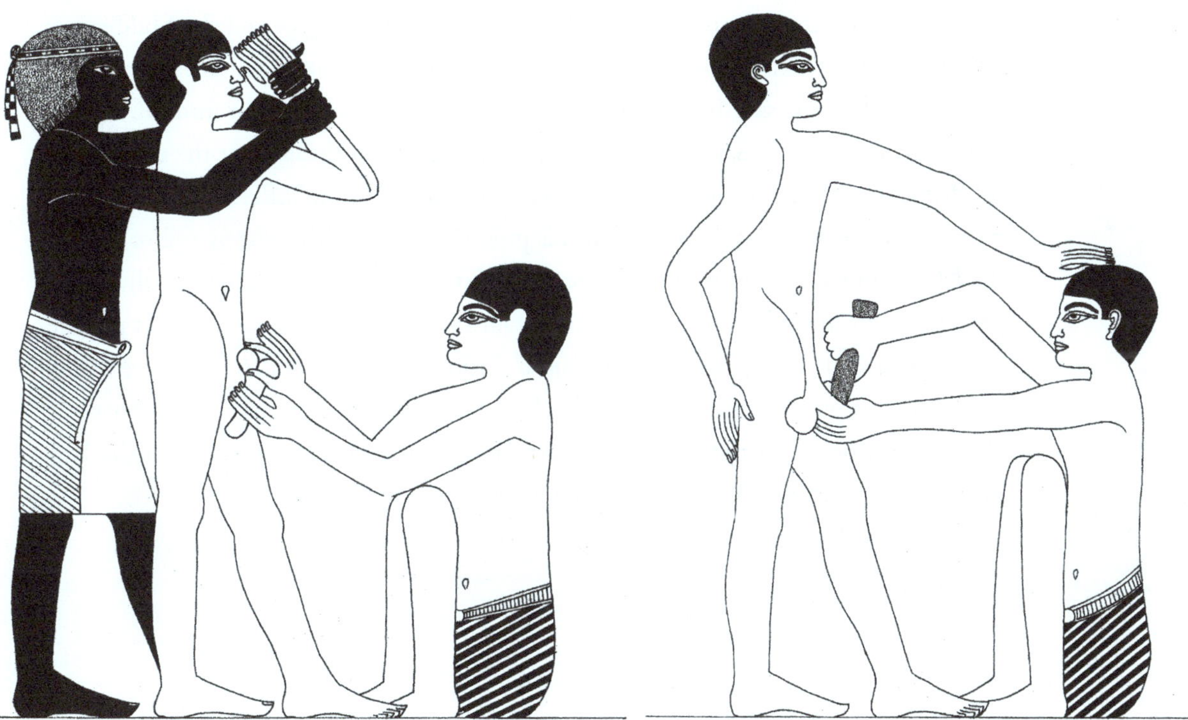

Figure 5.5: Scenes of a circumcision practiced on a young adult by a priest and not a physician, indicating this was a ritual act. The priest is also lavishing care on his patient with no indication as to whether treatment took place before or after the operation. The text "balloons" accompanying the scene inform us that the operation was performed by a funerary priest and that this latter is saying to his assistant: "Hold him firmly! Don't let him get soft!" From the evidence—and contrary to what has often been claimed—there was no anesthesia, which would have been in contradiction to the initiatory role of the operation. (Tomb of Ankhmahor, Saqqara, Sixth Dynasty.)

man's sexual activity. It does represent an attack on his physical integrity, though. Circumcision is still performed in Egypt and several other African nations, as well as throughout the Middle East.

There is nothing attesting to the practice of female circumcision, whether text or explicit image. Some rare writings do exist, however, that mention "young girls who have not yet been cut."[5] If we go back to the ardent desire of the "sister" in the love poems, we hesitate to consider female circumcision as a contemporary reality, given the fact that the operation definitively deprives the woman of complete sexual satisfaction. In the scene of the royal harem of Medinet Habu, the king is touching the sex organ of his favorite: does he want to see her reaction or to stimulate her romantic ardor? In the latter case, the gesture would be meaningless if the young woman had been "cut."

Just what does this "circumcision" of women consist of? This term is inadequate and clearly conceals an extremely traumatic and barbaric practice (both physically and psychologically) that originated in sub-Saharan Africa. The alleged "pharaonic circumcision" takes off the clitoris, a particularly sensitive and innervated part of the female sexual organs. It is still the custom with the Muslim population of Egypt and the Middle East, and in several African countries.[6] And yet, this excision, practiced without anesthesia or concern for hygiene save in large urban areas, is the most scaled-down form of this custom.[7] But what can be said of infibulation, still widespread throughout the countries of sub-Saharan Africa? It is much more painful and causes lifelong suffering for the women on whom it has been inflicted. In fact, this procedure cuts off the clitoris and/or sews up the labia minora, and even the labia majora, of the vaginal orifice, leaving only a small passageway for urine and menstrual blood. During the first sexual contact, this passageway must be enlarged, generally by incision![8] Infibulation does not seem to have existed in ancient Egypt. Let's make it perfectly clear that, from an anatomical perspective, the clitoris corresponds to the man's penis, the labia minora to the testicles, and the labia majora to the scrotum. What man would accept such mutilation?

CHAPTER SIX

Uncommon Sexual Practices

MALE AND FEMALE HOMOSEXUALITY

Male homosexuality is confirmed by illustrations and texts; female homosexuality is suggested by images, especially in the context of official and/or ritual depictions as well as those representing the lady of the house in the intimacy of her own home.

Male homosexuality was poorly regarded but tolerated and apparently fairly widespread. Society's attitude in this regard is well illustrated by the quarrels of Seth and Horus: the first is the aggressor and boasts of it without incurring the slightest reproach, whereas the second, the victim, is the object of general scorn. This attitude probably derives from the ancient practice of sexually humiliating a vanquished enemy. Figure 6.1 transposes this aggression into the animal kingdom. Atum embracing his son, Senusret I (fig. 6.2), is merely demonstrating well-deserved paternal recognition of the king. But the energetic gesture bringing the god Ptah and Senusret I into such a close embrace in figure 6.3 denotes a certain ambiguity in their relationship, an ambiguity that the stele representing Akhenaten and his successor, Smenkhkare (fig. 6.4), makes quite clear.

Among mere mortals, amorous affection between two men is also depicted in figure 6.5 according to the code of love we have already analyzed.

Figure 6.1: Sexual aggression between two bulls, a metaphoric image of aggressive male homosexual behavior. (Ostracon from Deir el-Medina, New Kingdom; Metropolitan Museum of Art, New York.)

Figure 6.2: Paternal and affectionate recognition of the king by his divine father, Atum. (Relief from a pillar of the processional pavilion of Senusret I, Karnak, Twelfth Dynasty.)

Figure 6.3: The god Ptah is firmly clasping his son, the king in his arms—barely emerged from his mummy-like sheath. The king is lifting his arm in an affectionate or protective gesture to support or caress the nape of the god's neck. The closeness of their faces resembles a "kiss of the nose." There is a certain ambiguity about this scene.

Figure 6.4: This scene, which has no accompanying text, poses a problem. Some believe it shows Akhenaten and Nefertiti, others feel that the two protagonists are the heretic king and his short-lived successor, Smenkhkare, who seems to have replaced Nefertiti at the end of the Amarnian reign. The hypothesis is plausible enough as the Aten is presenting a symbol of life to the faces of each partner, a representation formerly reserved for the royal couple alone. The image would therefore be a display of possibly ritual homosexuality. (Stele from Tell el-Amarna, Eighteenth Dynasty; Egyptian Museum, Berlin, no. 17813.)

A chance archaeological find has brought us a savory morsel of literature on male homosexuality. A palace servant accidentally witnesses the king Neferkare leaving his apartments at night alone for a stroll. His curiosity aroused, the servant follows His Majesty discreetly and has the surprise of discovering that the king is going to the home of his general, Sisene. Three hours later, Pharaoh leaves and sneaks back to the palace. The liaison is repeated for several nights in a row, and in the meantime everyone is obviously aware of it; what a fine scandal![1] The sage Ptahhotep had counseled in an earlier era (maxim 32): "Do not copulate with an effeminate adolescent, for you know you will thus be opposed to the water that is upon his heart (his semen). . . for never can you calm again what is within his belly! Do not allow him to spend nights doing that which is forbidden, as this is the way he will calm himself after having bested his desire. . . ."

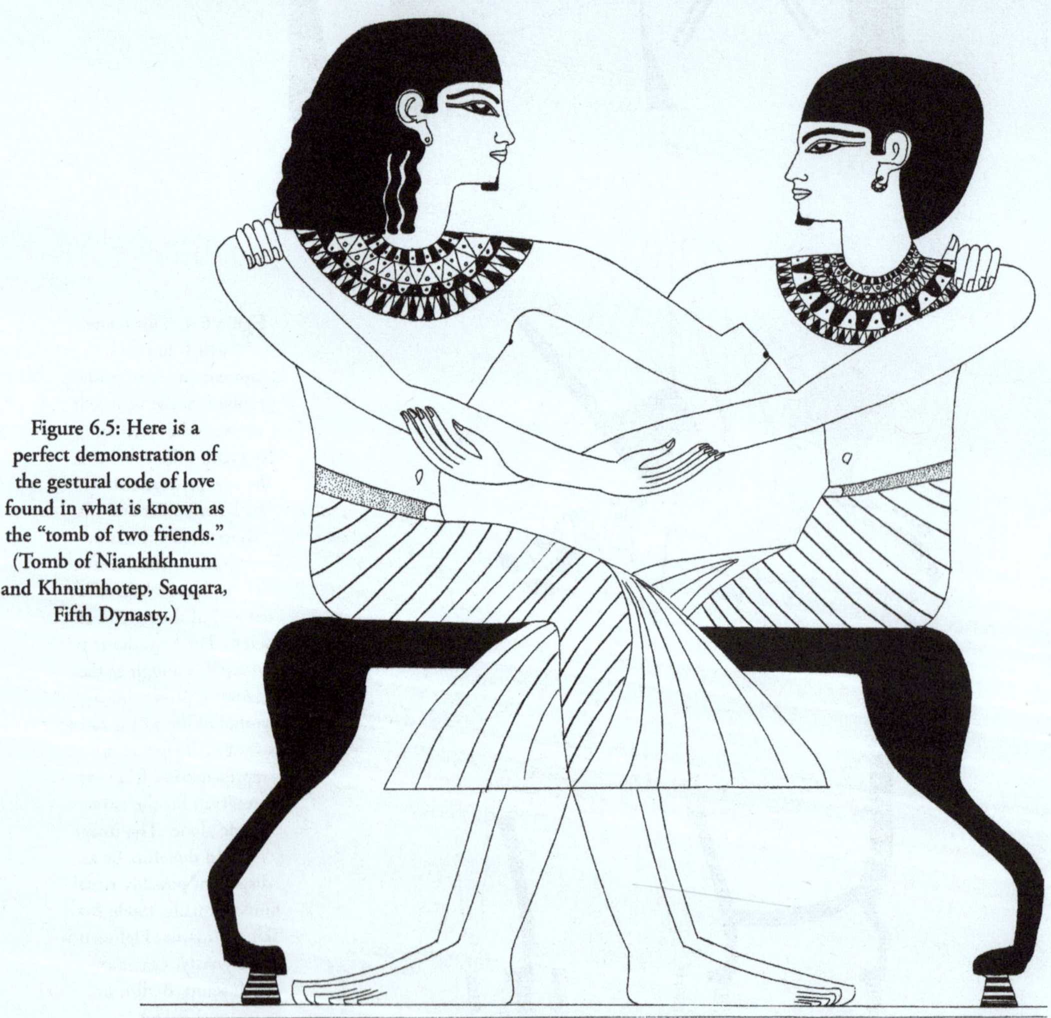

Figure 6.5: Here is a perfect demonstration of the gestural code of love found in what is known as the "tomb of two friends." (Tomb of Niankhkhnum and Khnumhotep, Saqqara, Fifth Dynasty.)

Excessive displays of affection, appropriate for the spirit of the gynaeceum (the private quarters for women), are discreetly, but frequently, suggested. The warrior goddess Neith (fig. 6.6) is the manly woman type, the Egyptian counterpart of the Syrian goddess Anat.

Two young Amarnian princesses, naked except for their jewels, are showing each other

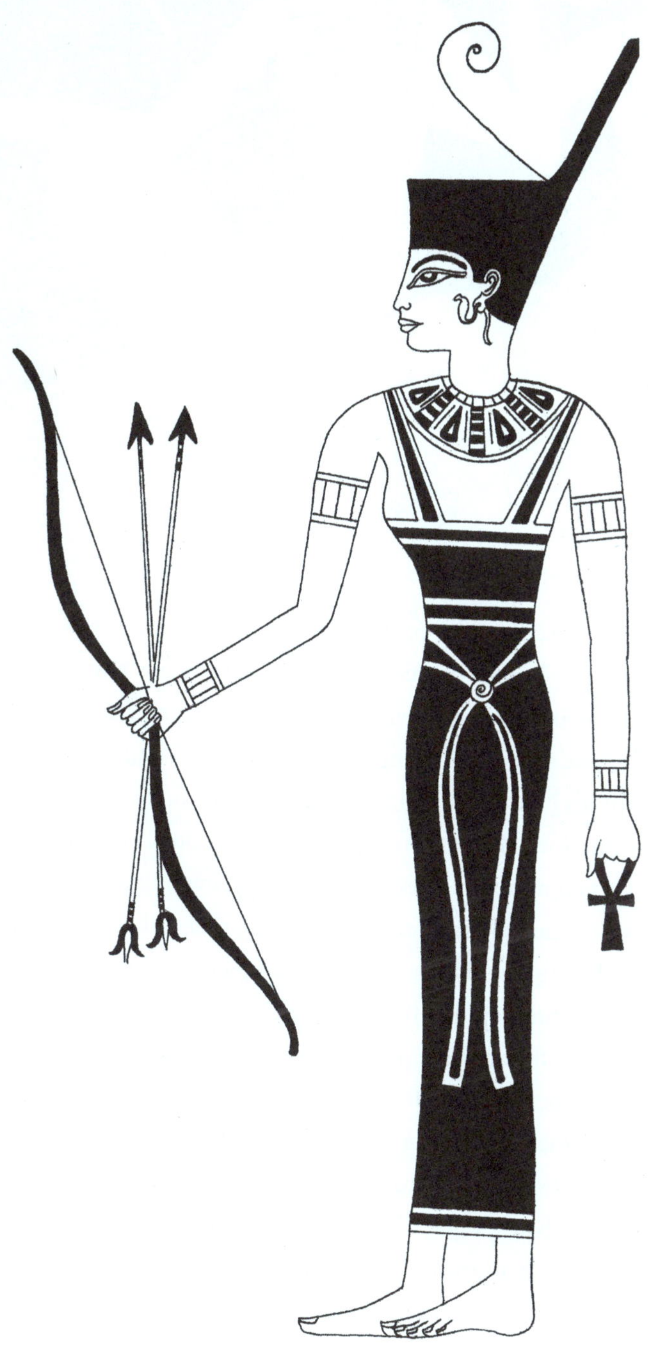

Figure 6.6: The goddess Neith, a veritable Amazon before the fact, seems nonetheless to value all forms of sexuality, as we have seen.

Figure 6.7: These two young Amarnian princesses are exchanging, within the intimacy of their apartments, some very affectionate gestures that may express nothing more than a still-childish friendship, but the harem atmosphere is clearly present in spite of their age. (Painting from royal palace, Amarna, Eighteenth Dynasty; Ashmolean Museum, Oxford.)

tender proofs of their affection (fig. 6.7). Depicted on her tomb, a noble woman is the object of a very attentive beauty make-over on the part of her feminine entourage (fig. 6.8). Retired within the intimacy of their apartments, or taking part in feasts, notably the funeral banquet, as here, women exchange flowers of intoxicating perfumes, mandrakes, caresses, and perhaps also jewels; the earring has a sexual connotation, like the ear itself. It is "the grotto" located within one of the body's erogenous zones (figs. 6.9 and 6.10). Two female musicians enjoy a very close union while providing a demonstration of their art; their elbows, hands, bodies, and feet are touching each other in the tradition of the amorous gestural codes (fig. 6.11). In another example, a mutually affectionate couple does not surrender its rights to publicly display affection when taking a stroll (fig. 6.12).

The documents on homosexuality, male as well as female, are quite numerous starting with the Ptolemaic period, which should not be a surprise for anyone.[2] The city founded by the Macedonian conqueror was particularly known for these practices, if we are to take Clement of Alexandria's word on the subject. But these took place throughout the land; even in the Theban temple of Amun a graffito has been found from 200 B.C. that is particularly insulting toward a certain Ptolemaios.[3] These practices became so common that a magistrate found himself prosecuted by a plaintiff because he did not pay

Figure 6.8: The toilet of a high-ranking woman by her servants and a friend who is very, if not overly attentive and affectionate. The lotus buds and flowers are the keys to the interpretation of this scene. (Painting, tomb of Ptahemhat, Theban tomb no. 77, Eighteenth Dynasty.)

any attention to his work and had his young lover, whom he lavished rich goods upon and caressed in public, accompany him everywhere. We are coming close here to a form of male prostitution. Furthermore, the custom of male bisexuality seems to have been so widespread that restrictions for the husband, in this regard, were stipulated in marriage contracts. For example, a contract from 92 B.C. (Tebtynis Papyrus 1.104) specifies that the future husband must not only commit to chiefly satisfying his wife's needs, but that he also agrees not to bring either a concubine or young male lover (a *païdikon*) into the house, not to have children by another woman during the lifetime of his wife, Apollonia, not to abandon the conjugal domicile, and, over all, not to put Apollonia out the door, nor insult or mistreat her.[4] No comment.

There is much that attests to the existence of lesbian practices during this era as well. It is intriguing to note that these documents can either be love charms provided by magicians or astrological reflections. The famous astronomer Ptolemy expounded at length on the influence of the conjunctions of the planets Venus and Saturn or Venus and Mars in

a

b

Figure 6.9 (a and b): Exchanges of equally obvious and codified gestures of love among guests at a funeral banquet; and (c) a chastely suggested love scene between two women of a certain rank, one of whom is young, ardent, and svelte while the other is of a more mature age. (From an anonymous tomb, Eighteenth Dynasty; British Museum, London.)

c

Figure 6.10: These two women (exchanging their jewelry) depicted in the intimacy of their home are touching each other amorously with easily decoded gestures. (Tomb of Horemheb, Theban tomb no. 78, Eighteenth Dynasty.)

Figure 6.11: Two female musicians enliven a festival with the sound of their instruments that stimulates them to share their keen reciprocal affection with gestures and gazes. (Tomb of Nakht, Eighteenth Dynasty.)

Figure 6.12: One of the two gleaners walking through a field got a thorn in her foot that the other is endeavoring to pull out as gently as possible. (Tomb of Menna, Theban tomb no. 69, Eighteenth Dynasty.)

a birth chart, which in the second case will produce either naturally effeminate men or masculine women (*Tetrabiblos* 4.5.187). In any event, these women lived publicly with their girlfriends in the same manner as heterosexual couples.[5]

OTHER PRACTICES

Incest and its foundations in pharaonic society were examined in chapter 2; there the role of incest in the transmission of royalty and several of its applications within the public domain were discussed.

Sodomy—that is, homo and/or heterosexual anal intercourse—is attested to in the Erotic Papyrus of Turin. The same term is sometimes used to designate zoophilia, sexual relations between a human—man or woman—and an animal.

There is no confirmation of pedophilia occurring among the ancient Egyptians.

Fellatio seems not to have been a sexual practice. The sole known example is the acrobatic autofellatio of Geb (fig. 1.10), something a god may achieve, but an improbable feat for a man.

The strange act of necrophilia, repulsive as it may be, was practiced by the embalmers, who were not themselves priests but simple thanatologists who provided the first treatments to the bodies of the newly dead. These humble assistants of Anubis smelled so strongly of corpses that, apparently, they could find no wives, and even prostitutes refused their business. So they were quite happy when a pretty young corpse came under their care, someone whose close relatives had neglected the elementary precaution—so far as this practice was a well-known fact—of delaying the delivery of the mortal remains.[6]

CHAPTER SEVEN

The Erotic Papyrus of Turin

This papyrus is famous within Egyptological circles, but hardly known by other archaeologists and is, naturally, unknown to the public at large, to whom it has not been accessible since 1946. Let's explain. This roll of papyrus entered the collections of the Turin Museum, with a series of other writings, at the beginning of the nineteenth century. It was already there in 1824 when Champollion wrestled with the problem that the collection of the Turin papyri brought to light. It is not our purpose to "unroll" here the eventful history of this papyrus, as our study only concerns the erotic portion of the scroll and not the so-called satiric scenes that bring animals into play, although it may prove necessary to refer to this portion on an ad hoc basis.

It was obviously the erotic part that prevented the publication of this document in its entirety until 1973.

The papyrus was already in a deplorable state when it fell under the eyes of Champollion, the brilliant decoder of the hieroglyphs, who was shocked by its images. On November 6, 1824, he wrote about it in these terms in a letter to his brother from Turin: "Here a piece of funerary ritual, . . . and the remnants of paintings of a monstrous obscenity that give me a very curious notion of Egyptian solemnity and wisdom."

Indeed, the content is pornographic, in the original sense of the word, as the action takes place in a brothel, which takes nothing away from its cultural interest. Up to now, this papyrus has remained unique in its genre, but it is not impossible, and it is even probable, that there were others like it, especially if we take into consideration the high number of erotic ostraca, reproducing the same themes and dating principally from the Ramesside era—which is also the date attributed to the Turin Papyrus based on iconographic, literary, philological, and historical criteria.[1]

What are these criteria? What was the artistic, social, and cultural motivation for such a work? What is its message? These are a lot of questions, to which it will not always be possible to give a reliable answer.

First, two apparently quite different themes figure on this papyrus, separated simply by the evocation of a plant. The satiric portion seems to have been shorter than the erotic part.

Next, while representations of couples in different poses is not too surprising in popular art (ostraca), their reproduction on papyrus, a costly material, is cause for reflection. Who could the owner, if not the person who ordered its creation, be? And couldn't these ostraca (fig. 4.8) be study sketches for works like the Turin Papyrus? For this papyrus is unquestionably work from the calamus of a single artist—the very personal, spirited, and confident line is evidence of this, and it is perceptible in spite of the mutilations of the material it is drawn upon. But why has this artist given the male characters faces of rare ugliness with features that look hardly Egyptian and inflicted them with such grotesque bodies?[2] The scathing nature of the drawing has spared the welcoming hostesses, although their faces denote a certain disillusioned vulgarity, unrelieved by any smile. Let's try to respond to these questions and to others, already raised, which also naturally flow from these considerations. The part representing the "dressed-up" animals, a theme of Mesopotamian origin, is a satire aimed at royalty and state hierarchy; this is widely confirmed.[3] The erotic part, in our opinion, fits into a similar context; however it is not the king, the court, or the country's administration that are being criticized, but the society, its insufficiencies and hypocrosies, and official religion and morality in relation to reality.[4] And this reality is depressing. We hold here perhaps a key, a motive explaining the staging of these hideous-faced men with the repugnant bodies who seem only to exist by and for their inordinately large penises, and to these expressionless women, acting in certain sequences like disjointed dolls. Did the ancient artist wish to show that these individuals were only pawns, placed any which way on the social chessboard? That behind the facade of respectability, forces beyond control declared themselves? Whatever the case may be, the two parts of this papyrus form an acerbic satire against the society of the period at the end of the New Kingdom. That said, it is obvious that the artist had a perfect understanding of the inner workings and the principal dogmas, as well as the religious iconography to which he referred for certain scenes; even here the "divine model" is present. But we do not believe that it is thereby necessary to consider these images as the descriptions of the frolics of a fallen priest with a singer of Amun whose charms are available at a fixed rate.[5] It must also be admitted that the presentation of the characters contains a drop of humor. Finally, this parade of positions implicitly constitutes an *ars amandi,* a domain in which the ancient Egyptians had the reputation of being connoisseurs. This is the aspect Stéphane Rossini wished to bring out by an esthetic approach conforming to that of Egyptian art in general, and not by reproducing these drawings exactly as they are.

From the archaeological point of view, however, we feel it necessary to give at least a glimpse of the document in its actual state, so that the reader may appreciate the unique air it gives off, but also have an idea about the state of the destruction of the document (which has been restored and completed by illustrators and Egyptologists in the nineteenth century and the beginning of the twentieth century, notably G. Seyffarth, G. Steindorff, and M. Tosi). For this purpose we have included here in vignette form (figs. 7.1 and 7.2) three relatively well-preserved scenes, as well as a sample from the satiric part (fig. 7.3). These drawings faithfully reproduce the state of the document, such as it has been published, with the exception of the color: the papyrus is painted in the conventional colors of Egyptian art, whose significance obeys a code that does not always correspond to reality (G. Seyffarth established a reconstituted and colored copy of the entire papyrus).

The beginning of the satiric section is lost. The erotic part is preserved in its entirety but has deteriorated greatly and is full of gaps.

The erotic section consists of twelve sequences that correspond here to figures 7.4 to 7.15. We will comment on it in detail as we go along.

Texts in very cursory hieratic characters are planted in and between the images. This arrangement indicates that the text was inserted after the drawings, contrary to normal procedure. The symbols were probably drawn by several scribes and are very poorly preserved. These texts provide no coherent indications, but it is clear they were meant to be remarks exchanged between the partners portrayed in the drawings or commentaries upon the scenes.[6]

To conclude this brief study of the erotic section of the Turin Papyrus, let's take a look at a very interesting inscription located on the verso of the document, on the back of the final scene: "Fan bearer to the right of the king (. . .), royal scribe, commander of the soldiers."[7] The placement of these lines on the verso, corresponding the end of the scenes on the recto, allows one to assume they were readable, once the papyrus was rolled shut. This prompted us to think that it would have been an identifying mark made by its owner. Even if the name is lacking, the inscription allows us to suppose that this exceptional document belonged to an important person's library. This hypothesis throws quite an unusual light on high society of the Ramesside era.

Plate 16. Scene from the Tomb of Ramses depicting a Ramesside pharaoh in ritual attire and crowned with the *atef,* making an offering to Amun-Re. The god is shown ithyphallic as Min-Kamutef, epithet meaning "Bull of his Mother" and referring to the god's self-creating sexual power. The god is assisted by Isis-Hathor. New Kingdom, 20th Dynasty. Valley of the Kings, Thebes-West.

Plate 17. Young woman, doubtless a professional musician, playing a small lute. She is completely nude save for her jewels. Her hair is carefully styled, perfumed, and studded with a lotus flower—other flowers are hanging from her arms. The girl is gracefully seated on a cushion in company of her familiar (very much so!) little monkey. A Bes figure is tattooed on her thigh. The lotus and papyrus bouquets as well as the grape vines create an Osirian atmosphere. This blue faience bowl might have been used during a funerary banquet (see fig. 4.30, p. 117). New Kingdom, 18th/19th Dynasty. Museum of Antiquities, Leyden.

Plate 18. Stele of the goddess Qadesh, the Syrian Hathor, standing on a lion passing between the gods Min-Amun-Re (left) and Seth-Baal (right) On the lower part, the two donors are shown worshipping those divinities. The kneeling man to the right is Djehuty, father of the young man on the left side. New Kingdom, 19th/20th Dynasty. Louvre Museum, Paris (see fig. 4.43, p.128).

Plate 19. Painted relief from the first hypostyle hall of the Abydos temple of Seti I showing the goddess Mut-Hathor nourishing the king-to-be-born. The divine child is already adorned with the blue khepresh-crown and wearing royal attire. It must be remembered that Pharaoh is the child of all divine powers which he is supposed to unite in his person. The goddess is seated on the cubic, archaic throne, which is decorated with the sema-tawy symbol. 19th Dynasty.

Plate 20. A ptolemaic queen giving birth to the "divine child," her son and future king she is supposed to have conceived by the demiurge. She is assisted by two Hathor goddesses, here in the role of midwives. Egyptian Museum, Cairo.

Plate 21. Detail from the erotic part of the Turin Papyrus. New Kingdom, 19th Dynasty. Werner Forman Archive, Egyptian Museum, Turin. (see also fig. 7.7, p. 156)

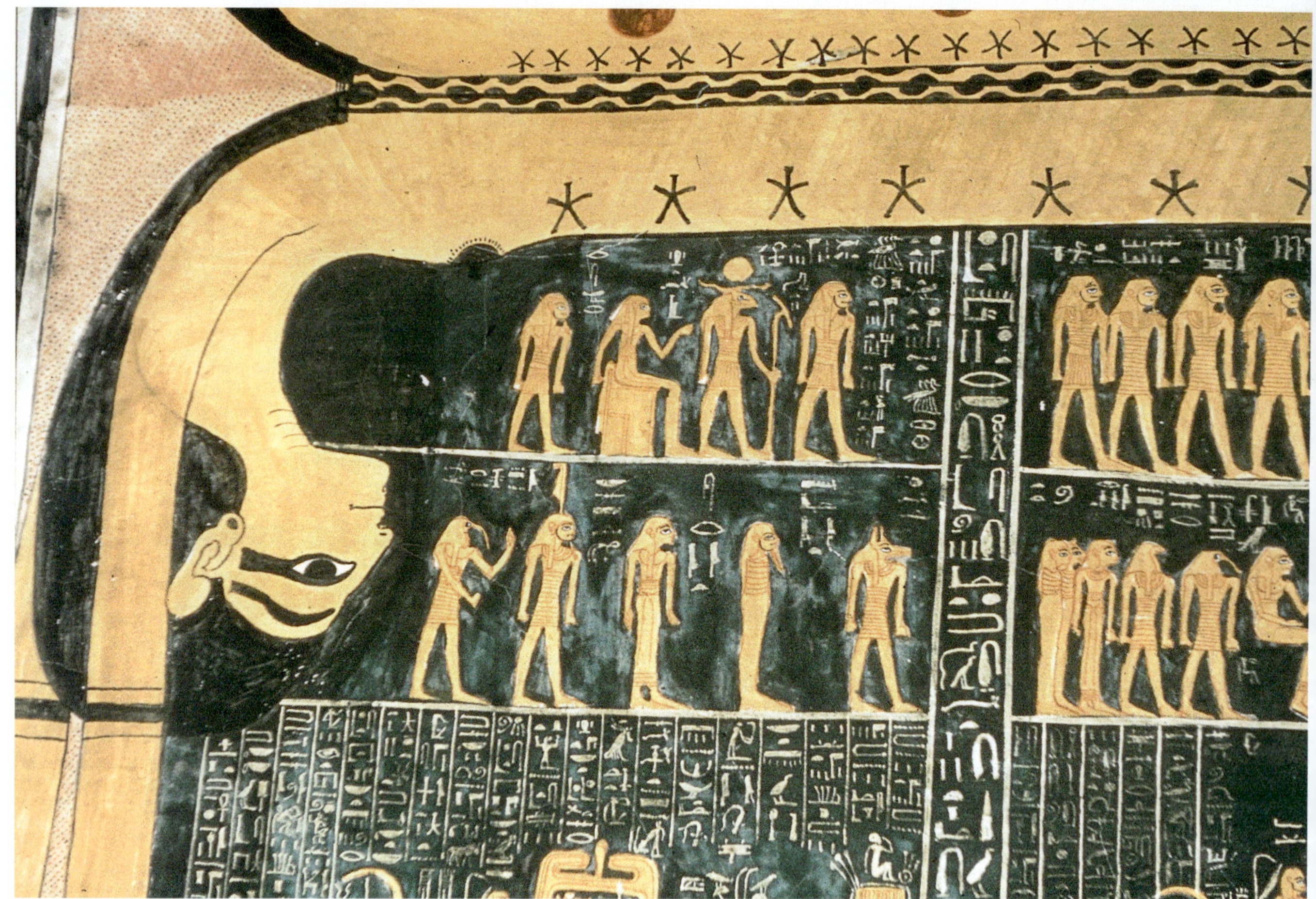

Plate 22. Image from the tomb of Ramses VI showing the sky-goddess Nut swallowing the sun in the evening and giving birth to it again in the morning. The star-spangled divine body is an X-ray vision that shows the progression of the sun inside the mysterious depths of the Universe. Numerous deities representing stars, constellations, decans, and time sections accompany and protect the event. This scene is an image of the cosmic cycle into which every being is integrated. Here it expands the divine magic over the sarcophagus of Ramses VI and guarantees his eternal life. Valley of the Kings, Thebes-West.

Plate 23. Ritual procession of two Bes and the hippopotamus goddess Taweret. These entities are beneficient genii, driving away all hostile demons and influences with tambourines, menacing roars, and knives. Their carved and gilt figures ornament the side-panels of an armchair found in Tutankhamun's tomb. It was a prophylactic gift from his cousin, princess Sat-Amun. New Kingdom, 18th Dynasty. Tutankhamun's treasure, Egyptian Museum, Cairo (See also figs. 4.21, p. 112 and 5.1, p. 133 for other roles of these divinities.)

Figure 7.1: This is the second sequence of the erotic part of the papyrus. The dotted lines represent restorations over lines that were still—but barely—visible, during the time when the copy was made. The broken lines indicate the completely destroyed portions. The man is holding a small lute in his right hand while a *sesheshet* sistrum is threaded over his right arm. He is coupling *a tergo* with the woman seated on the edge of the caisson of the chariot (her image is badly damaged) pulled by two young women. The intention of parodying a chariot outing by the royal couple seems obvious here (fig. 2.6).

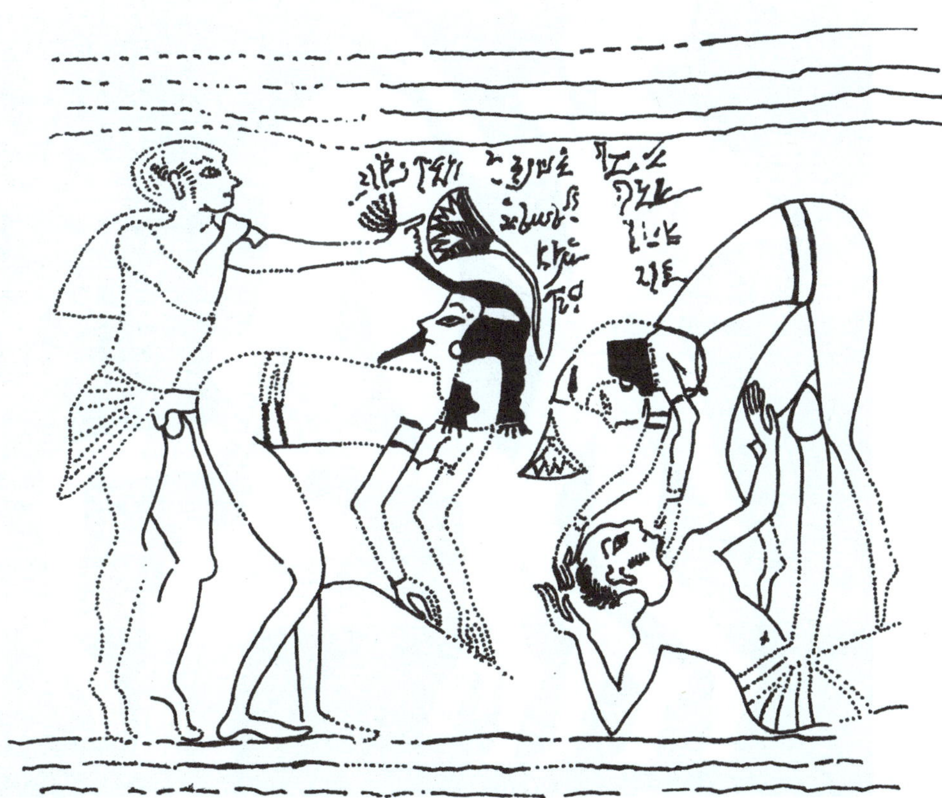

Figure 7.2: The figure represents, going from right to left, sequences 8 and 9 of the document. Sequence 8: The woman is preparing to impale herself on the penis of the man lying down, a position that inevitably recalls the embrace of Nut and Geb (fig. 1.13) in an ironic commentary on the dogma of the creation of the universe by a particularly degrading drawing of the man. Sequence 9: the original is destroyed for the most part. Nevertheless, J. A. Omlin thought it possible to establish the influence of rock drawings from Wadi Hammamat, some of which are quite erotic. The position of the two partners allows one to suppose sodomization; it is the sole example of this in the papyrus. Here the face of the woman is colored very strongly in red, likewise in sequence 7.

Figure 7.3: A scene occurring in the "satiric" part of the papyrus. The lion playing *senet* with a gazelle is a theme that often recurs in the popular drawings of this topsy-turvy world. The allusion to the scene of the harem under Ramses III (fig. 4.3) is obvious. A protome (head and neck) of the dorcas gazelle in gold-work adorns the headdresses of certain royal favorites. Triumph and greed can be read on the face of the lion-king. A cruel mockery.

Figure 7.4: Sequence 1 of the erotic part, redrawn by the modern artist on the basis of the original illustration. All twelve erotic sequences have been reworked this way; the texts have not been reproduced, but their translations follow sequence 12 (fig. 7.15). Here the couple is devoting their efforts to achieve a position *a tergo,* the man is standing, but why is he carrying a sack on his shoulder like a *shawabti?* Is he scared he might lose his balance? Or is this an allusion to those servants of eternity who have no free will? We see this detail again in sequence 9 (fig. 7.11). The woman is adopting a position that is as uncomfortable as it is astounding. If she is somewhat "arched like a vault" in imitation of the goddess Nut, her arms and head do not recall the goddess of heaven at all, but rather the attitude of the damned in the mythological depiction of hell (for example, in Seti I's temple in Abydos). Did the actors of this scene consider it this way? By the way, we doubt that such a position could actually have been performed.

Figure 7.5: Sequence 2 has already been analyzed (see fig. 7.1) and we noted there it parodied a chariot outing by the royal couple, who had to be Amarnian. While the royal couple embraced in public, the couple in this sequence clearly goes much further—and in a fairly crude fashion. The little princess who stung the rear ends of the horses with her wand is replaced by the monkey who is annoying the young women, harnessed in the place of the horses, by pulling on their reins. The sovereign's retinue, running breathlessly by the side of the chariot, is evoked by a little man carrying a curious purse reminiscent of those seen in depictions of the harvests of the Old Kingdom. There is no fan bearer, but the plant associated with women, erotic scenes, and the concubines of the dead, describes an elegant curve above the scene. Given that the vehicle is an Egyptian battle chariot, J. A. Omlin sees the woman as a "warrior of Venus."

Figure 7.6: The customer seems to be scared of his partner's fantasies. She is perched on a high stool with her legs in the air and seems to be gripping the man's phallus so she will not lose her balance. The *sesheshet* sistrum and lute beneath the stool could indicate that the young woman plied the trade of a musician as well. Is there a possible allusion to Iusaas that can be seen in the woman's gesture?

Figure 7.7: Sequence 4. This is no doubt the best-known image from the papyrus; it has been published often, but it is generally only reproduced showing the prostitute, who is putting on her makeup, from the waist up. Underlining the eyes was a very old custom, but rouge was not put on the lips. The circumcised man is pointing to the sex of the woman who is apparently installed upon a cone of perfumed fat (this is a hypothetical interpretation; it could also be an overturned vase). We see no classic parallel image, but have been able to establish a comparison with a small earthenware figurine from the Greco-Roman era, representing Isis seated in similar fashion upon a sow (see Erich Neumann, *The Great Mother: An Analysis of the Archetype* [Princeton: Princeton Univ. Press, 1974], and A. Piankoff *Mythological Papyri* 1 [New York: Bollingon Series 40, 1957], p. 3.).[8]

Figure 7.8: Sequence 5. The man is demonstrating his strength by seating his partner on his thighs. She is literally folded in half, with her legs on the shoulders of the man, who is holding her in position by the back and shoulder. In this case it is the man who is overseeing the maneuver. Corresponding evidence for this position can be found throughout the entire Mediterranean basin. The original drawing has been sufficiently preserved to allow one to note that the end of the man's nose has been cut off. We have seen (chapter 2, "Fidelity and Adultery") that the mutilation of the nose was a frequent punishment, especially in the case of transgressions of a sexual nature.

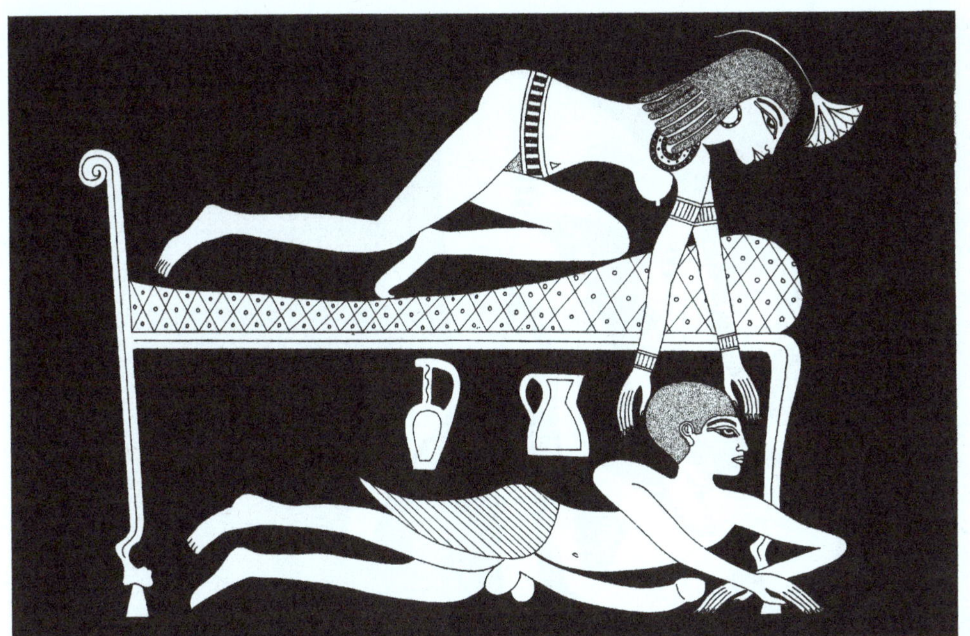

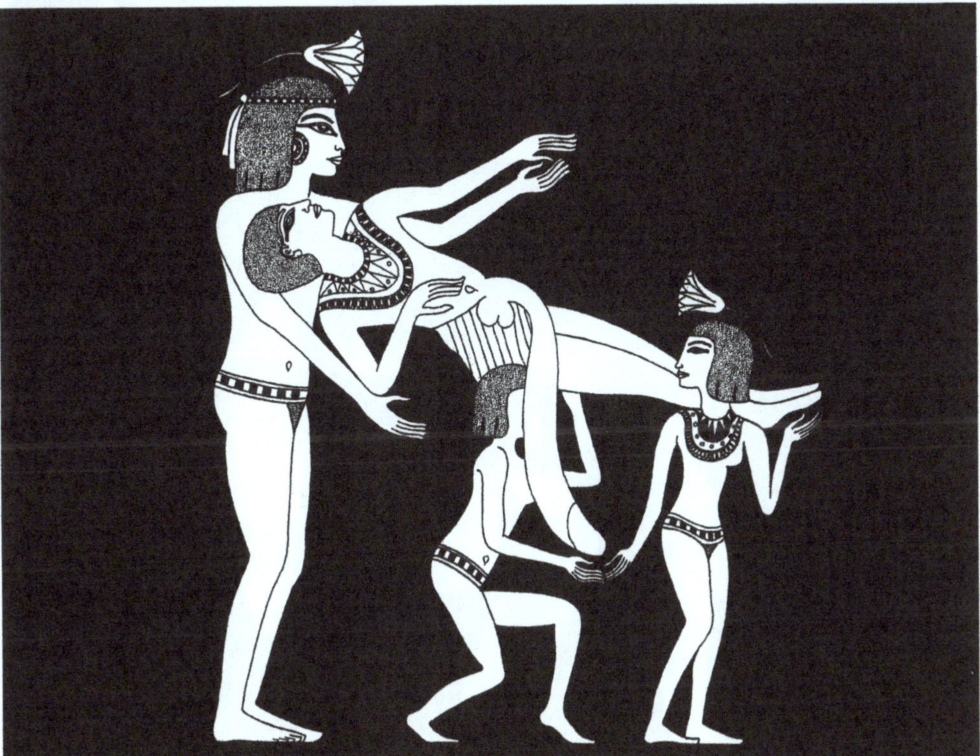

Figures 7.9 and 7.10: Sequences 6 and 7 are connected. We see no direct mythical allusion. On the other hand, to show a man who is impotent or worn out has always been a subject of mockery, which seems to be the case here. The woman on the bed (which resembles a simplified, ritual funeral bed nonetheless) seems to be trying to pick up the man who is lying down, unless she is in the process of ejecting him to make room for another totally exhausted customer, whom her colleague and two young servants are obliged to carry. One may ask if this faltering Priapus has fainted following sexual excesses or if he was drugged—or both at the same time? We have already discussed the use of narcotics for erotic purposes. Whatever the case, they are having a good laugh at his expense—but they are helping him anyway.

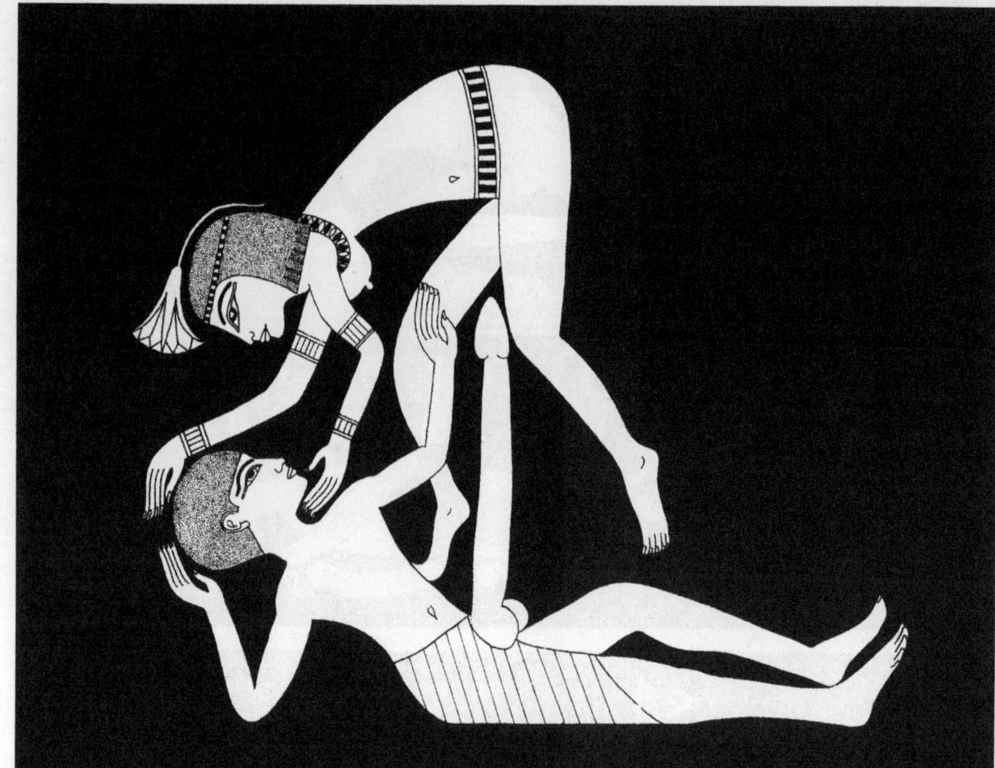

Figure 7.11: Sequence 8 has already been analyzed (see fig. 7.2). The intention of a blasphemous mockery is fairly clear: while the man does a fair imitation of Geb, the woman is a friendly caricature of the goddess Nut, with her feet floating in the air instead of being propped on Geb's body. This Nut's hands do not have an hieratic attitude either. A Nut who caresses the chin, mouth, and hair of her cosmic husband is unthinkable.

Figure 7.12: Sequence 9 has already been analyzed (see fig. 7.2). The original drawing is poorly preserved, but the junction of the genitals is still clearly visible and it can be safely declared that this is the sole example, in this papyrus, of sodomization. This practice does not seem to have been popular between homosexual partners (fellatio either, by the way—it does not appear in this document). For fans of technical terms let's specify that sodomization is medically defined as a *coitus posterior in situ posteriore,* and intercourse *a tergo* is also called *coitus anterior in situ posterior.* Omlin, *Der Papyrus 55001,* thinks this is not a representation of sodomy, but of coitus *a tergo.*[9]

Figure 7.13: Sequence 10. Coitus face-to-face on a comfortable mattress. This is the least sophisticated position in the collection—inserted as a reminder, if one may say so. The original image is terribly damaged; faint traces are all that remain of the woman, but the head, arm, and loincloth of the man are well preserved; in the original he is depicted as atrociously hairy and has obviously not shaved for several days.

Figure 7.14: Sequence 11. A rather sportive invitation to love! The young woman seems to be both a dancer and a musician, and uses her talents to demonstrate the original services she provides. She has made a pirouette while tossing a braid of her hair to her partner; this was a widespread gesture in ancient Egypt by those women seeking to attract a man's attention. The braids and curls of a woman's hair are a metaphor for the nets for hunting and fishing (see the love poems and the duck snared in the net, fig. 3.8). The ritual dancers in Hathor's service were well-trained acrobats. The man approaches the woman with a dance step that is quite appropriate under the circumstances. The lyre the woman is pretending to need for a prop is part of the original illustration, but the drawing is so damaged that the restorations differ and it is not possible to determine with any certitude if the animal heads represent ducks or horses, and at what level they are placed.

Figure 7.15: This scene ends the erotic portion of the document. The man's head, part of his body, his raised arm, and his legs have been nicely preserved. In contrast, the drawing of the woman is almost totally destroyed and it was necessary to refer to older restorations to do this illustration. The woman is lying on an inclined surface, upon which the man is resting one of his knees while getting support for his other leg on the woman's foot. A small figure on the original, perhaps ithyphallic like the man, seems to be hanging from the woman's arm, whose hand is holding a stylet. A stool is overturned beneath the slanted surface. This final scene does not depart from the principle observed by all the other illustrations: the environment is not defined but simply suggested by items of furniture that indicate all these events are taking place within a dwelling.

But how should we interpret the final sequence, presenting an act of *coitus anterior* in an unusual context, if not by seeking to find parallel instances? These can be found in mythology. In the *Book of Waht is in the Dat,* the twelfth hour ends with the awakening of Osiris, who is depicted sometimes sleeping on an inclined surface, sometimes on a slightly flattened mound, but always in a slanted position. The twelfth sequence is presumably related to this twelfth hour.[10] The emergence of Atum (fig. 1.5) uses a similar arrangement in another mythical context, but one related to sexuality as well, this time with regard to the creation of the universe.

What is the meaning of the little figure hanging from the arm of this beauty? We have not figured out just what significance to give it. The artist of the current work feels—no doubt out of professional solidarity—that it may be the figurative signature of his long-ago colleague, similar to the way that, keeping the respective difference in mind, Michelangelo signed his painting of the Sistene Chapel.

In his edition of the Turin Papyrus, J. A. Omlin subdivided the fragmentary inscriptions into nineteen groups, which he translated and arranged without assigning specific locations, as these texts are inserted between, above, and beneath the figures, wherever the scribes could find a place to jot down their later annotations to the drawings. Here is the list he came up with:

1. (. . .) the wrappings that you give.
2. So Thoth (. . .) Your
3. (. . .)
4. Sun! You have sought the heart of the (. . .) because of your movements (shudders), I am making the task pleasant (soft).
5. Do not be scared. What [could] I do to you?
6. The day (. . .)
7. The drummer (. . .)
8. He who retreats (. . .)
9. (. . .) see, come at me from behind with your love [the phallus]
10. Your phallus is with me, see! You will not bring me [my good reputation?]
11. [forms part of 10.]
12. O my brigand!
13. (. . .)
14. My bed is abandoned and me (. . .)
15. My huge phallus that is sick inside (. . .) [Would this be an STD?]
16. (. . .)
17. (. . .)
18. (. . .) Representing and I esteem myself [praise myself?]
19. Singer of Hathor.

These remarks, although full of gaps and disconnected, complete the atmosphere of these—Hathorian—encounters.

Conclusion

Hathor's secrets are numerous, varied, and often strange, but all derive from the first becoming, the divine creation of the universe, and commingle, on the terrestrial level, with humanity's history since its inception. Hathor the Golden One, the Sovereign of Love and Lady of Death, Mistress of Drunkenness, the ravaging Distant One and the tender Bastet, joyous Mistress of music and dance, the generous Celestial Cow, Lady of the Vulva and the womb of the world, Ra's burning eye, his untameable daughter, Uraeus who defends her father and protects the king, the Unique One with Four Faces, the Universal One who is always everywhere and nowhere, as ungraspable as love.

Hathor is the engine, the underlying, omnipresent energy of the history of Egypt since its remote beginnings until the end. The end? What end? We all know Egypt is eternal! But its pharaonic era came to an end—an end delayed momentarily by Hathor when Caesar and Cleopatra fell in love and formed a powerful couple capable of changing the face of the world. Their separation contributed to sealing the fate of the conqueror and the queen of Egypt. How, from this perspective, should we interpret the events that followed the Battle of Actium? The evidence is there—and without sinking into a disorderly mysticism, one must face the facts: the last pharaoh committed suicide because she knew her kingdom was lost with the destruction of her fleet. She, who was the "queen of Rome" at Caesar's side, could at no time imagine herself dragged behind the victor's chariot during his triumphal entry into the capital of the empire. She also lost her last love in this final, desperate battle. All that remained for her was the burning, mortal eye of Ra, the kiss of the serpent.

APPENDIX ONE

A Simplified Chronology

3300–2800 B.C.	**Early Dynastic Period** First Dynasty Pharoh: Narmer (Menes) Second Dynasty Pharaohs: Djed, Ka
2800–2200 B.C.	**Old Kingdom** Third Dynasty Pharaoh: Djoser Fourth Dynasty Pharaohs: Snefru, Cheops, Khephren, Menkaure (Mykerinus) Fifth Dynasty Pharaohs: Sahure (first king who was "Son of the Sun"), Unas Sixth Dynasty Pharaohs: Teti, Pepi I, Pepi II, the female pharaoh Nitocris
2200–2060 B.C.	**First Intermediate Period** Seventh Dynasty (fictional?) Eighth Dynasty Pharaoh: Ibi Nineth, Tenth, and the beginning of the Eleventh Dynasties (Parallel Reigns) Pharaohs of Upper Egypt: the Intef; Pharaohs of Lower Egypt: the Khety

2060–1785 B.C.	**Middle Kingdom**
	Eleventh Dynasty
	Pharaohs: the Menthuhoteps
	Twelfth Dynasty
	Pharaohs: the Amenemhats, Senusrets, the female pharaoh Sobeknefru
1785–1580 B.C.	**Second Intermediate Period (from the end of the Twelfth Dynasty to the beginning of the Seventeenth Dynasty)**
	Thirteenth Dynasty
	Pharaohs: the Sobekhoteps
	Fifteenth Dynasty
	Pharaohs: the Hyksos
1580–1090 B.C.	**New Kingdom** (the golden age of pharaonic civilization)
	End of the Seventeenth Dynasty
	Pharaohs: Tao, Kamose (liberators who drove out the Hyksos), Ahmosis
	Eighteenth Dynasty
	Pharaohs: the Tuthmoses, Amenhoteps, the female pharaoh Hatshepsut, Akhenaten, Tutankhamun, Horemheb
	Nineteenth and Twentieth Dynasties
	Pharaohs: the Seti, the Ramses (I–XI), the female pharaoh Tausert
1090–663 B.C.	**Third Intermediary Period** (decline of centralized power and the emergence of coexisting dynasties)
	Twenty-first Dynasty
	Tanite pharaohs of Lower Egypt: the Psusennes; Priest-Kings of Upper Egypt: Herihor, Pinedjem
	Twenty-second to Twenty-third Dynasties
	Libyan pharaohs: Sheshonq, Osorkon, Takelot
	Twenty-fourth Dynasty
	Princes of Saïs: Delta
	Twenty-fifth Dynasty
	Ethopian kings, the "black" pharaohs: Piankhi, Shabaka, Taharqa; the Divine Worshipers of Amun ruled over Upper Egypt: the

Amenirdis, Nitokris, Shapenipet

663–525 B.C.	**Sait Era**
	Twenty-sixth Dynasty
	Pharaohs: the Psammetiks (originally from the Delta)
525–333 B.C.	**The Late Period**
	Twenty-seventh Dynasty (First Persian invasion)
	Persian kings: Cambyses, Darius, Xerxes
	Twenty-eighth to Thirtieth Dynasties
	Last native pharaohs: Amyrtey, Nectanebo I, Nectanebo II (driven from power by the second Persian invasion); Persian kings: Artaxerexes, Darius II
333–31 B.C.	**Ptolemaic Era**
	Alexander the Great drives out the Persians; henceforth Egypt would be ruled by pharaohs of Greek origin, the Ptolemies and queens; Cleopatra VII is the last of the pharaohs.
31 B.C.–A.D. 395	Following the battle of Actium, ancient Egypt became part of the Roman Empire, where it remained until its collapse in A.D. 395. The Roman emperors were recognized as pharaohs by the Egyptians.
A.D. 395–640	Byzantine domination marks the end of the ancient Egyptian civilization.

APPENDIX TWO

Egyptian Deities

This list provides succinct descriptions of the Egyptian gods and goddesses mentioned in the text. The reader wishing more extensive knowledge of the Egyptian pantheon may consult the works cited in the bibliography.

Amun

Local Theban god who became god of the whole of Egypt starting with the Eleventh Dynasty, when Theban princes assumed power. He gradually supplanted the ancient Theban god, Montu. He forms a triad with Mut and Khonsu. Originally a god of the wind and air, he wears two long, straight feathers on his headdress. His celestial origin is reflected in his name, which means "the hidden." He is anthropomorphic, but can assume other forms, according to the aspect the image highlights (see fig.1.36). During the New Kingdom he was the principal god of Egypt, and absorbed or was assimilated by other deities under double appellations such as Amun-Ra, Min-Amun, and so forth. The goose and the ram are his sacred animals.

Anat

Asiatic goddess (Syrio-Phoenician), personification of the Moon, but also a warrior goddess assimilated to Astarte, one of the daughters of the Sun, Ra. During the Ramesside era she became one of the guardians of the pharaoh, notably in battle and all activities involving the handling of weapons. This role brings her close to Seth; in this capacity she is then considered his consort.

Anuket

Goddess of the first Nile cataract near Elephantine. She is probably of Nubian origin, judging by her coiffure. With Satis, ancient goddess of the region and associated, like Anuket, with the flood, she is a companion of the god Khnum, sometimes considered as his daughter. But this pseudo-triad hardly corresponds to the symbolism of these deities.

Anubis

The mummifying god, the black dog or jackal (Anubis, the Greek version of his name, comes from Inpu, meaning "young dog") is the master of the necropolis. The adulterine son of Osiris and Nephthys, he reassembled the corpse of his father which was then restored to life by the magic of Isis. This feat made him the patron god of funerary priests and embalmers. He guides the dead to the gates of the beyond, to which he appears to possess the key, something with which he is depicted during the later era. Anubis is depicted as a black dog, lying on a naos-tomb, or as a man with the head of a dog. He is also perceived as a form of the deceased in transformation.

Apophis

Infernal serpent and enemy of the Sun. See Seth.

Aten

Aten the Sun was worshiped as a cosmic body in Heliopolis. During the Amarnian era he became the one god, with no consort or offspring, as all creative and divine power was concentrated in him. Akhenaten worshiped the solar globe, honored by daily offerings placed on the 365 altars of the hypetros temple. During this time, Aten was depicted as a solar disk or globe, whose rays ended in little hands presenting the life symbol (the *ankh*) to the nostrils of the royal couple, responsible for transmitting the divine breath throughout the land and to all creatures. His worship disappeared with the return the the Amunian orthodoxy, but Ramses II used the religious concepts elaborated by Akhenaten for the benefit of his own deified person.

Atum

Demiurge of the beginning. Floating in the Nun, the abyssal waters to which he will return in the expectation of a new cosmic cycle, he had the shape of the primordial serpent. Having been nothing, he became all, thanks to his own creative power, which required a complementary trigger: the goddess Hathor, his daughter, his aura, who stimulates his sexuality, thanks to which he draws from himself through masturbation the seed of the universe, and, as a start, his children, the gods Shu and Tefnut. The goddess Nebet-Hetepet, or Iusaas, his hand, is, under these circumstances, the Hathorian form permitting the realization of the first stage of the Great Work. Atum is represented as a man, crowned with the *pschent* or a man with a ram's head *(Ovis longipes).* This is the form he takes when occupying a place in the barque of the Sun; he is the "divine flesh" that traverses the night sky while awaiting his resurrection as Ra, the day star. He is the head of the Heliopolitan Ennead.

Bastet

Cat goddess, the tamed but still uncontrollable form of Sekhmet. She was worshiped in her sanctuaries at Bubastis where the "bacchanals" took place that Herodotus witnessed. In her temple she was considered as the mother of the lion Miysis—she could transform herself naturally into a lioness, either as Maat or Sekhmet, because her teeth and claws were always ready for use! When depicted as a cat, she holds a sistrum and/or an aegis, and her forearm is threaded through the handle of a basket. She was the beneficial eye of Ra.

Bat

Idol of the seventh nome of Upper Egypt, about whom information is rare, because she was assimilated with Hathor at a very early date. In fact, her triangular feminine face with its bovine ears, curling horns, which is customarily viewed from the front and sits on a pedestal shaped like a handle, appears like the prototype of the Hathorian sistrum (see figs. 2.1 and 2.4).

Bebon

A little god and veritable Egyptian Priapus when he borrows human form, but can also be a monkey or a red dog (red is the color of Seth). He appears as early as the Pyramid Texts.

Bes

A guardian spirit, mainly of the gynaeceum or of women in labor. He has the form of a dwarf, with an immense head surrounded by a lion's mane. He sticks out his tongue, his short, stocky body is naked, save for a belt of serpents. His phallus hangs down to his feet and he has a tail coming out of his back. He is a figure whose ugliness is only matched by his benevolence, much worshiped by the people, with his consort, Beset. During the Late Period, he became a deity of the pantheon, containing in his person all the prophylactic attributes of the other gods. As a musician he is a member of the joyful retinue of Hathor and Hathor-Tefnut on the occasion of her return into Egypt.

The Distant One

See Hathor, Sekhmet, and Tefnut.

Ennead

Group of nine deities. The Ennead of Heliopolis consists of four divine couples, dominated by the demiurge Atum-Ra, whose children, Shu and Tefnut, are the first couple. They are the parents of Geb and Nut who, in turn, gave birth to Osiris and Isis, Seth and Nephthys. Horus, the elder, the fifth child of Geb and Nut, is not a member of the Ennead but was necessary to complete the cosmic myth of the solar year.

Geb

God of the fertile earth, son of Shu and Tefnut, the very amorous husband of Nut from whom he was separated by his father on orders from Ra in order to create a vital space where the Sun, Ra, could make his journey. The animal consecrated to Geb seems to have been the goose who is used to write his name and whose hieroglyph crowns the head of the god when he is depicted in anthropomorphic form. He was worshiped in Coptos, where Min also reigned. Grandson of Ra-Atum, he became his heir after the god's disillusioned departure for new horizons on the back of the celestial cow (see fig. 1.32).

Hapy

Personification of the Nile flood. He is represented as a man with an androgynous body that is naked save for the apron with boatsman's straps, bearing a platter of offerings symbolizing all the benefits of the flood. His head is generally surmounted by one of the heraldic plants of Egypt. As the land represents a united duality, the South and the North, there are two Hapy, he of the South adorned with the pseudo-lily, and he of the North wearing a tuft of papyrus as a headdress. Does this symbolic depiction conceal the reunion of the two Niles, the White Nile and the Blue Nile, that causes the flooded Nile to spill over its banks during the heart of the drought season?

Hathor

Goddess of multiple forms and functions. According to Heliopolitan cosmology, she came into existence at the same time as Atum-Ra, whose "hand" she is when personified by the goddess Nebet-Hetepet, or Iusaas. Yet Hathor is not a member of the Ennead. She has a husband, Horus of Edfu, but Ihy, her son with Tatenen, remains between light and darkness. She is the universal matrix, the grottolike womb of the world, whose cyclical renewal she assures. Following a mystical gestation, she is also the one who guides all the deceased, making them thereby her children, toward a new life on another plane, in another dimension. Her principal temple is in Dendara, of course, but she is also worshiped in other sanctuaries, especially in the Nubian *speoi* (grotto or cave temples), the same Nubia that was the source of the life-giving waters. Hathor is the image of the primordial feminine element, and she represents the two faces of love: life and death, heaven and hell. One could say that, at bottom, all goddesses are only her hypostases. Hathor is thus kind and gay, wine and music are her offerings, and she presides over the most unbridled of feasts. But it is dangerous to provoke her: the cat Bastet can become the lioness, the Distant One, Sekhmet-Tefnut; the benevolent solar eye, the green eye of Horus, can become destructive and fatal, when it assumes the form of the *uraeus.* During the Late Period her worship disappeared to a certain extent to the benefit of that of Isis, adorned, like Hathor, by the solar disk (or rather, globe) and lyre-shaped horns. Hathor's magical instruments are the two sistrums and the *menat; hut menat,* the "castle of the menat" designates her temple in Dendara.

Horus

It is no exaggeration to say that there are as many forms of Horus as there are sanctuaries in Egypt: Haaroëris, or Horus the elder; Horsaïsas, meaning Horus, son of Isis; Horhekenou (in charge of ointments); Harakhty or Horus the dweller on the horizon; Hor-nedj-itef, Horus, guardian of his father or father's image (?); Harpocrates or Horus the child; and, naturally, Hor-behedety, the form worshiped in Edfu, are the most important. A note on Horus the elder, the celestial god, whose eyes are the stars. In the event of the simultaneous eclipse of two celestial globes, he becomes Horus-with-no-eyes (Hormekhenty-en-irty), an aggressive form, but when the sun and moon reappear, he becomes Horus-who-has-eyes (Hor-khenty-irty), a benevolent form. Horus is generally represented either as a falcon-headed man or as a falcon. Horus, the heir of Osiris, his father, ruled Egypt, and all the pharaohs are considered to be reincarnations of Horus.

Hu

See Thoth.

Ihy

Son of Hathor, a young god, depicted with a naked black body. He shakes the *sekhem* sistrum, a luminous symbol of the birth canal, of the emergence into life under the sun. But Ihy remains on the threshold of two worlds. He is thereby the image of the dead in transformation. Ihy means "musician"—could the son of Hathor be called anything else?

Iosaas

See Hathor.

Isis

Twin sister and wife of Osiris, she was widowed before bearing any children. In fact her husband was assassinated by his brother Seth! But Isis was a magician and, aided by Nephthys, her sister, she found and reconstituted the body of her spouse with the assistance of Anubis. She magically revived his generative passions and in this way conceived a posthumous son, Horus. This notable and hardly edifying family history is a metaphor for the cycle of life and the action of the female element, which nothing and no one can prevent from achieving her ends of perpetuating the species. Isis is the model goddess of the wife and devoted mother. She has an irascible son, both violent and weak, who she nevertheless succeeds in seating upon the throne of his father, through deploying her gifts of intelligence, trickery, and magic. Isis is depicted as a woman coiffed in the hieroglyph of her name adorned by lyriform horns holding the solar disk, like Hathor. She was worshiped in several temples of Egypt, but her principal sanctuary was in Philae (transferred to Aghilka Island, before the rising of the waters caused by the construction of the Aswan Dam in 1965) facing Bigah, where the ritual tomb of Osiris, on whom Isis lavished all her ministrations, was located. The worship of this goddess spread throughout the Mediterranean basin right up to the northern boundaries of the Roman Empire.

Kamutef

The word means "bull of his mother," a metaphorical title of the demiurge.

Khepri

God of becoming, depicted as a scarab or a man with a scarab head, the image of the rising sun. Although an important deity, Khepri had no sanctuary of his own and received no worship.

Khnum

Ram god *(Ovis longipes)* with horizontal, wavily twisted horns (a race that has since vanished from Egypt), whose generative passion earned him the title of "handsome copulater." He is most often depicted as a ram-headed man. He was responsible for controlling the flood with his consort Satet and his consort Anuket, and had especially the task of fashioning human beings and their *ka,* as well all other creatures, out of Nile silt on his potter's wheel. He was worshiped in Elephantine and in Esna with Neith as his companion.

Khonsu

Ancient falcon god of the Thebaid, associated to the Amonian triad of the New Kingdom as the son. Khonsu is depicted as a young god, with the "curl of youth," a long tress falling down to his shoulders, and a lunar crescent and disk on his head, attesting to his role as a lunar god. He holds the two divine and royal scepters (the flail and the *heka* hook), as well as the *was* and sometimes the *djed;* the *menat* may sometimes grace his chest. His body, with the exception of his hands and forearms, is wrapped in a mummylike sheath. He was worshiped in a small distinctive temple, erected within the very enclosure walls of the great Amun temple at Thebes (Karnak).

Maat

Personification of balance, especially cosmic, but also moral and physical. She appears simultaneously with Hathor at the moment the demiurge becomes conscious of his desire to exist, a realization triggered by Hathor. In modern terms, we could say that the universe created in this way is the operating system run by the central processing unit, and that Maat is the software permitting it to be guided. A heavy responsibility! But the goddess is armed; the sarcophagus texts (Middle Kingdom) already incorporate her with the formidable Tefnut. She may also be the Uraeus in all her aggressiveness against the uncreated forces. Gods as well as men have need of this balance and are nourished by it. So the offering of Maat by the pharaoh makes that the culminating point of the divine office. These qualities make her the guardian of justice, of human and divine laws, the observation of which over the course of a lifetime will allow the candidate for eternal life to be judged as "righteous of voice," during the psychostasia. Maat can be depicted as an ostrich feather or as a woman wearing such a feather on her head, which is also the hieroglyph for her name. Maat was worshiped in all the sanctuaries of Egypt and was depicted on royal and noble tombs, and even upon the tombs of private citizens, but as she was the omnipresent cosmic flow, she had no temple of her own.

Min

An anthropomorphic, ithyphallic, and half mummylike deity, he was an ancient god of plants and fertility. His headdress is a round rigid cap in which two high straight feathers have been stuck. From the back of his cap (or headband) a long stiff ribbon hangs down to the ground. He is shown with one arm raised, holding the royal and sexual symbol of the flail, his other arm (not shown) is clasped tightly to his side, with his hand gripping his penis. Behind the god his "kitchen garden" plot is always depicted, which looks like it is planted with romaine lettuce; it also contains a small edifice, perhaps an archaic form of pavilion. His principal temples were in Coptos and Akhmim. Because caravan trails toward the Red Sea originated in these cities, he was the protector of desert travelers, and his oldest effigies are decorated with a specific form of maritime fauna. The "coming out of Min" and the "erection of the mast of Min" were the names of festivals celebrated in his honor, by Pharaoh and the queen, in the presence of the white bull of the god and with the participation of a great number of clergy. These festivities are related to ancient agrarian rituals.

Montu

Ancient warrior god of the Thebaid and notably Erment, also worshiped in Tod, Medamud, and to the north of Karnak. These four sanctuaries form, according to Drioton, the magic shield or palladium of Thebes. Montu is represented as an hieracocephalic man, coiffed with the solar disk and two tall, straight feathers; his brow is generally surmounted by two uraei. He was eclipsed by Amun during the New Kingdom.

Mut

A local Theban goddess of obscure origin who became the "mother" in the Amunian triad. Furthermore, her name means "mother" and is written with the hieroglyph of the vulture. She is depicted as a woman, wearing a feathered hide (like the queen mothers) upon which the *pschent* is placed, justifying her attributional title as Mistress of the Two Lands. She is also assimilated to the solar eye, in its benevolent and aggressive, even masculine, qualities, which gives her the rank of a demiurge (fig. 1.35). A sanctuary was dedicated to her at Karnak where presumably 365 statues of Mut-Sekhmet were erected around the sacred lake in the form of the half moon, the *isheru.* The celestial Mut clearly shares in the two cosmic elements, Sun and Moon, Amun-Ra and Khonsu, as well as the fluid of life, as is only appropriate for a mother goddess.

Nebet-Hetepet

See Hathor.

Nefertum

An anthropomorphic god depicted wearing a lotus-flower crown, seated within or standing upon a lotus (water lily) in his guise as the solar child—whereas officially he is the son of Ptah (god of natural treasures hidden deep within the bowels of the earth!) and a female form of the eye of Ra. He is the third element of the Memphite triad and the patron of pharmacists. In honor of his maternal genes, he can transform himself into a dreadful lion, guardian of the "gates" of Egypt.

Neith

Goddess of the city of Saïs, in the western Nile delta, she is depicted as a woman wearing the red crown of Lower Egypt, and holding a bow and arrows indicative of her warrior nature. She was considered androgynous, more male than female, and she also played the role of a demiurge; her seven arrows are the words of Neith, with which she created the universe. She was worshiped in her main temple at Saïs, and also in Esna, where she was the companion but not the spouse of the god Khnum. She had no children. She is one of the four guardian goddesses of mummified entrails, which were placed in canopic jars.

Nekhbet or **Nekabit**

Goddess originating in el-Kab, the former Nekheb, the Elleithiapolis of the Greeks. She is depicted as either a white vulture or a woman; in both forms she wears the white crown of Upper Egypt. She is the counterpart of the *Wadjet* of Lower Egypt; in this respect she is a guardian goddess of the pharaohs and is often shown flying above the king or perched on the heraldic plant of the South. In her city of origin, where the ruins of her temple are located, she was also considered a demiurge, who had created the cosmos—like Neith—with seven initial words. She has neither a consort nor children—but the king is also her mystical son, as he is of all the Egyptian goddesses, which is to say, of the preeminent divine female element.

Nephthys

Daughter of Nut, she is the sister of the other epagomenal children and the wife of Seth, with whom she had no children; on the other hand, she seems to have succumbed to the charms of Osiris, who gave her a son, Anubis. She is depicted as a woman wearing the hieroglyph of her name on her head. With Isis, she is one of the Two Weepers in the litanies and mysteries of Osiris, her martyred brother. With Isis, Neith, and Selket, she protects the mummified entrails of the deceased, in association with the Four Sons of Horus. A sanctuary was dedicated to her worship in Komir.

Nun

Container of the uncreated, personification of the energetic reserves of the cosmos, he contains the positive and negative forces of liquid magma, while awaiting the end of the universe and the dawn of a new world and a renewed demiurge.

Nut

Goddess of the sky, daughter of Shu and Tefnut, sister-wife of Geb, the Earth, she is the mother of the epagomenal children, examples of an Egyptian version of the house of Atreus. Separated from her husband by Shu on orders from Ra, she is depicted as a woman, holding herself arched above the earth that she barely touches with the tips of her toes and fingers (fig. 1.14). The barques of night and day circulate over her star-studded body. She swallows the sun every evening and causes its rebirth every morning. Ra is he "who appears between the thighs of Nut." Her image is depicted on the sarcophagus lids, which, when lowered over the deceased, thereby simulates the embrace of Nut and Geb-Osiris, with the hope of rebirth. Would not the countless stars be the souls of the deceased whom this goddess has welcomed? Nut can also take the form of a cow or a sow; she is depicted in the royal tombs as the celestial vault.

Ogdoad

Group of the eight divine forms contained in the Nun, consisting of four couples made up of male frogs and female snakes. The Egyptians were not mistaken about the antiquity of the part played by batrachians and slithery aquatic creatures in populating the world. According to the Hermopolitan cosmogony, these eight are presumed to have conceived and fashioned the primordial egg, a place of safe haven and site of real and symbolic gestation in which the sun was contained. The sun hatched in response to the call of the Great Cackler, the goose formed by Thoth, "He who presided over the Eight." Having completed its task, the Ogdoad was absorbed back into the abyss, the Nun (see fig. 1.3).

Osiris

The myth of Orisis has been presented in the work at hand. To sum up: Osiris is one of the "children of disorder" born of Nut during the epagomenal days with his brother, Seth, and his sisters, Isis and Nephthys. He reigned, with his sister-wife, over the fertile part of Egypt while Seth and Nephthys were stuck with the desert. The jealous Seth managed to murder his brother who had been imprisoned by a ruse within a chest, which he threw into the Nile. Isis, his faithful wife and childless, weeping widow, went in search of him accompanied by Nephthys and found the coffin—but Seth also saw it and in a rage took possession of the body of Osiris again, cut it into pieces, and threw them back in the river. The two goddesses were not discouraged by this but re-formed the body with the help of Anubis (fig. 1.19), and Isis reanimated it with her magic. She was thereby able to conceive Horus, her posthumous son in whom Osiris reincarnated (figs. 1.22, 1.24). Seth contested the rights to the throne with his nephew Horus and the two divine powers confronted each other by all available means and under various forms (figs. 1.26 and 1.28). When all was said and done, Horus gained the throne of Egypt, Ra gained the valuable services of Seth, and Osiris reigned over the Beyond, where he recharged his energies. Isis and Nephthys watched over the earthly tomb of Osiris. This pious link between the living and the dead engenders benefits for both parties; it is the model for worship of the dead, whom the living aim at resurrecting. All the dead buried according to these rites nourish the same hope. Mythically, Osiris is the black sun; he is also the source of the annual Nile flood, which allegedly transported the fluids emitted by his body. He is represented as a mummified man, wearing the white crown adorned by the feathers of Anedjty, a deity he had absorbed. His temple in Lower Egypt was located in Busiris, the one in Upper Egypt was in Abydos.

Ptah

Demiurge of the Memphis cosmogony who created the universe with his word, after having thought it in his heart. This dogma is close to that of Hermopolis. Ptah appears in human form, his head clasped in a skullcap, half of his body covered by a royal jubilee garment and half by a mummylike sheath, from which only his hands emerge, holding his interlocking attributes: the *ankh, djed,* and *was*. He is the patron of artisans. With Sekhmet and Nefertum he forms the triad worshiped in his principal Memphis sanctuary. He is a guardian of the royalty in the ancient holy city where the coronation initially took place.

Qadesh

Goddess of Syrian origin, depicted as a woman seen full-faced and either nude or clad in a form-fitting dress, standing on a moving lion. She holds snakes and sometimes scorpions in her hands, as well as lotuses. Her head is crowned by the lunar crescent and/or the lunar disk. She represents active female sexuality, and, for this reason, she is incorporated into Hathor. Her attributes also make her a protective deity against venomous animals, and she is a healer of the harm caused by their sting. Her worship was extended from Memphis during the time of the New Kingdom by the colonies of former war prisoners and Palestine-Syrian immigrants into Egypt. She is sometimes associated with Reshef, a warrior god who is also of Asiatic origin.

Ra

The most important divine manifestation of the solar demiurge, worshiped in Heliopolis, the ancient On. His different forms are Khepri at sunrise, Horus at the zenith, and Atum at sunset. His emergence took place over the original mound that ritually materialized in the *benben,* the raised stone that next became the obelisk, the image of his radiation, and a phallic symbol. He has been given various companions depending on the site of worship, such as Raït, the female Sun. He is depicted in anthropomorphic form wearing the solar globe as a headdress or as a hieracocephalic man with the same attribute; in this form he is identified with Horus. Associated with other deities, he lends them his brilliance and, in exchange, often borrows their appearance, such as is the case with Ra-Amun, Min-Amun, Ra-Horakhty. He presides over the great Ennead of Heliopolis and must confront the revolts and neglect of his own children, as well as of his own creatures—humanity. This is the tale told by the legends of the Distant One, of the vagabond eye, the container of his power, and of the Celestial Cow who takes pity on the weakness of the old demiurge. His "daughters," the female entities who came into existence with him and represent the counterpart of his sexual prowess are, principally, Hathor, Sekhmet, Tefnut, and the Uraeus. His sacred animal is the bull Mnevis.

Ruty

The Two Lions of the Horizon; see Shu and Tefnut.

Satet

Ancient goddess of the First Cataract, worshiped in her sanctuary at Elephantine. She is depicted as a woman wearing the white crown of the South, adorned by two antelope horns. She is associated with Khnum and Anuket.

Sekhmet

The dreadful lioness who is the daughter of Ra, companion of Ptah, and mother of Nefertum of the Memphis triad. She is depicted as a lioness or lion-headed woman. She represents the devastating aspect of the rays of the sun and her auxiliaries are particularly active during the epagomenal days, during which worshipers attempt to appease her with offerings, prayers, and litanies. Her acolytes are those putrid fumes that arise with the fouling of the waters before the flood's arrival. While she oppresses the land with illness and epidemics, she also has the power to heal them; her priests are physicians for whom she is a powerful patron. Her power is not only in the domain of health, but also in the defense of her father Ra's interests. She performs her mission with too much zeal, however, finding the taste of freedom to her liking, and ravages the Egyptian frontiers, a tale related by the legend of humanity's extermination. At the same time she gives free rein to her ravaging libido, thereby embodying dominant female sexuality. Following the appeals of Shu and Thoth, Hathor-Sekhmet-Tefnut returned to Egypt, where she assumed both her tame form as the cat Bastet and retained her virulent form as the Uraeus; this is how the balance of the world is preserved. Maat has been vigilant!

Selkis

The Greek form of her Egyptian name Sereket. The scorpion goddess, formerly a *Nepa rubra,* the water scorpion, hence her name: "She who causes one to take a breath." This origin was gradually obscured and the entity became a scorpion or a woman wearing a scorpion as a headdress. But if one closely examines the statuette of this goddess, seen protecting Tutankhamun's naos with canopic jars, it can be seen that it is not a scorpion but a *Nepa rubra* that she wears on her head. This role as guardian of the canopic jars is entrusted to her, as well as to three other goddesses: Isis, Nephthys, and Neith. Furthermore, while as a scorpion she can inflict cruel and even fatal wounds, she can also heal them, as she did for the child Horus in the Chemmis marsh.

Seth

The most turbulent of the children of Nut and Geb, brother and husband of Nephthys. He is depicted in the shape of an unidentified animal or as a man with the head of this animal. According to myth, he was the murderer of Osiris and the adversary of Horus. He compensates for these negative aspects of his personality by his role in the balance of the world, which cannot exist without this equilibrium between good and evil. Seth represents the untamed forces of nature, which are also displayed in his chaotic sexuality—nevertheless he remains sterile, like the desert over which he rules. Egypt's borders are also under this warrior's dominion (he was worshiped for his martial aspects during the Ramesside era). Ra valued him for the valiant way he acted in his struggle against Apophis, the serpent of the deeps, which the barque of the Sun must traverse. Popular piety and a certain portion of the clergy during difficult times in the history of the pharaohs combined Seth not only with the invader of the moment but also with this same Apophis—what fickle ingratitude! Seth and Horus are the emblematic figures of the two opposing and complementary aspects of the royal persona. Seth is the pharaoh's master of arms and, with Ra, Amun, and Ptah, the divine protector of the army. For failure to identify the animal in which he incarnates, ritual disgrace pursues those who have the misfortune to possess a reddish hide, namely dogs and donkeys.

Shu

According to Heliopolitan doctrine, Shu and Tefnut are the direct offspring of Atum, whose radiance they embody. Shu was charged by Ra-Atum to separate the Sky, Nut, from the Earth, Geb, so as to create the space necessary for the manifestation of the Sun. He is depicted as a man wearing an ostrich feather, the hieroglyph of his name, on his head. He can also, with his sister-wife, Tefnut, take the form of a lion, in which case they are the Ruty, the lions of the luminous horizon where the sun both sets and rises. Ra entrusted him, as well as Thoth, with the mission of bringing the Distant One back into Egypt. Shu fulfilled his charge under the symbolic name of Onuris, or Inher, "he who brings back the Distant One." When he left the world, Shu left the throne and government to his son Geb, who made poor use of his inheritance, sullied by the rape of his mother, Tefnut—a cosmic metaphor obviously.

Sia

Personification of the innate science of the demiurge; see Thoth.

Sothis

Greek name for Sepedet, "the sharp or pointed one," personification of the star Sirius, whose heliacal rising announced the return of the annual flood and a new solar cycle. She has been identified with Isis. In her temple of Abu Simbel, Nefertari, Great Royal Wife and beloved of Ramses II, was deified under the aspect of Sothis.

Tatenen

God of the subterranean space, traversed by the sun during its nocturnal course. As a cosmic entity, he was associated with the transformations of the deceased and with the Memphis demiurge, Ptah. He is the father of Ihy, forever enveloped by the dark shadows of his progenitor. He is depicted as anthropomorphic.

Tefnut

Daughter of Atum, sister-wife of Shu, and a luminous, ardent manifestation of the demiurge. She was worshiped with her brother at Leontopolis under the name of the Ruty. She assumes the form of the lioness along with Sekhmet; both are embodiments of the violent power of Hathor. Tefnut is the Distant One who left the demiurge for the heart of Africa in order to give free rein to her instincts as a savage lioness. She thereby deprived Atum-Ra of the essential aspect of his power, and it was vital that she be made to return to him. Shu and Thoth succeeded in achieving this feat. On her return, now tame, she became the charming Hathor or the gentle Bastet. This myth is the colorful description of the most vital of all events for the Egyptians: the annual return of the flooding of the Nile, which takes place when the sun enters the sign of Leo.

Thoth

Demiurge of the Hermopolitan cosmogony, who can be represented as either an ibis, an ibis-headed man, or as a hamadryas (baboon). (There was, incidentally, an ancient god, the white monkey, Hedj-ur.) Thoth is the god of all knowledge and learning. Thanks to the veritable font of knowledge, Sia, he was able to think Creation in his heart and have it realized by Hu, the Verb, for he is the Great Cackler with his enormous ibis beak. Hu and Sia are the hypostasis of Thoth and depicted as male humans. In Memphis, Thoth is considered as the tongue of Ptah. Thoth is thus the inventor of writing, the magic keeper of the scribe's palette, creator of mathematics and the calendar; there he was not quite successful, for every solar year is always missing one-fourth of a day, unless he did it on purpose. For his manipulation of time, which he introduced into the divine world (which would have liked to do without it), gave a greater importance to the Moon, to which the Sun is indebted for an enlarged space-time continuum—after all, Thoth is a lunar god who wears the the disk of the pale luminous body on his head. With his consort (who is not his companion) Seshat he looks after writings and libraries, and is the divine archivist who inscribes the names of the pharaohs and the duration of their reigns on the leaves and fruits of the sacred *ished* tree, recording the result of the psychostasia, as well as all protocol from divine get-togethers. His sagacity makes him the messenger and ambassador of the celestial cenacle, and he, as well as Shu, were naturally entrusted with the delicate mission of bringing the Distant One back into Egypt—something the two accomplices, transformed into monkeys for the occasion, managed to pull off quite successfully. He also provided medical services, for example, curing the wounded lunar eye of Horus, making it once more healthy, *wedjat,* and he procured a new head for Isis, who had been decapitated by her irascible son Horus. Thoth's renown spread throughout the eastern Mediterranean to the extent that Greeks incorporated him into their Hermes, under the name Trismegistus (thrice-greatest), which is only a poor interpretation of the Egyptian superlative. In all simplicity, Thoth is not "thrice-greatest" but simply the "greatest." His principal temple was built in Hermopolis, where Thoth was the first of the Eight, thus of the Ogdoad, which was thereby transformed into an Ennead. This hardly matters as the persona of Thoth caused the return of these four couples who assisted at the Creation to their original abyss. They took with them the gift of time, which gives them hope for an end to the world they helped create and the coming of a new cosmic cycle.

Taweret

In Egyptian, Ta-ueret means "the Great," the title of several goddesses. Taweret was the gravid hippopotamus goddess who protects pregnant women and women in labor.

Uraeus

This Latinized term is a masculine noun; it comes from the Egyptian word *iaret,* which is feminine, obviously appropriate for a cobra goddess with multiple implications, but always under the form of a snake, even when she is the savage eye of Ra. She rises over the foreheads of the demiurge and certain gods, as well as the king, whom she protects against his enemies until death or rather transformation. The new pharaoh, Horus incarnate, will find her faithfully at her post. She only ever refused her service to Geb, little appreciating his behavior toward his mother, Tefnut, one of whose most violent manifestations is the uraeus. Her involvement is implied in all the cosmic myths, representing fire as the solar eye and water, transported by virtue of the return of the equally enraged Distant One.

Weuret-Hekaou

Personification of magic power, as her name, "Great of Magic," indicates. She is often incorporated into Isis, among whom she became an attributive hypostasis. The divine entity furthermore represents the qualities of the royal crowns: her power could equally manifest under the form of the Uraeus.

Useret

"The Powerful One," personification of an epithet of the uraeus.

Wadjet

Cobra goddess originating in Buto, where her sanctuary was located. She is the protector of the royalty of Lower Egypt and wears, for this reason, the red crown, although her name means "the green," in this case the green of vegetation and vitality. She is the counterpart of Nekhbet, the vulture of Upper Egypt. The serpent is either depicted raised on its coils above a clump of papyrus or coiled around the stem of that plant. The two tutelary goddesses of the royalty are the Two Ladies of the royal titulary: the second of the great names of the king is always introduced by this reference.

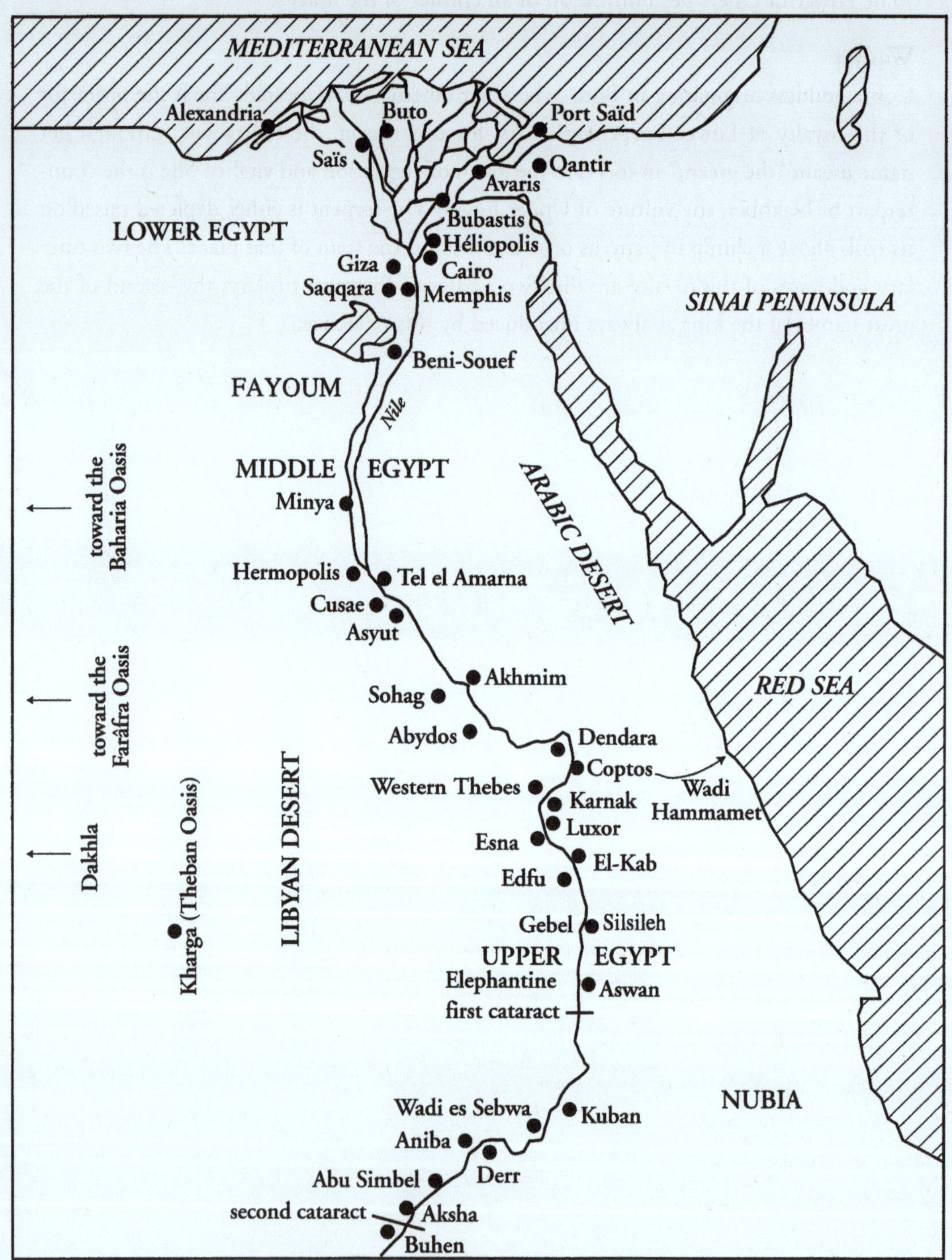

Map of Egypt from the Delta to the Second Cataract

APPENDIX THREE

Egyptian Place-Names

This list contains only the sites mentioned in the book.

Abydos

City of Upper Egypt, where a sanctuary for the ancient funerary god, Khentamentiu, was located. This god was absorbed by Osiris, thereby making Abydos his principal temple in the South (see Busiris).

Agilkia

New archaeological site to which were transferred the monuments of the island of Philae, in an international undertaking by the joint venture for "Salvaging the Monuments of Nubia" under the aegis of UNESCO, in order to prevent the loss of these treasures of the heritage of world patrimony following the construction of the Aswan High Dam (1965).

Amarna

Tell el-Amarna, the archaeological site of the capital constructed on virgin soil by the "heretic" pharaoh Akhenaten, of the Eighteenth Dynasty. The location was destroyed by his successors.

Biga

Island to the west of Philae where the mystic tomb of Osiris is located and ritually maintained by Isis. Its monuments were also transferred to a neighboring island to save them from the waters of Lake Nasser.

Buto

Symbolic religious capital of Lower Egypt, home of the sanctuary of the goddess Uto or Wadjet.

Bubastis

City of the eastern Nile delta, the modern Tell Basta, location of the principal sanctuary of the cat goddess Bastet and site of the unbridled festivities celebrated in her honor that Herodotus described.

Busiris

City of the Delta where Anedjty was worshiped, a god later absorbed by Osiris. This made Busiris the principal place of worship and pilgrimages for Osiris in Lower Egypt.

Canopus

City on the Delta, where, according to legend, Canopos, the pilot of Menelaeus, died on his return from Troy. An Osirian idol (?) was worshiped there in the form of its characteristic vase, prompting archaeologists to compare it to the containers that hold mummified viscera, hence "canopic jars."

Chemmis

Mythical location in the Delta, where Isis secretly raised her son Horus while Seth was lurking about seeking to do him harm.

Dendara

City of the principal temple (still in quite good condition) of the cult of the goddess Hathor in Upper Egypt. She formed a triad there with Horus of Edfu and Ihy, who was considered the son of Horus.

Edfu

The ancient city of Behedet, an important place of Horus worship. The magnificent temple from the Ptolemaic and Roman eras is still very well preserved.

Elephantine

Ancient captial, near Aswan, of the first nome of Upper Egypt, where Khnum and his consorts Satis and Anuket had their sanctuaries. These are gone today, having fallen victim to the lime ovens in the nineteenth century, but they were seen and drawn by the scholars of the Bonaparte expedition.

Erment

Principal temple (significant ruins of it remain today) of the warrior god Montu, protector of the Thebaid.

Esna

City of Upper Egypt. An important modern urban center surrounds what remains of a well-preserved temple from the Greco-Roman era. It was consecrated to Neith, a demiurge like her companion in this temple, Khnum—her associate but not her husband, but to fulfill the principle of the triad, he was nonetheless the father of the god of magic, Heka. Furthermore, the "handsome copulater" had two goddess-wives here, Nebetu and Menhyt.

Heliopolis

The city of the Sun, the ancient On, Yunu of the Egyptians, was a religious capital of the first importance. Today it is no more than an archaeological site to the north of Cairo, a souvenir of the brilliant city of the Great Ennead.

Hermopolis

City of Thoth, the former Khemenu, meaning "City of the Eight," an allusion to the primoridal Ogdoad. The sanctuary was allegedly constructed on the first mound, the one from where the sun rose for the "first time" at the beginning of time.

Karnak

See Thebes.

Luxor

See Thebes.

Memphis

The ancient religious and royal capital, to the south of Cairo, was located, like its modern sister, at the "balancing point of the Two Lands," the hinge between Upper and Lower Egypt. Only ruins remain of the imposing capital where Ptah and his family ruled, near the contemporary village of Mit Rahina. It faces the most prestigious necropolis of ancient Egypt, the names of whose sites—Giza, Saqqara, Maidum, and Dahshur, evoke the splendors of the past, the site of the only one of the seven wonders of the ancient world still standing: the pyramids.

Philae

Island at the First Cataract, where sanctuaries of Isis and complementary deities, as well as Hathor, were erected. All of these well-preserved monuments were transferred to the island of Agilkia to protect them from the waters of Lake Nasser.

Punt

Land of incense and plants that were unknown in Egypt. It has not been identified with any certainty, but it is thought it may well have been Somalia.

Saïs

Ancient city of the eastern Delta where the goddess Neith was worshiped as a demiurge and mother of the Sun.

Thebes

The Waset of the Egyptians was, from the time of the Middle Kingdom, an important religious and administrative center and became during the New Kingdom the capital of the vast Egyptian empire. The modern towns of Karnak and Luxor are districts of the ancient "hundred-gated Thebes," a title referring to the impressive number of pylons erected there. It was placed under the protection of the god Amun and his very powerful clergy, as well as under that of Montu. Ptah, Mut, Khonsu, and Sekhmet also had sanctuaries in this immense religious complex, which is still today the great temple of Amun, and where even the heretic king Akhenatan left his mark. The harem of the South—the Ipet-sut—designates the temple of Luxor, a main tourist attraction, where festivals for renewing the generative powers of the demiurge took place in antiquity. The necropolis located facing it, on the west bank of the Nile, is only slightly less splendid than that of Memphis. It includes the so-called funeral temples, the "palaces of millions of years," of the great sovereigns of the New Kingdom on the sites of Deir el-Bahari, Qurna, the Ramesseum, Medinet Habu, as well as their richly decorated tombs in the Valley of the Kings, and those of the queens, princes, and princesses, in the Valley of the Queens.

Valley of the Kings

See Thebes.

Valley of the Queens

See Thebes.

APPENDIX FOUR

Egyptian Hieroglyphics

A SHORT SELECTION OF TERMS RELATING TO LOVE AND SEXUALITY IN PHARAONIC SOCIETY

This small vocabulary should, beyond its linguistic aspect, reveal to the reader the twists and turns of thought of the ancient Egyptians in the particular field of the present study. All the elements of the celestial, human, animal, plant, and mineral world are translated into images, without exception. Assembled to form words, they magically take on life through handwriting and pronunciation. This latter partially escapes us, because ancient Egyptian only took note of consonants and semivowels; the suggested pronunciations here are thus only an approximation (see Stéphane Rossini, *Egyptian Hieroglyphics: How to Read and Write Them* [New York: Dover, 1989]).

The reader will find beneath every word in hieroglyphs its international transcription (which takes into account the difficulty of this transcription by using diacritics), a suggested pronunciation, and the translation of the term, topped off, if need be, with semantic observations. The vocabulary is not listed in alphabetical order but thematically.

FAMILY AND SOCIETY

1. *s* es man as opposed to "woman"

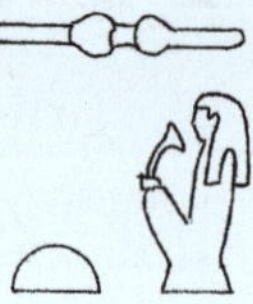

2. *st* set woman as opposed to "man"

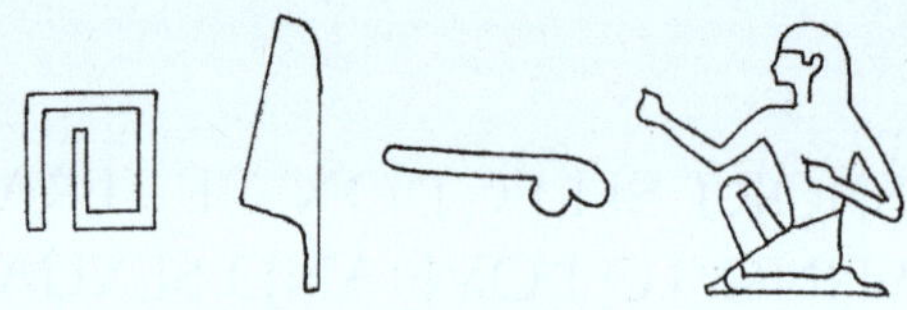

3. *hi* hi husband

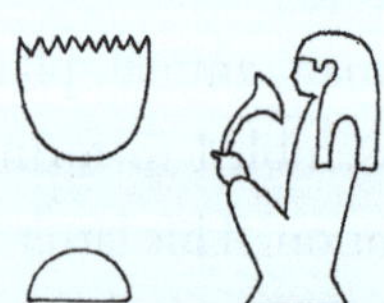

4. *ḥmt* hemet spouse, wife

5. *ẖnmw* khenemu the married couple; literally the neighbors, the interdependent ones, the joined ones

---

6. *ꜥḳ r pr* aq er per to contract a marriage, literally to enter into a house

---

7. *mwt* mut mother

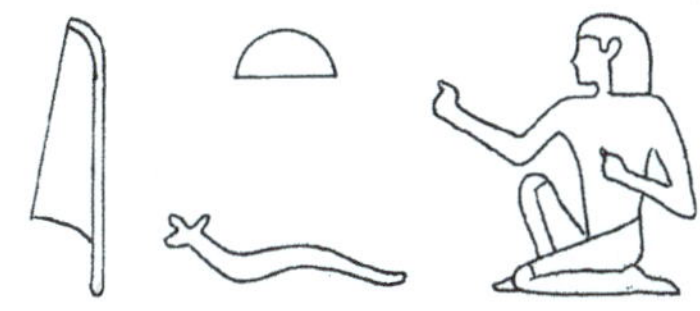

8. *it* it father

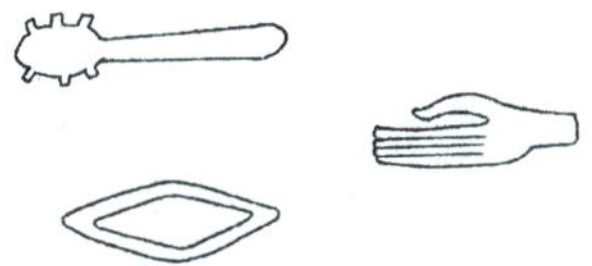

9. *ẖrd* khered child

10. *sꜣ / zꜣ* sa/za son

11. *sꜣt / zꜣt* sat/zat daughter

---

12. *sn* sen brother, also lover, "beloved," and even "husband"

---

13. *snt* senet sister, as well as "beloved" and even "wife"

---

14. *mt ḥnt* met henet concubine

---

15. *ḫnr* khener harem, derived from the word "prison"

16. *ḫnrt* kheneret lady of the harem, concubine

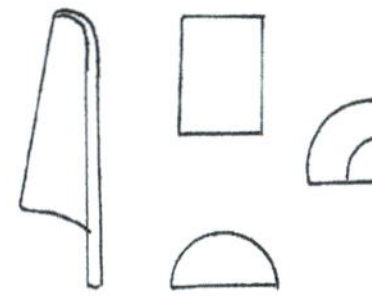

17. *ipt* ipet house of women, by extension "harem"

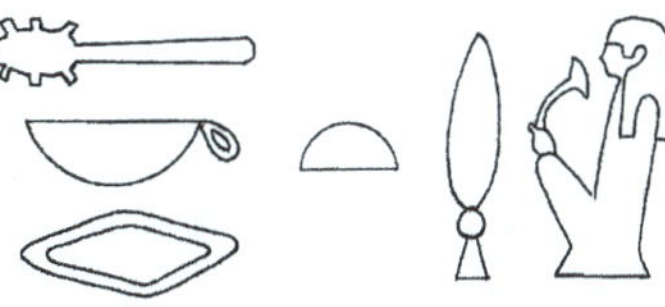

18. *ẖkrt* khekeret lady of the harem; the term is derived from the word "ornament," "decor," hence "ornament of the king" for "favorite"

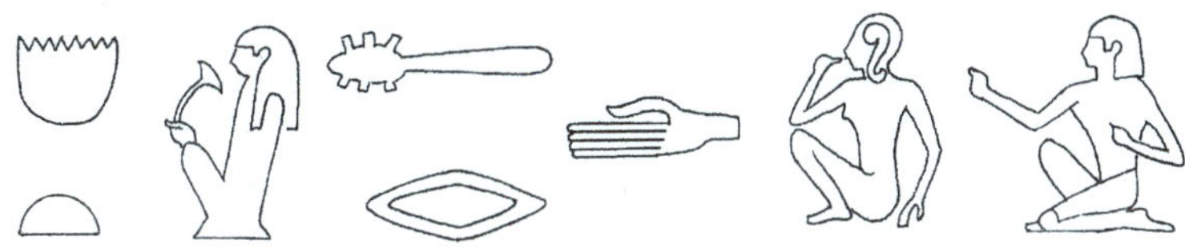

19. *ḥmt ẖrd* hemet khered ephebe, transvestite (?)

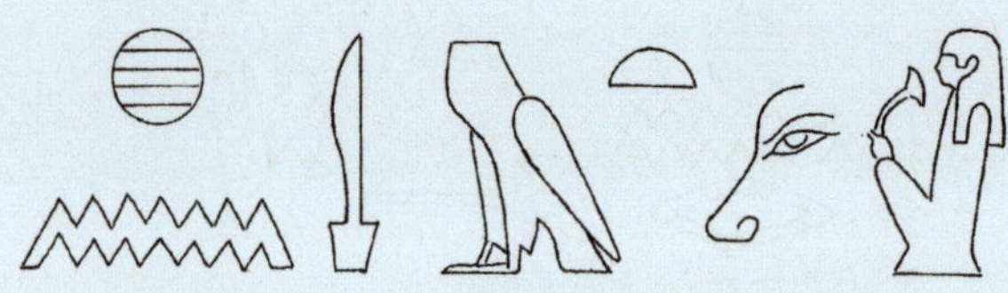

20. *ḫnmt* khenemet prostitute; the same word designates a nurse, a child's nanny, but the writing changes; the sign of the nose, suggesting the perfume used by an "easy woman" is omitted

---

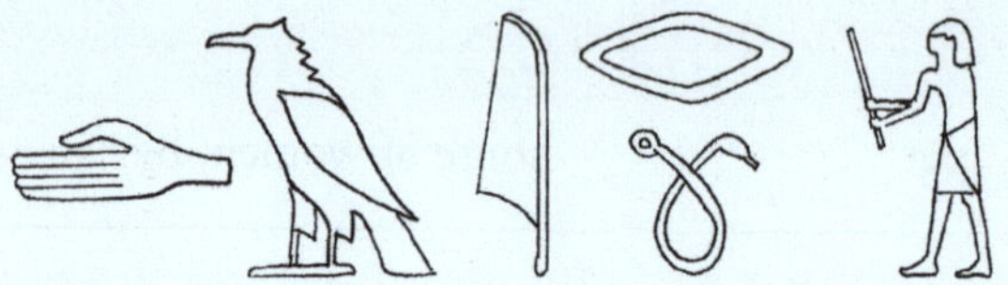

21. *dꜣ(i)r* da(i)r to subjugate, to force with violence, to rape

---

22. *nk ḥmt ṯꜣty* nek hemet tchaty to commit adultery with a married woman

---

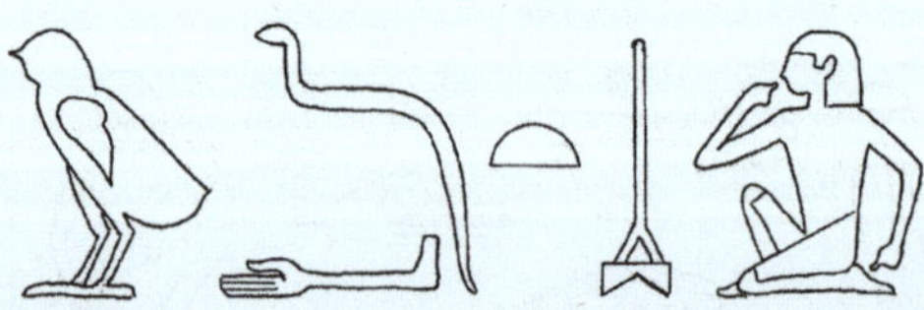

23. *wḏꜥt* wedjat divorce by judgment for man or woman

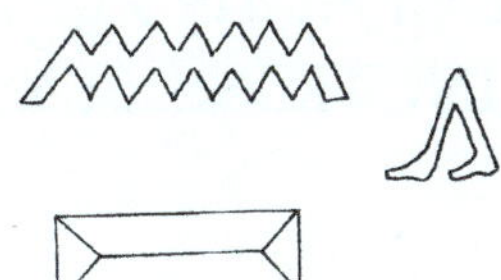

24. *nš* nech to repudiate his wife, to divorce; literally, "put outside," "chase off"

25. *fḫ(t) m ṯꜣm* fekh em tcham circumcise; literally, "take away the foreskin"

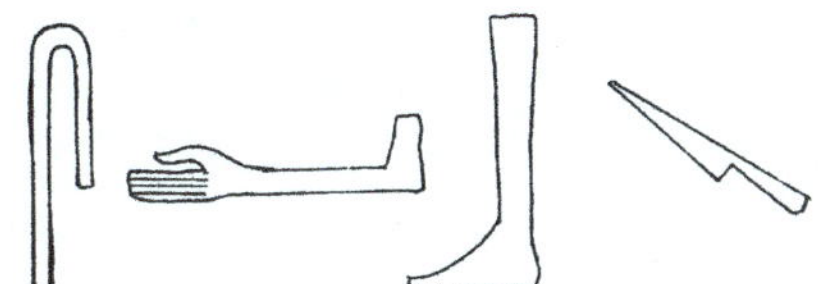

26. *šꜥb* sab to castrate an animal; ox, castrated animal; by extension, a eunuch?

EROGENOUS ZONES AND THEIR FUNCTIONS, SEXUAL ORGANS

27. *bꜣḥ* bah phallus; urethra, the front

28. *ḥnn* henen prick; also donkey's sex organ

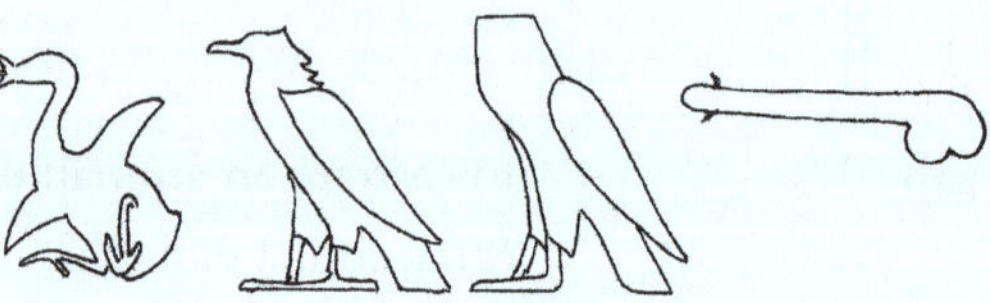

29. *ṯꜣm* tcham foreskin (see circumcise)

30. *ẖrwy* kherouy testicles

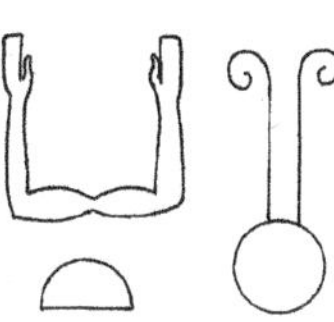

31. *kꜣt* kat vagina, vulva

32. *ḥmt* hemet uterus; derivative of a word for "receptacle," is synomous with woman

---

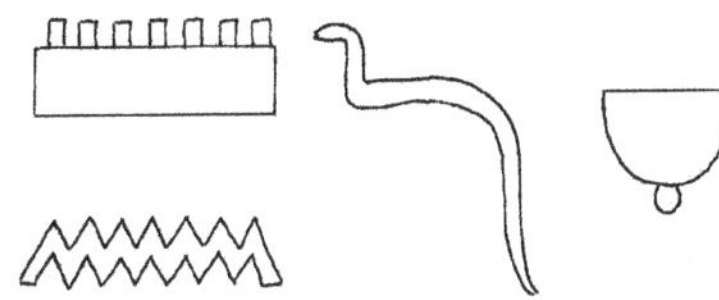

33. *mnḏ* menedj female breast

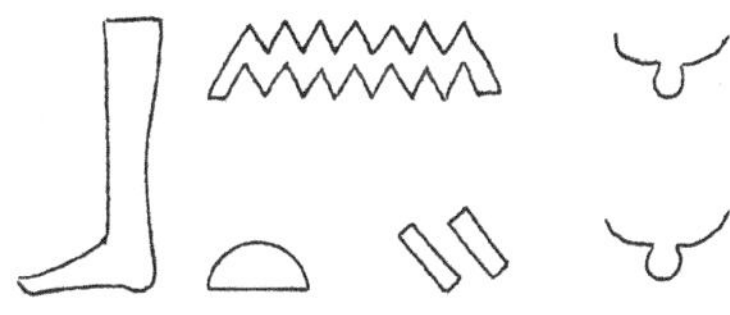

34. *bnty* benty the two breasts, tits; literally, "the two daughters" (the two boobs!)

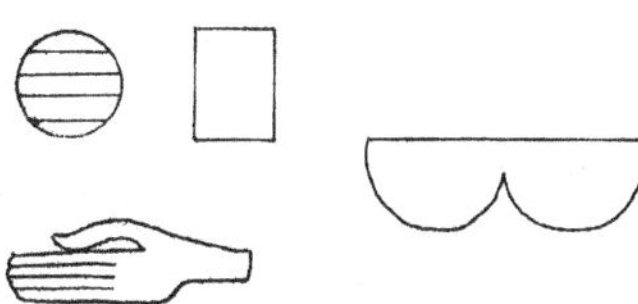

35. *ḫpd* kheped buttocks

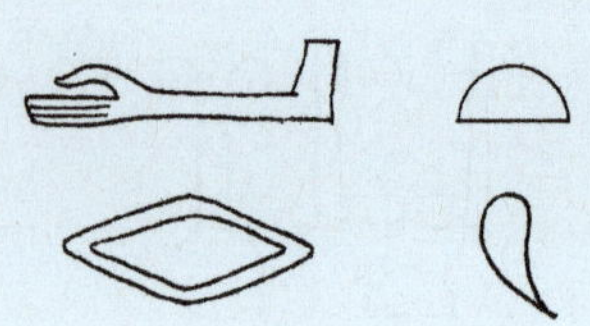

36. *ʿrt* aret anus

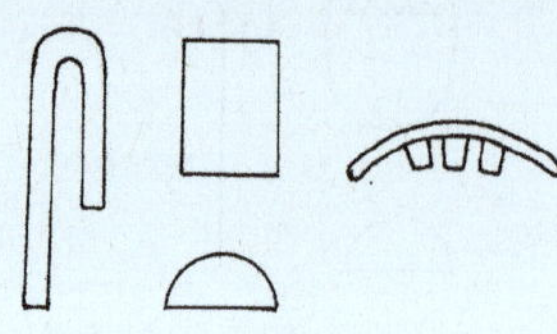

37. *spt* sepet lip

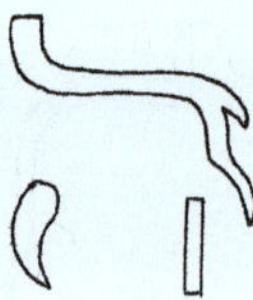

38. *nś* nes tongue

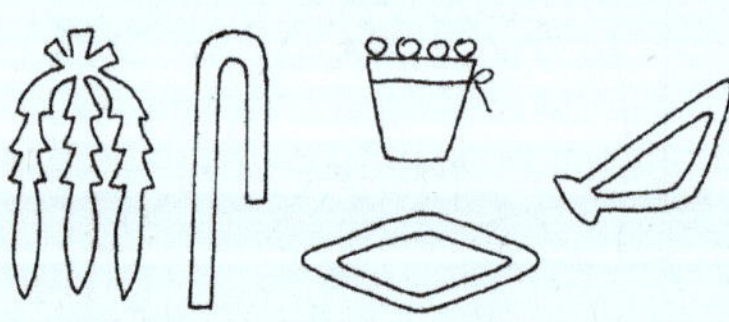

39. *mśḏr* mesdjer ear

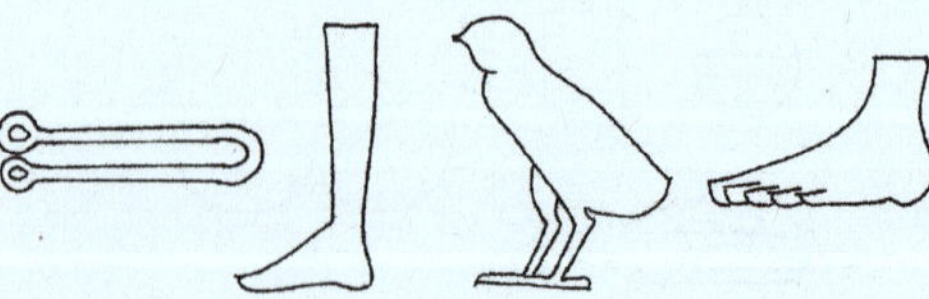

40. *ṯbw* tchebu sole of the foot

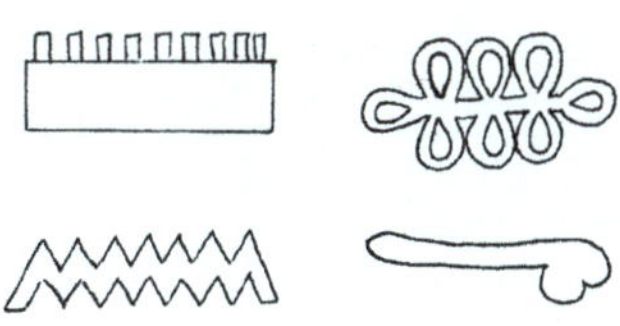

41. *mnśꜣ* menesa erection

42. ꜥꜣꜥ sperm (divine), seed

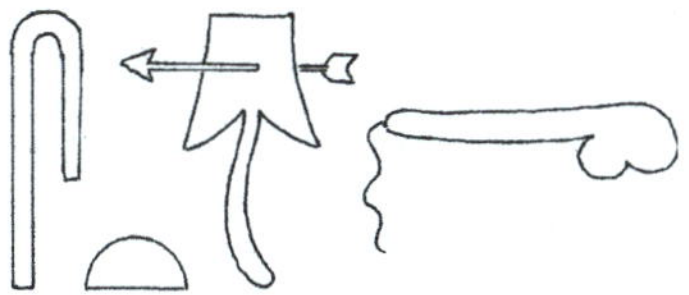

43. *śti* seti ejaculate, engender

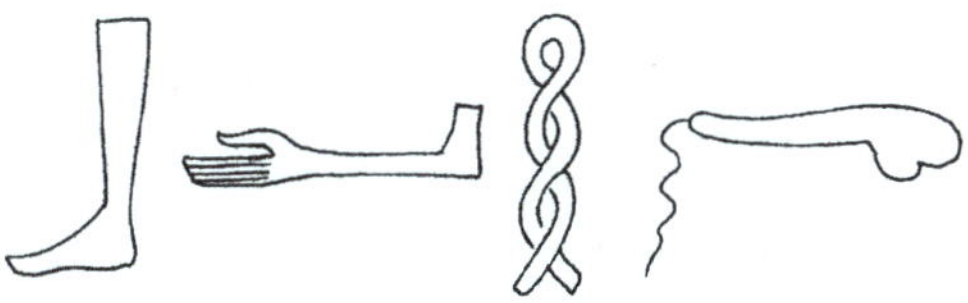

44. bꜥḥ bah ejaculation, flood (reference to the god Sobek)

45. *iwr* iur to concieve a child; embryo (human)

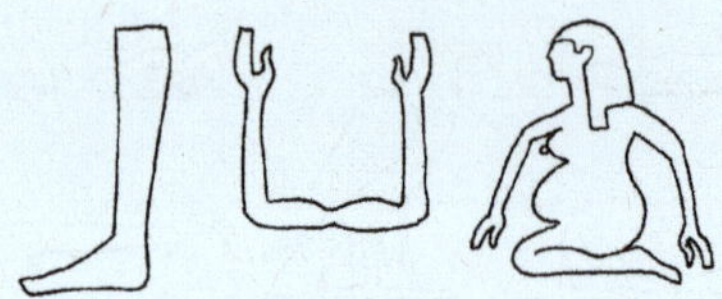

46. *bkꜣ* beka to be pregnant

47. *mśwt* mesut birth

48. *msw* nesu those who are born, offspring; children (in general)

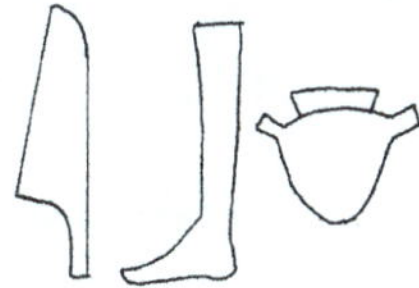

49. *ib*	ib	heart

50. *mrwt*	merut	love

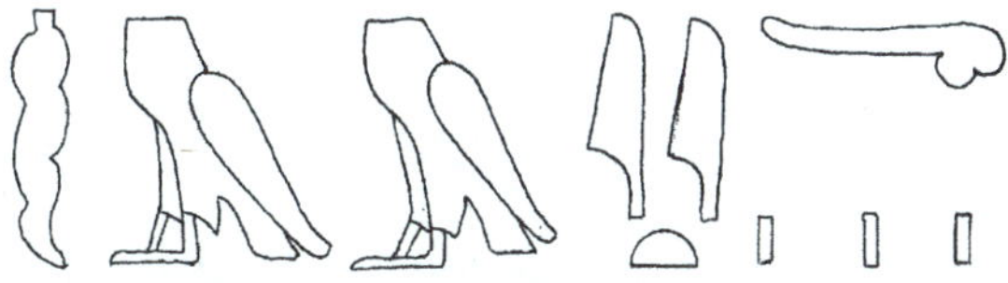

51. *nḏmmyt*	nedjemmit	passion

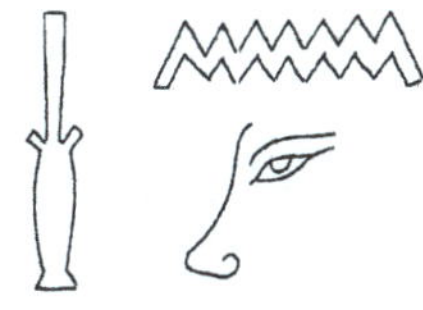

52. *śn*	sen	to give a kiss (nose, mouth); literally, "to feel and/or smell" (odor, touch)

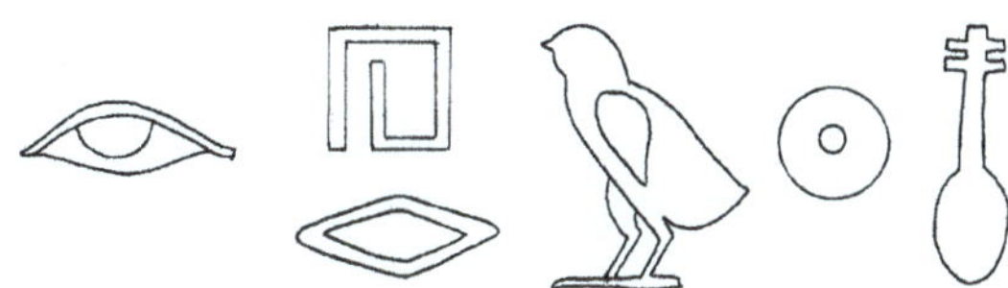

53. *ir ḥrw nfr*	ir heru nefer	to spend an enjoyable day

54.	*ir nḏm*	ir nedjem	to take sexual pleasure

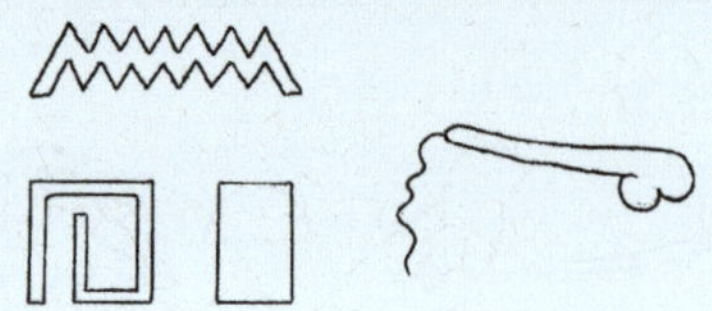

55.	*nhp*	nehep	copulate, coitus

56.	*dꜣ*	da	to copulate violently; derivative of "hurl to the ground" (enemies, etc.)

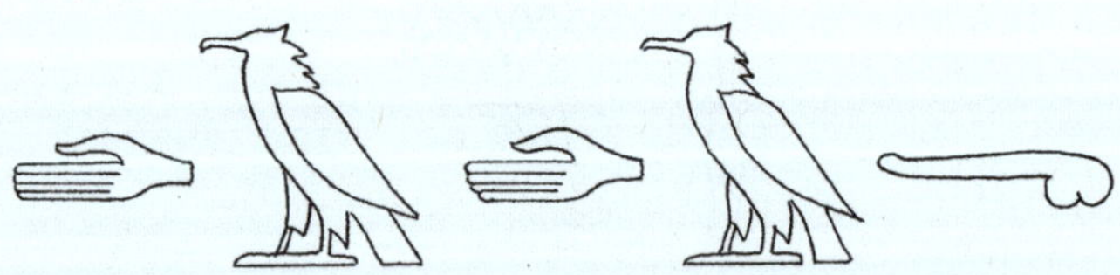

57.	*dꜣdꜣ*	dada	to rape (see 21); sodomize (?)

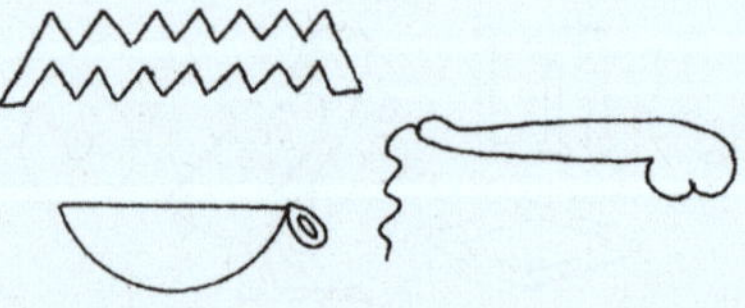

58.	*nk*	nek	copulate, to fornicate, (the most common term)

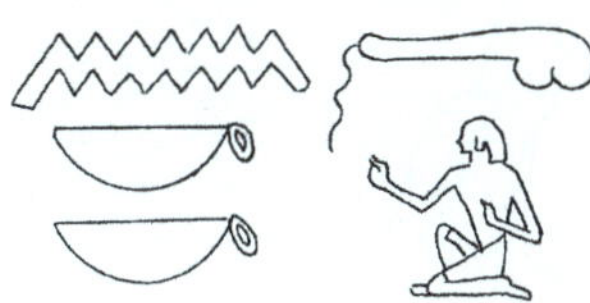

59. *nkk* — nekek — "cute"; homosexual (apparently there is no specific word for homosexuals)

60. *nk nkk* — nek nekek — to copulate with a homosexual, sodomize

---

61. *ḥmty* — hemety — a "woman-man" homosexual; coward, impotent; "sekehety" is restricted to the religious texts of the Old and Middle Kingdoms

---

62. *ḥ3dt* — hadet — sexual excitation

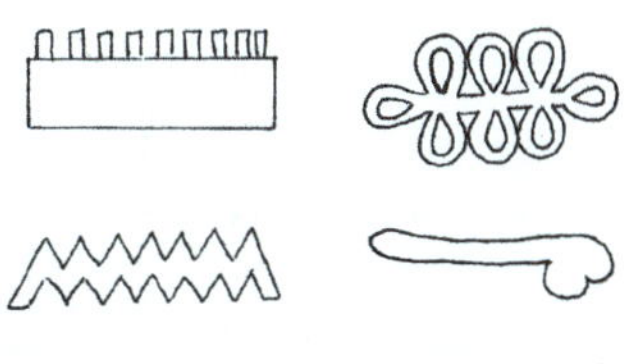

63. *mnš3* — menesa — erection (see 41)

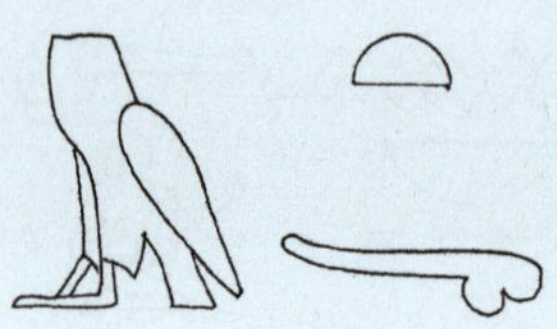

64. *mt* met virile, synonym for man

65. *bꜣꜣwt* baaut virility, sexual prowess

66. *mbꜣḥ* em bah in the presence of, in the front (see 27)

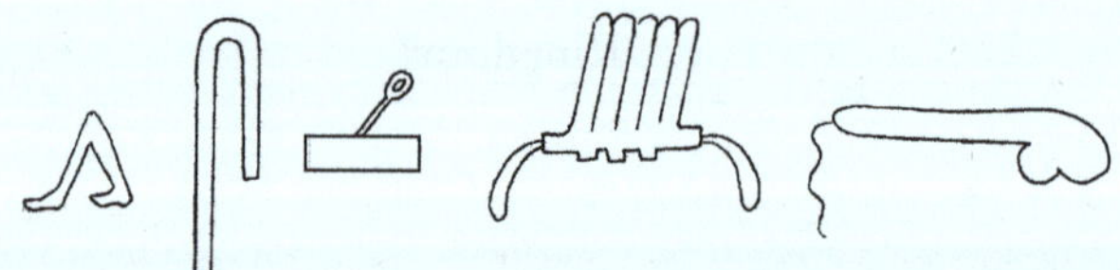

67. *iwsꜣw* yusau masturbator (epithet for Atum)

Notes

INTRODUCTION

1. Herodotus (484–425 B.C.), *Histories,* Cambridge: Loeb Classical Library, 1920; and Diodorus Siculus (first century B.C., in Egypt from 60–57 B.C.), *Bibliothèque historique,* partially inspired by Hecataeus of Miletus (circa 300 B.C.), who lived in Egypt under Ptolemy I. *Translations of Diodorus Siculus* (Paris: Hoeffer, 1846); C. H. Oldfather, *Diodorus of Sicily,* (London, 1968); *Bibliothèque historique,* trans. M. Casevitz (Paris: Societé d'èdition "Les Belles Lettres," 1972).

CHAPTER ONE

1. The Pyramid Texts date from the Fifth and Sixth Dynasties. They adorn the walls of the sarcophagus chambers, annexes, and corridors of the pyramids of Unas, last king of the Fifth Dynasty (the oldest), and the principal kings of the Sixth Dynasty: Teti, Pepi I, Merenre, and Pepi II. They were discovered in 1881 and published by Kurt Sethe (Leipzig, 1908–10). Several texts figure in the pyramids of a King Ibi of the Eighth (?) Dynasty; they were brought to light in 1920 and others even more recently, all on the Saqqara plateau. They constitute a collection of incantations for the resurrection of the pharaoh, which reflect the religious concepts already formed in that era and probably also the then current power struggles, presented under a mythical format.
2. C. Desroches-Noblecourt, *Toutankhamon: À la découverte de l'Égypte éternelle,* CD-ROM, (Paris: Syrinx, 1997).
3. P. Derchain, *Hathor Quadrifrons* (Istanbul, 1972), p. 42 and n. 52.

4. Thoth was considered the inventor of the calendar. The game with the moon is a myth that metaphorically explains the adaptation of the lunar calendars (the more ancient, agrarian, and closest to reality) and the solar (the more recent, administrative, and official) calendars. For more on this subject see P. Derchain, *La Lune: Mythes et rites,* Sources Orientales 5 (1962); C. Desroches-Noblecourt, *Amours et fureurs de la Lointaine* (Paris: 1995), pp. 37–40; and S. Cauville, *Le Zodiaque d'Osiris,* (Leuven/Louvain, 1997), p. 68ff.

   Thoth was not completely successful with his introduction of time into the divine sphere, because Ra escaped with a quarter of a day annually. The result on earth was that the solar calendar was staggered with respect to the seasons and did not fall right except every 365 × 4 = 1,460 years, a gap that the Egyptians called the "Sothian era," in reference to the goddess Sothis, personification of the star Sirius. In fact, this star rises anew a little before the sun, after a disappearance of seventy days, a lapse of time that ritually corresponds to the duration of the embalming of all the "Osiri." This event takes place around July 19–21 in the modern calendar and coincides with the beginning of the annual flood of the Nile, directly after it has hit its lowest levels when nature hovers between life and death, before resurrecting and providing fruits, like Osiris following his revival by Isis. For more on this subject see D. Meeks and C. Favard-Meeks, *Les Dieux égyptiens* (Paris: 1993), p. 156ff, where the reader may find the corresponding bibliography; and Desroches-Noblecourt, *Amours et fureurs,* pp. 41–45.

5. The number 16 (sometimes 14) is related to the flood of the Nile, whose optimal rise was 16 cubits, measured by the nilometers at the temples that marked off the course of the river. A flood that was too weak meant famine, an overly strong flood devastation. The flood was supposedly derived of the liquids from the body of Osiris; it carried "all the fathers and mothers" of Egypt.

6. The pterophoric (winged) goddesses depicted on the sarcophagi encircling the deceased with their wings echo this myth. See Desroches-Noblecourt, *Toutankhamon.*

7. The battles between Horus and Seth are fully described in the Pyramid Texts. A summary and an interpretation of the different myths can be found in the work of J. G. Griffith, *The Conflict of Horus and Seth* (Liverpool, 1960).

8. A. H. Gardiner, *The Chester Beatty Papyrus, I* (London, 1931), contains a story on the adventures of Horus and Seth, "The Contendings of Horus and Seth," preserved on this papyrus from the reign of Ramses V. Regarding this text, Gustave Lefebvre says, rightfully, that "one is struck by the not only familiar but irreverent tone of the tale. The author spares no sarcasm for his divine characters; he gleefully emphasizes their weaknesses and their ridiculous traits, he highlights their defects; he shamelessly exposes [. . .] the indecent actions he attributes to them." He wonders "what esteem the Egyptians [. . .] had for such vulgar gods" and if the religion was not, for the most part, "the belief in the efficacy of the magic." G. Lefebvre, *Romans et contes égyptiens* (Paris, 1949), p. 179.

9. A plant that remains unidentified. See J. Vandier, *Le Papyrus Jumilhac III,* 1–6 (Paris, 1961).

10. Gardiner, *Chester Beatty Papyrus, VII,* verso 1, 5–11, 3.

11. Gardiner, *Chester Beatty Papyrus, I,* 11, 2–13, 3.

12. Papyrus *Sallier IV,* 2, 6ff; and the *Chester Beatty Papyrus,* 1, 8, 9ff. concerning the ritual killing of a male hippopotamus, a form of Seth (whereas the sacred female animal of the benevolent goddess Thueris is taboo). For more on this subject see T. Säve-Söderbergh, "On Egyptian Representations of Hippopotamus Hunting as a Religious Motive," *Horae Soederblomianae,* 3, (Uppsala, 1953).

13. The first part of this composite myth is also the most ancient. It is known by the title "The Book of the Cow of Heaven," including the "Destruction of Men." This chapter was subsequently joined to the "Myth of the Beyond." The text of the title "The Book of the Cow of Heaven" is engraved, more or less in totality, in five royal tombs of the New Kingdom: those of Tutankhamun, Seti I, Ramses II, Ramses III, and Ramses VI, but the text probably dates from the Middle Kingdom, transcribed into neo-Egyptian. Publications by C. Maystre, *BIFAO* 40 (1941), pp. 53–115 (pp. 58–73 concern the destruction of mankind); A. Piankoff, *The Shrines of Tut-ankh-Amon* (New York, 1955); E. Hornung, *Der Ägyptische Mythos von der Himmelskuh,* OBO 46 (Göttingen, 1982).

    For more on "The Myth of the Distant One," see H. Junker, *Der Auszug der Hathor-Tefnt aus Nubien* (Berlin, 1911), and K. Sethe, *Zur Altägyptischen Sage Sonnenauge, das in der Fremde war* (Leipzig, 1912); M. Lichtheim, *Ancient Egyptian Literature* 2 (Berkeley and Los Angeles, 1976), pp. 197–99; C. Lalouette, *Textes sacrés et textes profanes de l'ancienne Égypte* 2 (Paris, 1987); for a new interpretation see Desroches-Noblecourt, *Amours et fureurs,* p. 20ff.

14. J. Vandier, "Iousâas et (Hathor)-Nébet-Hétépet," *Revue d'égyptologie* 16 (1964), 17 (1965), and 18 (1966) assembled the documentation on these particular forms of Hathor and studied them in detail.

    Iusaas, in Egyptian, *iu.s, aas,* can be translated as "she arrives, she grows," an expression no doubt referring to the hand and the phallus (the hand is a feminine noun in Egyptian, but the standard term for phallus, *bah,* is not; however, in the Book of the Dead, the term used for phallus, *djet,* is feminine). For an account of this matter, see J. Leclant, *Lexikon der Ägyptologie* 2 (Wiesbaden, 1977), col. 813–15.

15. On the subject of the "Spouses of the God" and the "Divine Worshipers" one should consult C. E. Sander-Hansen, *Das Gottesweib des Amun* (Copenhagen, 1940); M. Gitton, *L'Épouse du dieu Ahmès Néfertari* (Besançon-Paris, 1975); *idem,* "Le clergé féminin au Nouvel Empire," Actes du 1er CIE au Caire, 1976 (Berlin, 1979), pp. 225ff; *idem,* "Le rôle de la femme dans le clergé d'Amon," *BSFE* 75; *idem, Les divines épouses de la XVIIIe dynastie* (Besançon, 1984); J. Yoyotte, *Le Harem virginal de la Divine Adoratrice,* Academie Inscript. Belles-Lettres (1961–62). For the list of the divine worshipers and their socioeconomic role, see M. Gitton and J. Leclant, *Lexikon der Ägyptologie* 2 (Wiesbaden, 1977), col. 792–805; E. Graefe, *Untersuchungen zur Verwaltung und Geschichte der Institution der Gottesgemahlin* (Wiesbaden, 1981); and C. Desroches-Noblecourt, *La Femme au temps des pharaons* (Paris, 1986), pp. 67–68, 115–21, and 288, n. 15, underlining their political and religious importance.

16. Gardiner, *Chester Beatty Papyrus I,* 3, 13–44, 3.

17. Extract from the ceremony of the two kites, the speech of the Two Women with Braids, from

the P. Vernus translation in *Chants d'amour de l'Égypte antique* (Paris, 1992), pp. 106–7.

18. Ibid., pp. 120–21, no. 293, extract from the hymn to Hathor by the king Intef II (Eleventh Dynasty).

19. Ibid., pp. 101–2, n. 208, 210.

20. C. Desroches-Noblecourt, *Un lac de turquoise*. . . Monuments Piot 47 (Paris, 1953), pp. 23–50.

21. Chassinat, *Le Temple de Dendara* I-V (Cairo, 1935–52), and Chassinat-Daumas VI (Cairo, 1965); *Dendara* III, p. 174, and 11, p. 175, n. 2; from Derchain's translation, *Hathor Quadrifrons,* p. 9, n. 41, 42.

22. *Dendara* III, p. 157, from Derchain's translation, *Hathor Quadrifrons,* p. 9, n. 40.

23. Rochemonteix and Chassinat, *Le Temple d'Edfou* IV (Cairo, 1897–1934), pp. 379, 18–380; from Derchain's translation, *Hathor Quadrifrons,* p. 9, fn 43.

24. *Le Temple d'Edfou* VI, pp. 265, n. 10; from Derchain's translation, *Hathor Quadrifrons,* p. 8, n. 38, quote taken from a litany to Sekhmet, who is introduced by the appeal to the lioness eye of Ra, so that she may show herself under the appearance of Hathor: "Come! Appear as Hathor with her four faces, who Ra loves to gaze upon."

25. *Dendara* III, pp. 157, 9110; from Derchain's translation, *Hathor Quadrifrons,* p. 9, n. 39, 40, as well as p. 5, n. 14, where the author explains the reasons that led him to translate, in certain cases as here, the word *akhet* not as "horizon," "solar horizon," or "luminous horizon," but as "empyrean" and the goddess as "the empyreal one." He created this term in reference to the element of fire and the radiation of gold, attached to the eye of Ra, an incandescent aura. The term was picked up anew by I. Franco, *Mythes et dieux. Le souffle du soleil* (Paris, 1996), p. 49, n. 7.

CHAPTER TWO

1. J. C. Goyon, "Nombres et univers: Reflexions sur quelques données numériques . . . " in *Magia in Egitto* (Milan, 1987); P. Barguet, *Le Livre des morts des anciens Égyptiens (*Paris, 1967), chap. 130–36 and 140–43; S. Rossini and R. Schumann-Antelme, *Becoming Osiris: The Ancient Egyptian Death Experience* (Rochester, Vt.: Inner Traditions, 1998), p. 46, ill. 30, and pp. 84–85. Englarged and translated edition of the French book *Osiris, Rites dimmurtalité de l' Egypte pharaonique,* Laraur: Ed. Trismegiste, 1995.

2. The question is worth posing because the title of a stolist priest, *sema(ty),* as one who is the overseer of this type of ritual garment, for Min as well as Horus, is vouched for, as well as that of a "stolist, head of the ritual habits of the *sed* festival of Ra" (inscription on a Middle Kingdom fake door stele). It is not impossible that the protection of the virile organ of the king, being a god incarnate, like all his ritual clothing, would be put under the guardianship of a priest, a high ranking courtier. For more on this theory see the article by B. Grdseloff in *ASAE* 43 (1943), pp. 357–66.

3. Theogamy scene from the temple of the female pharaoh Hatshepsut at Deir el-Bahari, Eighteenth Dynasty. Text extract from the translation by Vernus, *Chants d'amour,* pp. 133–34.

4. Hatshepsut is the best known of the female pharaohs, but not the only one: Nitocris (Neith-Ikeret) lived at the end of the Sixth Dynasty; Nefru-Sobek ruled at the end of the Twelfth

Dynasty and Ta-Useret (or Twoseret) ascended to the throne at the end of the Nineteenth Dynasty. It will be noted that with the exception of Hatshepsut, whose long reign (a quarter of a century) took place during the prime of the Eighteenth Dynasty, the other female sovereigns ruled during the closing days of their respective dynasties as the link between two royal families.

5. For more on the subject of marriage, see S. Allam, *Lexikon der Ägyptologie 1* (hereafter cited as *LÄ*), col. 1162–81.

6. For more on the organization of different royal harems, see E. Reiser, *Der Königliche Harim im alten Ägypten und seine Verwaltung* (Vienna, 1972), and Desroches-Noblecourt, *La Femme au temps des pharaons,* pp. 78–83.

7. C. Desroches-Noblecourt, *Ramses II: La véritable histoire* (Paris, 1966); *idem, Ramses II,* CD-ROM (Paris: Syrinx, 1998). C. Leblanc, in *Néfertari: L'Aimée de Mout* (Paris, 1999), pp. 299–312, lists 48 attested sons and 60 attested daughters—not to mention the unacknowledged children. The tradition that attributes more than 100 children to this great king is therefore no exaggeration. We can still ask ourselves though if all this progeny was exclusively the result of the pharaoh's exceptional vigor.

   On polygamy, see W. K. Simpson, "Polygamy in Egypt in the Middle Kingdom," *JEA* 60 (1974), p. 100ff.

8. The harem plot against Ramses III is known from the records of the trial against the guilty and the merciless verdicts that were handed down. The Judicial Papyrus of Turin, the Rollin Papyrus, the Lee Papyrus. De Buck, *JEA* 23 (1937), pp. 152–164; Goedicke, *JEA* 49 (1963), pp. 71–92; other writings have been assembled by Sauneron and Yoyotte, *BIFAQ* 50 (1952), pp. 107–17. A summary of it can be found in Desroches-Noblecourt, *La Femme au temps des pharaons,* pp. 92–96.

9. See Allam, *LÄ* 1, col. 1162–81, and Desroches-Noblecourt, *La Femme au temps des pharaons,* pp. 92–96.

10. Westcar Papyrus, Berlin no. 3033, from the end of the Second Intermediate Period (Hyksos); see G. Lefebvre, "Le conte des deux freres," *Romans et contes,* pp. 137–58.

11. D'Orbiney Papyrus, British Museum no. 10183, Ramesside era; see G. Lefebvre, "Le conte des deux frères," pp. 137–58.

12. Deir el-Medina Papyrus 27; see Allam, *LÄ* 1, col. 1162–81.

13. Diodorus Siculus, see above, chap 1, n. 1; Allam, *LÄ* 1, col. 1180.

14. Allam, *LÄ* 1, col. 1162–81.

15. Diodorus Siculus, 1.27; J. Cerny, *JEA* 40, (1954), p. 23ff, makes mention of the rarity of such unions in ancient Egyptian society.

16. W. Hinz, *Das Reich Elam* (Stuttgart, 1964), p. 76.

17. For Bintanath, Great Royal Wife, and her tomb no. 71 in the Valley of the Queens, see Desroches-Noblecourt, *La Femme au temps des pharaohs,* pp. 46, 65; R. Schumann-Antelme, *BSAK* 4 (Munich, 1990); C. Leblanc, *Néfertari,* p. 185ff.

18. Westcar Papyrus, "Le conte des rameuses," in Lefebvre, *Romans et contes,* pp. 77–80.

19. A. Gardiner and K. Sethe, *Egyptian Letters to the Dead* (London, 1925); Gardiner, *JEA* 16 (1930), p. 19ff; and Gunn *JEA* 16 (1930), p. 147ff. These "letters to the dead" are inscribed on earthenware containers (two famous bowls, one in the Louvre Museum and the other in the Berlin Museum), *ostraca,* cloth, and even papyrus.

20. Desroches-Noblecourt, *La Femme au temps des pharaons,* pp. 100–2.

21. Strabo, XVII.1.46. Cited by L. Manniche, *Sexual Life in Ancient Egypt* (London, 1987), pp. 14–15, according to the translation of H. L. Jones, *The Geography of Strabo* (London, 1959).

22. Herodotus, I.182.

23. J. Vandier, "Iousâas et Hathor," n. 16.

24. On divine worshipers, see above, n. 15.

25. "Maxims of Ani," Desroches-Noblecourt, *La Femme au temps des pharaons,* pp. 272–73.

26. L. Manniche, *Music and Musicians in Ancient Egypt* (London, 1991), pl. 18, British Museum no. 48658.

27. D. Montserrat, *Sex and Society in Graeco-Roman Egypt* (London and New York, 1996).

CHAPTER THREE

1. L. Störk, *LÄ* V (1984), col. 634, citing Aman, *Behaviour Today* 10, no. 40 (1979).

2. Only the Ani text has been given the title, "Beginning of an Educational Teaching," the others are simply "teachings," *sebait.* The text is preserved on five incomplete Ramesside-era papyri and four ostraca in Cairo. Sheshonq, demotic, Late Period, British Museum papyrus no. 10508, London; Kagemni and Ptahhotep, Prisse d'Avennes Papyrus, Old Kingdom (Sixth Dynasty) Paris, Bibliothèque nationale; Merykare, text on three papyri, all from the Eighteenth Dynasty, the Hermitage 116A, Saint Petersburg, Moscow 4658, Carlsberg VI; Djedefhor, the oldest wisdom text known, Old Kingdom, Fourth Dynasty.

   We have primarily used the translations of M. Lichtheim, *Ancient Egyptian Literature* I (Berkeley, Los Angeles, London: Univ. of California Press, 1973), 2 (1976), and 3 (1980). For more detail and a list of all the authors who have wrestled with these texts, see *LÄ* (Wiesbacen, 1980), col. 964–92.

3. Ptahhotep (see above, n. 2), extract from Lichtheim, *Ancient Egyptian Literature,* I, p. 68, n. 18 and p. 69, n. 21.

4. Ani, (see above n.2) extract from M. Lichtheim, *Ancient Egyptian Literature* II, pp. 136, 137, and 143.

5. Vernus, *Chants d'amour,* p. 173, n. 1. Gardiner, *Chester Beatty Papyrus I.*

6. Vase coming from Deir el-Medina; translated by Vernus, *Chants d'amour,* p. 186, n. 127.

7. *Chester Beatty Papyrus I,* translation by Vernus, *Chants d'amour,* pp. 63–73.

8. An allusion to the heliacal rising of Sirius, the goddess-star Sothis, announcing the beginning of the flood that itself marks the beginning of the year.

9. The hair of the gods was presumed to be this color, if not actually consisting of this stone.

10. The Unique One is one of the titles of the goddess Hathor.

11. Harris Papyrus 500, Nineteenth Dynasty, extracts from Vernus, *Chants d'amour,* n. 56 and pp. 74–82.

12. Vase coming from Deir el-Medina; Vernus, *Chants d'amour,* n. 127 and p. 88.

13. Turin Papyrus no. 1966, Twentieth Dynasty, Vernus, *Chants d'amour,* pp. 83–86.

14. *Chester Beatty Papyrus I,* rearranged extracts from the translation by Vernus, *Chants d'amour,* pp. 70 and 71; B. Mathieu, *La Poésie amoureuse de l'Égypte ancienne: Recherches sur un genre littéraire au Nouvel Empire, IFAO* (Cairo, 1966); and on love literature in general, S. Schott, *Altägyptische Liebeslieder* (Zurich, 1950), French translation by P. Krieger; A. Hermann, *Altägyptische Liebesdichtung* (Wiesbaden, 1959).

CHAPTER FOUR

1. An overview of this architectural complex was published in eight splendid folio volumes by the Oriental Institute of Chicago from 1930 to 1970. Volume VIII contains scenes of the *migdol,* a Hebrew term for "tower," because this tall and massive gate was reminiscent of Canaan fortifications.

2. On the game of *senet* see Desroches-Noblecourt, *Toutankhamon,* pp. 94–232, pl. 49b, 272–73. Catalog from the exhibition, *Ramsès le grand* (Paris, 1976), funerary hearse of Khonsu, p. 195ff (Ruth Schumann Antelme).

3. These cosmetic spoons had a ritual function as an offering (primarily myrrh) reflected by their decorations: ankh, mandrake, lotus and papyrus (the aquatic element)—all the symbols of rebirth reunited around the feminine element. But there were also, though more rarely, figures of men and servants represented as bearers of the cup for cosmetics, perfumes, incense, and unguents. For daily use, unguents were kept in receptacles in the apotropaic shapes of certain animals (lion, ape) or plants (palm trees); alabaster was preferred for fragile unguents, for they kept well at a relatively cool temperature.

   Cosmetics were used by both sexes, especially for highlighting, but also for treating or protecting the eyes. Coloring agents were primarily ochre, malachite, and galena, not to mention henna, whose use has even been confirmed in prehistoric times. Cheek rouge did not appear before the New Kingdom (tomb of Nefertari). Ointments, on a base of animal fats and oils, also contained active products for physical health care. All these products belonged to the very rich pharmacopoeia of Egypt; they were placed under the divine protection of Nefertum, Horhekenu, and Bastet.

4. Derchain, "La Perruque et le cristal," *Studien zur altägyptischen Kultur* 2 (1975), pp. 55–74.

5. L. Manniche, *An Ancient Egyptian Herbal* (London, 1989, 1993), p. 48. The oil of the decoction had the froth skimmed off, was filtered, and placed in flasks that were then sealed. It required an enormous quantity of flowers to make the very valuable oil of lily; in order to obtain three liters of this strongly perfumed oil, one needed at least one thousand flowers! So

it is not surprising that the tomb pillagers first object of choice was ointments and perfumes which are still exorbitantly expensive today. The existence of aromatic solutions in alcohol is not confirmed until 400 B.C.

6. Dioscorides, *De materia medica* I, p. 72ff. Modern Egyptian solid perfumes are manufactured with roses, which were unknown to ancient Egypt.

7. V. Loret, "Le Kyphie," *Journal asiatique* 10, (1887), pp. 76–132; R. Germer, *Untersuchungen über Arzneimittelpflanzen in alten Ägypten* (Hamburg, 1979), introduction.

8. Punt incense came from southern Arabia and the Somalian coast in the form of resinous "pearls" harvested from trees of the Boswellia family. Myrrh comes from the Commiphora bush.

9. Fermentation occurred rapidly in the hot climate—too hot for hops, which were unknown to the Ancients.

10. Various extremely sweet (maybe mulled) wines were particularly esteemed; thousands of potsherds found at the sites of archaeological digs testify to the heavy consumption of intoxicating beverages—to the great joy of the archaeologists, because the inscriptions in ink make these jar fragments a veritable archive on the Egyptian economy and lifestyle. They also provide precise dates on the length of the life and reign of certain kings.

11. The erogenous zones of the body are well known and utilized in Tantric practices, and their application is revealed by countless reliefs on Indian temples. Acupressure is a medical treatment based on this knowledge. Furthermore, modern medicine confirms that these touchings or pressures at precise locations activate the corresponding nervous systems and can also discharge certain hormones. The interlaced hands (fig. 4.14, *left*) constantly figure in sculpture in the round and, especially, on the reliefs of tombs and temples in which the deity takes either the king, the queen, or simply the deceased, affectionately by the hand to guide them. Figure 4.14 *right* is the reproduction of a relief on a *talatat* from Karnak, Akhenaten era.

    For the coded meaning of the erogenous zones, see M. Eliade, *The Forge and the Crucible*, (Chicago and London, 1978), p. 38.

12. The reader interested in musical instruments may refer to the fundamental works on the subject by H. Hickmann, *General Catalog, Cairo Museum* (Cairo, 1949); *idem, Musicologie pharaonique* (Kehl, 1956); *idem, 45 siècles de musique dans l'Égypte ancienne* (Paris, 1956); E. Hickmann and L. Manniche, "Altägyptische Musik," in *Neues Handbuch der Musikwissenschaft* 2 (Laaber, 1989), chap. 2, pp. 31–75; L. Manniche, *Ancient Egyptian Musical Instruments, MÄS* 34 (Munich, 1975); *idem, Music and Musicians in Ancient Egypt* (London, 1991); C. Sachs, *Die Musikinstrumente des alten Ägyptens* (Berlin, 1921; English edition, 1942, 1944), on the history of musical instruments in ancient times; C. Ziegler, *Les instruments de musique égyptiens au musée du Louvre* (Paris, 1979).

13. The male loincloth worn by these dancers recalls a similar costume (but on dancers who have long braids terminating in disks) depicted in the mastaba of the vizier Mehu, Fifth Dynasty, Saqqara. With regard to the dwarf in the center of the group of dancers, see E. Brunner-Traut, "Neger-und Zwergentänze im Alten Ägypten," *Nikephoros* 6 (1993), pp. 23–32.

14. For more on this subject, see also F. Daumas, *ZÄS* 95 (1968), who compares this dance to the *zikr,* still performed in Egypt, and notes that these movements, repeated to an accelerated beat, produce an altered state of consciousness in accordance with the ritual. This ancient tradition was maintained until the Greco-Roman era and implies the performance of certain dances by the king. A ritual dance for Hathor can be found in the goddess's temple at Dendara: "Pharaoh comes to dance, he comes to sing. Sovereign, look how he dances! Wife of Horus, look how he leaps!" cited (in German) in ibid., p. 28. On dance in general in ancient Egypt, see E. Brunner-Traut, *Der Tanz im alten Ägypten,* 3rd edition (Hamburg-Glückstadt, 1992); and "Tanz," *LÄ* 6 (1986).

15. From the English translation by E. F. Wente, *The Tomb of Kheruef.* The end of the prayer brings to mind "God save the king (. . .) make him victorious, happy, and glorious, long to reign over us, God save the king," For an interpretation of the mystical and political role of Hathor, see A. Roberts, *Hathor Rising: The Power of the Goddess on Ancient Egypt* (Rochester, Vt.: Inner Traditions, 1997).

16. This plant is *Aristolochia clematitis* L. For more information on this plant, see chapter 5, note 3.

17. Found toward the end of the nineteenth century, according to the museum's numbered inventory records, this object was prudishly "improved" and the phallus taken away. Thanks to old photographs, the drawing could be reconstituted. It was published this way by Manniche, *Sexual Life,* ill. 17.

18. Dr. William Emboden, an associate researcher in botany at the Los Angeles Museum of Natural History, and researcher in the biology department at the State University of California. He published some of his results in an article entitled "The Sacred Journey in Dynastic Egypt: Shamanic trance in the context of the narcotic water lily and the mandrake," which appeared in the *Journal of Psychoactive Drugs* 21, no. 1 (January–March 1989). Bouquets composed of water lilies (blue lotus), mandrake, and papyrus (for symbolic reasons) constitute a perfect combination of plants for giving out strong narcotic substances capable of inducing a trance state were used in certain rituals, and also for certain medical purposes. Both are founded on the principle of the dissociation of the spiritual part (the *ba*) from the physical part *(ka)* of the human being. These techniques were applied for the regeneration of the living (for example, the king during the *sed* festival) and the dead for rebirth on another plane. For more on this, see P. Barguet, *Le Livre des Morts égyptiens* (Paris, 1967), introduction and particularly the chapters 112–115; S. Rossini and R. Schumann-Antelme, *Becoming Osiris* (Rochester, Vt.: Inner Traditions, 1997); R. Schumann-Antelme, *Bulletin de IANDS-France,* no. 5 (June 1997) on NDE and altered states of consciousness in ancient Egypt; M. Bon, *Des mort singulières* (Paris, 1997), on the status of the question about these practices in different civilizations; M. Eliade, *Shamanism: Archaic Techniques of Ecstasy* (Princeton: Bollingen Series LXXVI, 1964).

19. Reports generously communicated by the Bibliothèque Interuniversitaire de Médicine, Paris, Station 5, "Drugs in Ancient Populations," reports of the cytological and molecular examinations, by N. Moore, D. Brothwell, and M. Spigelman (May 1993) of mummies from Egypt, North and South America, and Europe: "Recently drugs (cocaine, hashish, and nicotine) were

extracted from skin and head hair of Egyptian mummies." In 1994, on the other hand, other examinations concerning objects from the tomb of Kha (Turin), Eighteenth Dynasty, did not reveal the presence of opiates. In 1994, A. and Z. Fleisher studied the taste and smell of the mandrake mentioned in the Bible (Gen. 30: 14–16). Their analyses identified 55 odoriferous elements that form "bizarre" chemical combinations in the particular aroma of the mandrake. The biblical texts make clear that this fruit did not play a role in the rituals but was esteemed for its perfume, taste, and aphrodisiac qualities *(Mandragora officinarum).* Between 1986 and 1991 no less than four theses (two medical, two pharmaceutical) were written on the mandrake in France!

20. Balout, Roubet, et.al., *La Momie de Ramsès* 2, CNRS/RSC (Paris, 1985).
21. Extracts of magical formulas from the publication by F. Lloyd Griffith and H. Thompson, *The Leyden Papyrus: An Egyptian Magical Book* (London, 1904; New York, 1974).
22. The Louvre Museum collection houses such magical objects, see P. du Bourguet, "Un ensemble magique de la période romaine d'Égypte," *MIFAO* 104 (Cairo, 1981), pp. 225–38. See also J. F. Borghouts, *The Magical Texts of Papyrus Leiden I* (1971), p. 348; Y. Koenig, *Magie dans l'Égypte ancienne* (Paris, 1994), which deals with this subject in its entirety.
23. The fundamental publications on amulets are: G. A. Reisner, "Amulets" I and II, *General Catalogue of the Cairo Museum* (1907 and 1958); K. A. Wiedermann, *Die Amulette des Alten Ägypten* (1910); W. M. Flinders Petrie, *Amulets* (London, 1914); F. Lexa, *La magie* 1 (Paris, 1925); E. A. W. Budge, *Amulets and Talismans,* (reprint, New York, 1961); Bonnet, *Reallexikon der ägyptischen Religiongeschichte* (Beylih, 1952), "Amulet"; bibliography and classification of amulets by A. L. Klasens in *LÄ* 1 (1975), col. 232–36.
24. On these amulets, see E. Winter, *Untersuchungen zu den Ägyptischen Tempelreliefs* (Vienna, 1968), and I. Franco, *Mythes et dieux* (Paris, 1996), p. 209, n. 29.

CHAPTER FIVE

1. On medicine in general, see G. Lefebvre, *Essai sur la médecine égyptienne à l'époque pharaonique* (Paris, 1956); H. Grapow and W. Westendorf, "Grundriss der Medizin," in *Handbuch der Orientalistikl* 1, (1970), pp. 212–19.
2. N. E. Himes, *Medical History of Contraception* (Baltimore, 1936). Grapow and Westendorf, *Handbuch* IV, p. 277 and V, pp. 476–78; *Médecine et Hygiène,* no. 820 (Geneva, April 1968), p. 429, confirms the effectiveness of acacia sap as a spermicide.
3. This climbing plant was considered to be a *convolvulus,* but we believe with Manniche *(Egyptian Herbal)* that it would rather be the *Aristolochia clematitis* L., whose gynecological qualities were also esteemed in the West, as indicated by its English common name, birthwort. Unfortunately, the ancient Egyptian name for the plant has not been determined, in spite of Dioscorides (III.6) who referred to it under the name *"sobo(i)eph."* Its characteristics (leaves, vines), however, are sufficiently evident in the depictions dealing with birth, and the mother and child. Theophrastus (370–287 B.C.) reports in his *Treatise on Botany* (IX.13.2; IX.20.4) on several uses of the plant as a remedy for headaches, snakebite, and its use as a soporific. But

primarily, he notes its use as a lotion, to be applied topically, against all the ills of the uterus and vagina, mainly prolapse of the womb.

4. The origin of this custom is lost in the depths of time and was not exclusively practiced in Africa and the Near East. It is also witnessed in the New World, in Australia (the Aboriginal populace), but not in the Far East. Male circumcision seems linked to rites of initiation, but not to dogmatic requirements properly speaking, whatever the religion; these notions developed later. The first Christians were circumcised, and it was Saint Augustine who had this custom suppressed among the faithful, in order to distinguish them from the Jews. Thanks are owed to him, because his exhortations also spared Christian women from this operation. Insofar as Islam is concerned, circumcision is not demanded by the Koran, but is preached by certain Islamic schools; moreover, it is not practiced in certain Muslim countries (Saudi Arabia, Turkey, Tunisia, and Iran, for example). On the other hand, circumcision is rooted in the Old Testament and is still regularly practiced among Jews.
5. Desroches-Noblecourt, *La Femme au temps des pharons*, p. 200, and *LÄ* 1 (1975), col. 728–29, also indicated as source is *CT* VII 450d = Kees, *Totenglauben,* 301; WB I, 185, 13, although it remains a fairly aleatory one.
6. Feminine "circumcision" (clitoridectomy) is still very widespread in Africa—that is, in Egypt, Somalia, Sudan, Nigeria, Ethiopia, etc.
7. This form of operation, also called "pharaonic" or "sunnite" circumcision, a lesser one though it may be, often entails irreparable damage, all the more as it is practiced on increasingly younger girls, between four and six years of age, whereas in sub-Saharan Africa, it was a rite of adolescence. The worst that can happen is fatal hemorrhaging; persistent infections of the genital organs are frequent. The poorly performed ablation can afflict the victim with permanent incontinence by a lesion of the sphincter, and the haphazard scarring of these innervated tissues leaves them either insensitive or hypersensitive, provoking sharp pains at the slightest touch.
8. For more on the barbaric form of sexual mutilation known as infibulation, one can find documentation thanks to the following works: Fran Hosken, which is the best documented. In the context of the United Nations' Decade of the Woman (1980–1990), numerous reports have been written on these disastrous practices: Belkis Wolde Giorgis, *Female Circumcision in Africa,* African Training and Research Center for Women (Addis Ababa, 1981); Dr. Fawiza Assad, former professor at the Ain-Shums University of Cairo, currently in Geneva, who exposes in the *Revue de l'OMS* (1982) the medical and psychological consequences of this "custom," which is a crime according to our laws, that currently affects around 50 to 70 million women and creates, according to modest estimates, at least 500,000 new victims a year throughout the world. See also in this regard B. de Rachewitz, *Black Eros* (1965), pp. 212–19.

   The work of Bruno Bettelheim, *Symbolic Wounds: Puberty Rites and the Envious Male* (London: Thames & Hudson, 1955), is a classic work on the history and psychological approach of rituals touching on sexuality.

CHAPTER SIX

1. G. Posener, *RDE* 11 (1957), pp. 119–37; Brunner-Traut, *Märchen der Weltliteratur,* no. 24 (Dusseldorf: Diedricks, n.d.).
2. Montserrat, *Sex and Society.*
3. *Graffito* about Ptolemaios, *ASAE* 23 (1923), p. 139, and Montserrat, *Sex and Society,* pp. 154–55.
4. Montserrat, *Sex and Society,* pp. 155–56.
5. Ibid., pp. 158–59.
6. Necrophilia is alleged for by Herodotus, *Histories* II, p. 89: "The wives of the lords or women of great beauty are not immediately delivered into the hands of the embalmers, but only three or four days after their death; this is done so that the embalmers will not practice coitus with them. It is said that one embalmer, surprised by his colleagues in full coitus with the corpse of a newly dead woman, was denounced." The historian does not talk about what punishment the guilty party may have incurred.

CHAPTER SEVEN

1. J. A. Omlin, *Der Papyrus 55001 und seine satirisch-erotischen Zeichnungen und Inschriften* (Turin, 1973). The papyrus is in generally poor condition. The so-called satiric part is the smaller of the two, the erotic part being longer. The two parts are now kept separate. The average width of the papyrus is 21.5 centimeters, its current total length is 259 centimeters. Out of this, 174 centimeters are taken up by the erotic part, leaving 85 centimeters for what remains of the satiric section, which must be missing at least 60 centimeters, if we use the standard-size scroll of the Ramesside period as a guide. The dimensions of the leaves of papyrus used are an element considered in dating them. The papyrus was drawn on with a very black ink, and then colored in yellow, red, and green. The artist was very sure of his drawing abilities, for no sign of a grid or of underlying sketches are visible. Over time the background has become brown. The scenes unroll from right to left, according to the system of writing on papyrus. We present them here in the opposite order, according to our own system of writing and reading, by "cutting up" the document as we would imagine it.
2. Desroches-Noblecourt, *La Femme au temps des pharaons,* op. cit., p. 315 when referring to the Turin Papyrus, feels that the men depicted are "visibly Syrian."
3. For an analysis of animals used in a satiric context and the Mesopotamian origin of this practice, see E. Brunner-Traut, in *Zeitschrift für ägyptische Sprache und Attertumskunde* 80, p. 20ff.
4. Omlin is quite critical with regard to the position held by women in pharaonic society. We would like to qualify this position by advancing the view that woman was lawfully almost man's equal and that she was probably much freer and more independent than her sisters today. But the field of sexuality was primarily reserved for men. The Turin Papyrus is the cruel parody of this, showing man caught in the snare of his own making within a disillusioned society.

5. For the view that situates the erotic part of this papyrus within a clerical milieu, see G. Maspero (1887), G. Farina (1929), W. Wolf (1975), and J. Yoyotte (1965), all quoted by Omlin, *Der Papyrus 55001,* pp. 23–26.
6. The reading and translation of these very fragmentary texts were established by Seyffarth, Erman, Pleyte, Rossi, as well as by Omlin, with several clarifications and improvements by G. Posener. Gaps and differences in readings reveal the progressive deterioration of this document, which now seems to enjoy sufficient protection.
7. The reading and restoration of the "label" of this papyrus are the work of G. Posener (not published).
8. E. Neumann, *The Great Mother—An Analysis of the Archetype,* p. 140 (Princeton: Bollingen, 1971); and A. Piankoff, *Mythological Papyri,* 1 (New York: Bollingen Series XL, 3, 1957).
9. Omlim, op. cit., thinks that this is not a case of sodomy but rather an act of *coitus a tergo.*
10. A. Painkoff, op. cit., pl. 1, Papyrus of the Lady Her-uben.

Glossary

This list includes some terms that are not normally found in a modern dictionary.

abaton

The mound, or tomb, of Osiris on the Island of Biga; the waters surrounding that island. In general it means purifying, mystical waters.

Amarna, Amarnian

Tell el-Amarna is the modern name of the ancient capital of Akhenaten in Middle Egypt. The adjective "Amarnian" refers to the site, the monuments, and objects of the Atonian religion as well as the religion itself and to the distinctive art style of that period (Eighteenth Dynasty).

ankh

Hieroglyph meaning "life."

apotropaic

Adjective signifying "protector," "protective," in a preventive capacity.

Ba

Spiritual component of the personality of gods as well as human beings. This entity who, for mortals is revealed by virtue of the funeral rites, constitutes the divine spark, the link between creator and creature, that we may, relatively speaking, consider as the soul. The *ba* of the gods is an object of worship; it is represented as a human-headed bird, or possessing the head of the deity it enhances. His statue-abode is exposed at certain times to the rays of the sun, so that it may recharge its energies.

benben
Standing stone (or stonework) in the form of a squat obelisk topped with a pyramidion. The prototype, worshiped in Heliopolis, of the obelisk; it is both a solar and phallic symbol.

criocephalic
Ram-headed.

crowns
The gods and pharaohs possessed several crowns. Those of the pharaoh are the white crown *(hedjet)* of Upper Egypt and the red crown *(deshret)* of Lower Egypt; the two crowns united, one inserted within the other, form the *pschent,* a name that means "the two powerful ones." Pharaoh may also sport the blue crown, the *khepresh.*

divine worshiper
Title of the priestess attached to the cult of Amun as the mystical wife of the demiurge.

djed
Pillar or column, an emblem of Osiris signifying "stability."

epagomenal days
Literally, "the days above the year," those it was necessary to add to bring the solar year from 360 to 365 days. The Egyptian calendar had no leap year.

hieracocephalic
Falcon-headed.

hypostasis
This term designates a personified manifestation of a specific power of a demiurge; for example, Sia, representing knowledge, as an emanation of the demiurge Thoth, is a hypostasis.

Ka
Personification of the vital forces of every human being, its counterpart of spiritual and sexual energy, which is inseparable but invisible during earthy existence. At the moment

of death, the deceased, who has become an Osiris thanks to the rituals, finds himself faced by his *Ka,* who continues to assist and complete him, and to feed him, as he makes the funeral offerings assimilable. The gods also have one or more *ka* (the plural is *kaou*)—Ra has fourteen!—in the same way as the king; this latter can see and feel the activity of his *Ka* during his terrestrial existence.

karnata

The phallic sheath used in the ancient civilizations of the Middle East.

leontocephalic

Lion-headed.

mammisi

House of birth where the divine child should enter the world; a construction added to certain temples, notably Dendara (consecrated to Hathor) and Philae (consecrated to Isis).

menat

Emblem and magic instrument of Hathor, which transmits life.

nome

Administrative subdivision of ancient Egypt. The heads of the twenty nomes of Upper Egypt and the twenty-two nomes of Lower Egypt were nomarchs, who mostly belonged to princely families.

***ostraca* (singular is *ostracon*)**

Pieces of pottery or limestone shard used by students to practice writing or by artists for preparatory sketches. They are also the medium of choice for popular artists.

pallacidia

Sacred prostitute attached to a temple in ancient Greece.

pschent

See above, Crowns.

psychostasia

Word of Greek origin meaning "weighing of the soul." In Egyptology it is understood to mean the judgment of the dead person by the weighing of his heart as the seat of knowledge and awareness. The heart is placed on the plate of the scales with the counterweight on the other plate being the feather of the goddess Maat, symbol of cosmic order, balance, and justice. The weighing took place at the divine tribunal before Osiris. The result was recorded by Thoth. If the deceased was "righteous of voice," which is to say, he had not lied to the forty-two judges and that his heart was balanced with Maat, he was accepted into the kingdom of Osiris. In the opposite case, infernal torments awaited him.

pterophoric

Having wings; the goddesses often depicted this way are Isis, Nephthys, and also Sereket (Selket) and Neith as guardians of the canopic jars (vases containing embalmed internal organs), as well as Maat.

Ptolemies, Ptolemaic

The Ptolemies are the pharaohs of Greek origin who ruled over Egypt from the time of the conquest of Alexander (332 B.C.) to the death of Cleopatra VII (31 B.C.). The adjective refers to characteristics of the artistic style, language, and writing of that era.

quadrifrons

Latin word meaning "with four faces."

scepters

The scepters of Osiris and the king are the flail *(nekhakha),* a sort of whip, and the hook *(heka),* a curved staff like that of a shepherd's, whose form and symbolic meaning still exist in the bishop's cross. The *sekhem* scepter, which means "power," is used for the consecration of offerings. It is also an insignia of office.

sed*-festival** or ***heb-sed

Egyptian name for the pharaoh's jubilee, which allegedly mystically renewed the sovereign's forces.

sema-tawy

Egyptian expression for the "reunion of the Two Lands," meaning Upper and Lower Egypt, which forms part of royal ritual. The symbol of this reunion is the hieroglyph for reuniting, reunion, and the depiction of the two heraldic plants of Upper and Lower Egypt with their stems knotted around the sign "reunion." These plants are the pseudo-lily for Upper Egypt and the papyrus for Lower Egypt.

shawabti

A small funerary statuette who is allegedly obligated to magically perform certain tasks in the beyond when called upon to do so by the deceased. They must answer the call by responding, "Here I am." Hence, their later name meaning "the answering one(s)"—*ushabtiu* (singular *ushabti*) in ancient Egyptian, according to chapter 6 of the Book of the Dead.

shendjit

Egyptian name for the simple male loincloth.

speos (plural is speoi)

A rock temple, hollowed out of the mountain in the image of a grotto, the universal womb.

talatat

Arab word, "a third," or "by threes," designating the size of carved stones used for the constructions undertaken at Karnak by Akhenaten. They were demolished by his successors and have become over the years, objects of restoration by archaeologists.

theogamy

Mystical (and naturally fictitious) marriage between the queen and the god Amun, who adopts the features of the king, the terrestrial husband of the queen, so as to unite with her. In this way the heir to the throne is the legitimate descendent of the god incarnated by the pharaoh. Reliefs depicting theogamy can be found in the temples of Luxor and Deir el-Bahari.

triad

Association of three deities, who vary according to the site of worship and the doctrines. In general, these three entities form a family, one male god, the demiurge, the indispensable female principle, and a young god in the role of son, the guarantor of cyclical renewal, the reincarnation of divine forces, transferred to the king. The main triads are: Osiris-Isis-Horus (Abydos); Ptah-Sekhmet-Nefertum (Memphis); and Amun-Mut-Khonsu (Thebes).

usekh

"Wide" and designates, by extension, the large and very elaborate gorget worn by men and women for festivals and other exceptional occasions. The king and queen are generally depicted wearing this piece of jewelry.

wadj

"Green" in ancient Egyptian. The term does not only designate the color, but also includes the notion of being in good heath and being sexually green [the French word *vert,* whose most common meaning is the color "green," can also mean "spry" or "sexually active"—translator.] On the other hand, the word is not employed to mean green with fear or envy.

was

Hieroglyph and scepter, the symbol of power.

***wedjat* (or *udjat*)**

The eye of Horus, mistreated by Seth and healed by Thoth. It's name means "healthy," "complete."

Bibliography

The reader will find here a list of works generally relating to the themes discussed in this book. The books, articles, and so forth concerning specific points have already been listed in the notes.

Abbreviations of Egyptological Works and Journals

ÄA	*Ägyptologische Abhandlungen*
ASAE	*Annales du Service des Antiquités de l'Egypte,* Cairo
BIFAO	*Bulletin de l'Institut Français d'Archéologie Orientale,* Cairo
BSAK	*Beiträge zum Studium des altägyptischen Kultur,* Munich
BSFE	*Bulletin de la Société Française d'Égyptologie,* Paris
CGC	*Catalogue Général du Musée du Caire,* Cairo
CIE	*Congrès International des Égyptologues,* Actes
JEA	*Journal of Egyptian Archaeology,* London
LÄ	*Lexikon der Ägyptologie,* Wiesbaden
MÄS	*Münchner Ägyptologische Studien,* Munich and Berlin
RÄRG	*Reallexikon der ägyptischen Religiongeschicte,* Berlin
Rev. Eg.	*Revue d'égyptologie,* Société française d'égyptologie, Paris
SAK	*Studien zur altägyptischen Kultur,* Hamburg
W.B.	*Wörterbuch der Aegyptischen,* Berlin
ZÄS	*Zeitschrift für Ägyptische Sprache und Alterumskunde,* Leipzig and Berlin

DEITIES AND MYTHOLOGY

Bonnet, *RÄRG,* Berlin, 1952.

Barguet, *Le Livre des morts,* Paris, 1967.

———. *Textes des sarcophages égyptiens du Moyen Empire,* Paris, 1984.

Derchain, *Hathor quadrifrons,* Istanbul, 1972.

Daumas, *Les Dieux d'Égypte,* Paris: "Que sais-je?" 1965.

Erman, *La Religion des Égyptiens,* Paris, 1952 (German edition, 1905).

Faulkner, *The Ancient Egyptian Book of the Dead,* Austin, Texas: Univ. of Texas Press, 19, 1992.

Franco, *Mythes et Dieux,* Paris, 1996.

Goyon, *Rituels funéraires de l'ancienne Égypte,* Paris, 1972.

Hornung, *Les Dieux de l'Égypte,* French translation, Monaco, 1997.

James, *Ancient Egypt: The Land and its Legacy,* Austin, Texas: Univ. of Texas Press, 19.

Rossini and Schumann-Antelme, *Becoming Osiris: The Ancient Egyptian Death Experience,* Rochester, Vt.: Inner Traditions International, 1998.

Rossini and Schumann-Antelme, *Nétèr, Dieux de l'Égypte,* Lavaur, 1992.

Sethe, *Die altägyptischen Pyramidentexte,* Berlin, 1901, reprinted Darmstaadt, 1960.

Vandier, *Iousâas et Hathor-Nébet-Hétépet,* Rev. Eg., 1964, 1965 1966.

LOVE, EROS, AND SEXUALITY

Desroches-Noblecourt, *Amours et fureurs de la Lointaine,* Paris, 1995.

———. *La Femme au temps des pharaons,* Paris, 1986.

Hermann, *Altägyptische Liebesdichtung,* Wiesbaden, 1959.

Manniche, *Sexual Life in Ancient Egypt,* London, 1964.

Omlin, *Der Papyrus 55001 und seine satirisch-erotischen Zeichnungen und Inschriften,* Turin, 1973.

Rachewiltz de, *Black Eros,* London, 1964.

Roberts, *Hathor Rising: The Power of the Goddess in Ancient Egypt,* Rochester, Vt.: Inner Traditions, 1997.

Robins, *Women in Ancient Egypt,* London, 1993.

Schott, *Altägyptische Liebeslieder,* Zurich, 1950.

Störk, "Erotik," in *LÄ* II, Wiesbaden, 1975.

Vernus, *Chants de l'amour de l'Égypte ancienne,* Paris, 1992.

Vorsberg, *Ars erotica veterum: Das Geschlechtsleben im Altertum,* Hanau/Main, 1968.

Wenig, *Die Frau im alten Ägypten,* Berlin.

DANCE

Brunner-Traut, *Der Tanz im Alten Ägypten,* Glückstadt, 1938.

Wild, "Les Danses sacrées de l'Égypte ancienne," in *Les Danses Sacrées, Sources Orientales* 6, Paris, 1963.

MAGIC

Borghouts, *Ancient Egyptian Magical Texts,* Leyden, 1978.

Koenig, *Magie et magiciens dans l'Égypte ancienne,* Paris, 1994.

MEDICINE

Erman, *Zaubersprüche für Mutter und Kind,* Berlin, 1901.

Grapow and Westerndorf, "Grundriss der Medizin," *Handbuch der Orientalistik* 1, Leiden, 1970.

Hosken, *Les Mutilations sexuelles féminines,* French translation, Paris, 1983.

Leca, *La Médecine égyptienne au temps des pharaons,* Paris, 1971.

Lefebvre, *Essai sur la médecine égyptienne à l'époque des pharaons,* Paris, 1956.

Pillet, "Scenes de naissance et de circoncision . . . ," *ASAE* 52, 1952.

MUSIC

Anderson, Cat. Antiquities British Museum, III, "Musical Instruments," London, 1976.

Hickmann, C. G. C. *Instruments de musique,* Cairo, 1949.

Hickmann and Manniche, "Altägyptsche Musik," *Neues Handbuch der Musikwissenschaft,* Laaber, 1989.

Manniche, *Music and Musicians in Ancient Egypt,* London, 1991.

Ziegler, *Les Instruments de musique égyptiens au musée du Louvre,* Paris, 1979.

PLANTS AND PSYCHOTROPICS

Germer, *Untersuchungen über die Arzneimittelpflanzen im alten Ägypten,* Hamburg, 1979.

Germer, Flora des phaaraonischen Ägypten, Mayence, 1985.

Keimer, *Die Gartenpflanzen im alten Ägypten,* Berlin, 1924 and Mainz, 1985.

Manniche, *An Ancient Egyptian Herbal,* London and Austin, Texas: Univ. of Texas Press, 1993.

Schultes and Hofmann, *Plants of the Gods,* Rochester, Vt.: Inner Traditions International, 1997.

Index

Numbers in italics indicate illustrations.

abaton, 25, 216
Abydos, 183
Abydos triad, 220
adultery, 15, 57–58
aegis, *49*
Agilkia, 183
Ahmose, king, 60
Ahmose-Neferetari, 54, *56*, 60, Plate 15
Akhenaten
- death of daughter, 61, *61*
- family life, *62*, Plate 8
- incestuous marriages of, 60
- Nefertiti and, *55*, *100*, *101*, Plate 13
- performing official duties, *100*
- possible homosexuality of, *141*
- the "heretic," 52–54, 99, *101*
- use of iconography, 99
- worship of Aten, 52, 54

Amarna, 183, 216
Amenhotep II, 60
Amenhotep III, 57, 110–12
Amenhotep IV. *See* Akhenaten
Amenirdis, 66
amulets, 129–31
Amun
- as demiurge, 26, *28*
- described, *56*, 166, Plate 15
- singers of, 65, 112–13, *114*

Amun. *See also* theogamy
Anat, 166–67
Ani, 66–67, 72, 74
ankh
- as amulet, *130*
- described, 52, 54, 216
- Maat with, *11*
- for rebirth ritual, *48*, Plate 7
- as symbol of life, *10*, *20*, *33*, *54–56*, Plate 15

Ankhesenamun, *124*, *125*
Anubis, 15, *15*, 167
Anuket, *136*, 167, Plate 19
aphrodisiacs, 119
Apophis, 167. *See also* Seth
apotropaic, 216
art. *See* figurative art; ostraca
astrology, 145–46
Aten, 52, 54, *55*, *62*, 167
Atum
- cosmic children of, 11–13
- creation and, *7*, *8*, Plate 2
- as demiurge, 8, 27
- described, 167–68
- embracing his son, *139*
- as Min, 26, *29*
- at the moment of creation, *9*
- reinvigoration of, *10*
- *See also* Ra

ba, *40*, 43, 216–17
Bastet, 25, *26*, 49, *49*, *122*, 168
Bat, 52, *52*, 53, *53*, 168
Bebon, 168
benben, 217
bennu, 49, *49*
Bes, 36, *36*, 68, 102, *112*, 168, Plate 5
Biga, 183
birth
- houses for, 42, *48*, 218, Plate 7
- overview, 134–35, *134*, *135*

bisexuality, 145
blue lotus, *104*, 119, *120*, *122*, 126
Book of Amdwat, 160
Book of the Dead, 121
bride of the god, 31, 65–66, 217
Bubastis, 107, 184
bull's eye, 53
Busiris, 184
Buto, 184

Caesar, 162
Canopus, 184
celebrations
- of Amun, 26
- festivals, 43, 44–45, 107, 110–12, 219
- for the Lady of Drunkenness, 25–26

ceremonies
in honor of Hathor, 43, 44, 45
for "the gold of reward," *100*
chakras, 107
Champollion, Jean-François, 1, 68, 150
Chemmis, 184
Chester Beatty Papyrus, 31, 34, 75, 105
chronology, 163–65
circumcision, 137–38, *137*
clematis, 112, *113*, 134, *135*
Cleopatra VII, 162
clothing
eroticism of, 102
shendjit, 51, *53*, *109*, 220
skirt of King Narmer, 52, *52*
skirt of Tuthmosis III, 53
code of love
in figurative art, 94–102
for the five senses, *56*, 102–7, *108*, Plate 15
for magic and amulets, 126–31
for music and dance, 107–18
for psychotropic agents, 118–26
contraception, 133, 135
cosmetics, *67*, 156, *156*
cosmetic spoon, 104, *104*, Plate 14
cosmic soup, 3, 4, *4*, 6, 8, 174
creation myths, 2–15, *4–14*
criocephalic, 217
crocodile, 84, *86*
crowns, *48*, 51, 217, Plate 7
Curly-haired One, 34, *34*. *See also* Hathor
cursing, 70–72, *70*

dancers. *See* music and dance
demiurge, 8, 22, 26, 27, *27*, *28*, 30
Dendara, 44, 48, 184
Diodorus Siculus, 44, 58
Distant One, myth of, 24–26. *See also* Sekhmet
divine conception, 54–55
divine worshipers, 31, 65–66, 217
divorce and remarriage, 59
djed, *130*, 131, 217
Djedefhor, prince, 72
drinking customs, 36–37, 107
dwarfs, *92*, *109*

earth god. *See* Geb
Ebers Papyrus, 132
Edfu, 43–44, 184
Edwin Smith Papyrus, 132
Egyptian Hieroglyphics: How to Read and Write Them (Rossini), 187
Eight of Hermopolis. *See* Ogdoad
Elephantine, 184
embalmers, 149
Ennead, 14, 18, 21, 169
epagomenal days, 217
Erment, 185
erogenous zones, hieroglyphics for, 194–98
eroticism
clothing and, 102
in freestyle art, 102
hieroglyphics for, 199–202
on ostraca, 102, *103*, *111*, 151
of the Papyrus of Turin, *103*, 152, *153–59*, 160, *161*
in royal art, 97
See also love poetry
Esna, 185
eternity, image of, 7
eye of Atum, 27
eye of Horus, 18, *20*, *38*, 127, 129, *130*, 221
eye of Ra, 22–26, *24*. *See also* uraeus
fairies of fate, 42
family
code of love for, 62, *62*, Plate 8
hieroglyphics for, 188–93
fellatio, 148–49
festivals
at Bubastis, 107
of Hathor-Tefnut, 44–45
in honor of Hathor, 43
sed-festival, 110–12, 219
figs, 87, 95, *95*
figurative art, 94–102
civil, 99–101
freestyle, 102, *103*
royal, 94–99, *95*, *96*
for tombs, 64, *64*, Plate 9
fish, 85, *85*
floral scepter, *54*
Freud, Sigmund, 71
funeral banquets, 100, 121, *123*, *146*
funerary magic
images of, *85*, *86*, *90*
offering for, 104, *104*

Geb
caricature of, 158, *158*, Plate 22
described, 11, 24, 169
union with Nut, *12*, Plate 4
gods and goddesses
insulting of, 71
list of, 166–81
See also specific deities
Golden One, 34, 78. *See also* Hathor
gold of reward ceremony, *100*
graffiti, 102
Great Royal Wife, 55, 57
gynaeceum, 68, *135*, 143
gynecology and obstetrics, 133–36

hand of god, *9*, 30, 31, *31*, 32, *32*
Hapy, 27, 30, *30*, 169

harems
  of the demiurge, 65–66
  of the pharaoh, 57, *95*
Hathor
  about, 162, 169–70
  as bovine-headed woman, 52, 54, *54*
  as celestial cow, *24*, *38*
  as Curly-haired One, 34, *34*
  as eye of Atum, 27
  as goddess of love, 8, 110
  as goddess of the sycamore, 89, *90*
  as Golden One, 34, 78
  as hand of god, *9*, 30, 31, *31*
  as image on jewelry, *104*
  as Lady of Drunkenness, 25–26, 36, 89, 107, *119*
  as Lady of Life, 39
  as Lady of Song, 36
  as Lady of the Vulva, 34
  menat and, 46, *46*, *48*, Plate 1, Plate 7
  as protector of pharaoh, 51
  sacred objects of, 44
  tame form of, 49
  welcoming Nefertari, *40*
  young woman form of, 31, *33*, *43*
  See also Bat
Hathor-Tefnut, 25–26
Hatshepsut, queen, 55
hearing, code of love for, 105
heart, hieroglyph for, *75*
heaven and earth. *See* Geb; Nut
heb-*sed,* 219
Heliopolis, 185
Heliopolitan
  cosmogony, 14, 169
  creation myths, 3–15, *4–14*
hermaphrodite vs. demiurge, 27, 30
Hermopolis, 185
Herodotus, 1, 44, 65
Hidden One. *See* Amun
hieroglyphics, 187–202, *188–202*
  for erogenous zones, *194–98*
  for family and society, *188–93*
  for the heart, *75*
  for love, eroticism, and sexuality, *77*, *199–202*
Holy Summit, 65
homosexuality, 18, 19, 68, 139–48, *140–48*, 158
Horus
  described, 14, *14*, 170
  eye of, 18–19, *20*, 22, *38*, 127, 129, 221
  with Isis, *19*
  Osiris and, 17–22, *17*, *18*
  Seth and, *20*, *21*
Hu. *See* Thoth
hypostasis, 217

Iby, 170
iconography. *See* figurative art
Ihy
  approaching the light, *119*
  described, 39, 44, 170
  at rebirth ritual, *48*, Plate 7
  on threshold of birth, *41*
Ihy-Osiris, 39
immortality and the gods, 14
incense, 106
incest, 11, 15, 18–19, 59–61
inheritance, 59
insults, 70–72, *70*
Intef II, 37, 39
Iosaas. *See* Hathor
Isis
  described, *13*, 126, 171
  with Horus, *19*
  knot of, 56, *56*, *130*, 131, Plate 15
  Nephthys and, 34–35, *35*
  Osiris and, 15–22, *17*, *18*, 42, *42*
Isis-Hathor, 21, 39
ithyphallic deities, *10*, *23*, 26, *27*, *28*
Iusaas, 30–31, 32, *32*

jewelry
  earrings, 144
  eroticism of, 102, *105*
  Hathor's image on, *104*
  Usekh, 47, *47*, 220
jubilee ceremony. *See sed*-festival

ka, 36–37, 44, 123, 217–18
Kamutef, 171
Karnak. *See* Thebes
karnata, 51, 218
Karomama, 66
Khepri, 171
Khnum, 171
Khonsu, 171–72
knot of Isis, 56, *56*, *130*, 131, Plate 15

Lady of Drunkenness, 25–26, 36, 89, 107, *119*. *See also* Hathor
Lady of Life, 39. *See also* Hathor
Lady of Song, 36. *See also* Hathor
Lady of the Vulva, 34. *See also* Hathor
leontocephalic, 218
letters to the dead, 62–63
libido, increasing, 119
literature, 69–93
  Chester Beatty Papyrus, 31, 34, 75, 105
  creation text, 8, *8*
  on homosexuality, 142
  on morality, 72–75, 142, Plate 11
  Papyrus of Turin, *103*, 150–61, *153–59*, *161*, Plate 21, Plate 22

poetry, 66–67, 75–93
Pyramid Texts, 3, 17, 70
Westcar Papyrus, 58
writing mediums used for, 69–70
loincloth. *See* shendjit
lotus of rebirth, *85*
love
between husband and wife, 61–63, *63*
girl dreaming of, *80*
hieroglyphics for, *77*, *199–202*
See also code of love; eroticism; love poetry
love poetry
about, 75
examples of, 76–93
images for, *80*, *82–86*, *88*, *90–93*, Plate 12
Luxor. *See* Thebes

Maat, *11*, 49, 52, 172
magic, 126–32
amulets, 129–31
goddesses and gods of, 126, 129
love spells, 126
medicine and, 132
revenge spells, 129
Maketaten, 60, *61*
mammisi, 42, *48*, 218, Plate 7
mandrake, *37*, *104*, *112*, 119, 121, *122*, *124*, *125*
marriage
contracts for, 59, 74–75, 145
incestuous, 59–61
laws and customs for, 51
sex before or outside of, 50–51
medicine and sexuality, 132–38
gynecology and obstetrics, 133–36
medical texts on, 132
sexual mutilations, 137–38
veneral diseases, 147
Medinet Habu temple of Ramses III, 94
Memphis, 22, 185
Memphis triad, 22, 220
men
bisexuality of, 145
circumcision of, 137–38, *137*
insulting of, 71
as prostitutes, 68
menat
dancers with, 110, *110*
described, 44, 54, 218
Hathor and, *24*, *38*, *43*, 46, *46*, 47, *47*, *48*, Plate 1, Plate 7
Mendes, 106
menstruation, 64
Min, 26, *29*, 172–73
mirrors, 102, *105*
monkeys, *25*, *88*, *92*
Montu, 173
moral literature, 72–75, Plate 11
music and dance
Bes and, 36, *36*, 68, *112*
celebrating a birth, *113*
code of love for, 107–18
dancers with *menat,* 110, *110*
during worship, 37
flutists, *113*, *115*, *116*, *147*
harpists, 68, *91*, *117*, *118*, Plate 10
lutists, *37*, 113, *115*, *117*, Plate 17
lyre player, *113*, *115*
ritual dances, 108–12, *109–12*, Plate 16
singers of Amun, 65, 112–13, *114*
tambourine players, *37*
tambour players, *104*, 113, *114*, Plate 14
women clapping rhythms, *116*
Mut, 26, *27*, 173
muu dancers, 108, *109*, Plate 16

Narmer, king, 51, 52, *52*
Nebet-Hetepet, hand of god, *9*, 30, 31, *31*, 32, *32*
Nebmaatre. *See* Amenhotep III
necrophilia, 149
necropolis, 64–65, 185
Nefertari, queen, *40*, 65
Nefertiti, queen, *55*, 60, 61, *61*, *62*, *100*, *101*, Plate 8, Plate 13
Nefertum, *9*, 22, *23*, 42, 132, 173
Neith, *56*, *143*, 173–74, Plate 15
Nekhbet, 174
Nephthys
described, 13, *13*, 15, 174
Isis and, 34–35, *35*
Osiris and, *17*, 42, *42*
nest of Isis, 56, *56*, *130*, 131, Plate 15
nome, 218
nose kiss, *101*, *141*
Nun, 3, 4, *4*, 6, 8, 174
Nut
caricature of, 158, *158*, Plate 22
children of, 13–14
described, 174–75
reinvigoration of Atum, *10*
union with Geb, *12*, Plate 4

Ogdoad, the, 3, *6*, 175. *See also* creation myths
olive branch, *106*
Omlin, J.A., 160
opet celebration, 26
Osiris
awakening of, *17*, *18*, *101*, 160

described, *13*, 14–15, *14*, 175
germinating, 16, *17*, Plate 3
with Isis and Nephthys, *42*
myth of, 15–22
rebirth and, 121
tribunal of, *16*
ostraca, 2, 69–70, 75, *103*, *111*, 151, 218
oxyrhynchus, *16*, 126

pallacidia, 218
papyri
Chester Beatty Papyrus, 31, 34, 75, 105
Ebers Papyrus, 132
Edwin Smith Papyrus, 132
use of, 69, 151
Westcar Papyrus, 58
See also Papyrus of Turin
Papyrus of Turin, 150–61
caricature of Nut and Geb, 158, *158*, Plate 22
erotica in, *103*, 152, *153–59*, 160, *161*
as pornography, 150–51
as satire, 150, 151, 152, *154*
pedophilia, 148
perfumes, 106
phallic sheath, 51, 52, *52*, 218
pharaoh
as a god, 51, 52, 54, 94, 99
harems of, 57, *95*
rebirth of, 51
sepulchers of, 64
women as, 55, 60
Philae, 106, 186
phoenix, 49, *49*
poetry
on love, 75–93
on prostitution, 66–67
See also love poetry
polygamy, 55, 57
pomegranates, 95, *95*
poppy, 125–26, *127*
popular art. *See* ostraca
pornography, 150–51
pregnancy and birth, 134–35, *134*, *135*
priestesses
as bride of Amun, 65–66
as divine worshipers, 31, 65–66, 217
as singers of Amun, 112–13, *114*
as virgins, 66
priests, ritual purity for, 63
primordial couples. *See* Ogdoad
promiscuity, 50–51
prostitution, 65, 66–68, *67*, 145, Plate 10
pschent, *48*. *See also* crowns
psychostasia, *16*, 218–19
psychotropic agents, 118–26
blue lotus, *104*, 119, *120*, *122*, 126
drinking of, *123*
mandrake, *37*, *104*, *112*, 119, 121, *122*, *124*, *125*
poppy, 125–26, *127*
white lotus, 119
Ptah, 22, 176
Ptahhotep, 72–73, 142, Plate 11
pterophoric, 219
Ptolemaic temples, 42
Ptolemies, 219
Ptolemy, 145–46
Punt, 106, 186
Pyramid Texts, 3, 17, 70

Qadesh, 126, *128*, 176, Plate 18
quadrifons, 219

Ra
creation and, 8, 13
described, *10*, 176
eye of, 22–26, *24*
See also Atum
Ramses II, 40, 57, 60, 94, 99, 119
Ramses III, 60, 94, 99
Ramses IX, 7
rape, 59
rebirth
lotus of, *85*
magic of, *120*, 121
menat and, 46, Plate 1
pharaoh as a reincarnating god, 51
phoenix and, 49
playing *senet* and, 98
symbols of, 104, *104*
recluses of the god, 63–64
Rekhmire and his wife, *63*
ritual prostitution, 65
ritual purity, 63–65
Rossini, Stéphane, 152
rowers of Snefu, 61
royal art, code of love in, 94–99, *95–98*
Ruty, the, *11*. *See also* Shu; Tefnut

Saïs, 186
Saqqara plateau, 68
Satet, 177
scarab
as amulet, 129, *129*
as hieroglyph for becoming, *28*
as image of eternity, 7, Plate 2
Khepri as, 171
scepters, *20*, *54*, *63*, *122*, 219, 221
sed-festival, 110–12, 219
sekhem scepter, *63*, *122*
sekhem sistrum, 22, *43*, 44, 45,

45, 47, *47*, Plate 6
Sekhmet, 22–26, *23*, *24*, 132, 177
Selket, *56*, 177, Plate 15
sema-tawy, *124*, 219
senet game, 96, 97, *97*, 98, 99
Senusret I, *140*, *141*
sepulchers of the pharaohs, 64
sesheshet sistrum, 44, 45, *45*, Plate 6
Seth
  bestiality of, 71
  described, 14, *14*, 15, 178
  opposing Horus, *20*, *21*
  Osiris and, 15–22
  sacred crocodile of, *86*
Seven Hathors, 42
sex
  before or outside of marriage, 50–51
  hieroglyphics for, 194–202
  practices of married couples, 63, *64*, Plate 9
  uncommon practices, 139–49, *140–48*
sexual freedom, men vs. women, 51
sexual insults, 71
sexual mutilations, 137–38
sexual organs, hieroglyphics for, 194–98
Shapenipet, priestess-queen, 66
shawabti, 219
shendjit, 51, *53*, *109*, 220
Shu
  children of, 11–12
  described, 178
  as lion of the solar horizon, *11*
  returning Tefnut, 25
  rule of, 24
  separating Nut and Geb, *12*
  tame form of, *31*
Shut-re sanctuaries, 99
Sia, 178. *See also* Thoth
sight, code of love for, 102–4
singers of Amun, 65, 112–13, *114*
Sirius-Sothis, a form of Isis-Hathor, 53
sistrums, 22, *43*, 44, 45, *45*, 47, *47*, *49*, Plate 6
Sky goddess. *See* Nut
slaves, 67–68
smell, code of love for, 105–6
Smenkhkare, *141*
society, hieroglyphics for, 188–93
sodomy, 148, 158, *158*
solar child, *9*, 22, *23*, 42, 132, 173
solar disk, *38*, *54*
solar egg, 3, *6*
solar eye. *See* eye of Ra
song of the harper, 91
Sothis, 178–79
space and time, creation of, 13–14
speos, 220
Strabo, 65
succession to the throne, 57, 60
sun god. *See* Atum; Ra
sycamore tree, 88, 89, *90*
symbol of life. *See ankh*
symbol of power. *See* scepters
syrinx, 64

talatat, 220
talismans, 129–31
taste, code of love for, 107
Tatenen, 179
Taweret, 126, 133, *133*, 180
Tefnut
  as Bastet, 25, *122*
  children of, 11–12
  described, 24–25, 179
  lion form of, *11*, *25*
  tame form of, 25, *31*
Tefnut-Sekhmet, 24–25
tet, 56, *56*, *130*, 131, Plate 15
Thebes, 64–65, 66, 186
Thebes triad, 220
theogamy, 54–55, 56, *56*, 60, 220, Plate 15
Thoth
  creation and, 3, 13, 14
  described, 6, *6*, 179–80
  monkey form of, 25, *25*
Tilapia nilotica, *85*
time and space, creation of, 13–14
tomb art, 64, *64*, Plate 9
tombs
  for queens, 121
  syrinx, 64
touch, code of love for, *56*, 107, *108*, Plate 15
trance states, inducing, 104, *104*, 110, *110*, 119
trees, 88, 89, *90*
triad, 22, 220, Plate 23
Turin papyrus. *See* Papyrus of Turin
Tutankhamun, 123, *124*, *125*
Tuthmosis I, 54
Tuthmosis III, 53
Two Divine Weepers, 34–35, *35*
Two Lions of the Solar Horizon, *11*. *See also* Shu; Tefnut
Two Women of the Braids, 35, *35*

uraeus, 23–24, *24*, *33*, *41*, 44, 180
Uret-Hekat, 126, 180
Usekh, 47, *47*, 220
Useret, 181

Valley of the Kings. *See* Thebes
Valley of the Queens, 64–65. *See also* Thebes

venereal diseases, 137
virgins, 66

wadj, 97, 99, 129, 220
wadjet (cobra goddess), 181
was scepter of power, *20, 122,* 221
wedjat, 18, *20, 38,* 127, 129, *130,* 221
Westcar Papyrus, 58
whabti, 219
wigs, 102, *105, 116*
women
  circumcision of, 138
  Great Royal Wife, 55, 57
  insulting of, 71
  as lesbians, 145–46
  as pharaoh, 55, 60
  as priestesses, 31, 65–66, 112–13, *114,* 217
  private quarters for, *135,* 143
  as property, 74–75
  rebirth and, 121
  as recluses of the god, 63–64
women. *See also* harems
word balloons, 70, 118
writing. *See* literature; papyri

zoophilia, 148